Destination Weddings For Dummies®

Contacting Major Airlines

To arrange discounted airfares for a wedding party, call airlines directly rather than booking online.

- Aer Lingus: 800-223-6537; www.aerlingus.com
- Aero Mexico: 800-237-6639; www.aeromexico.com
- Air Canada: 800-247-2262; www.aircanada.com
- Air France: 800-237-2747; www.airfrance.com
- Air Jamaica: 800-523-5585; www.airjamaica.com
- Alaska Airlines: 800-252-7522; www.alaskaair.com
- Alitalia: 800-223-5730; www.alitalia.com
- Aloha Airlines: 800-227-4900; www.alohaair.com
- American Airlines: 800-433-7300; www.aa.com
- British Airways: 800-247-9297; www.britishairways.com
- Continental: 800-523-3273; www.continental.com

- Delta: 800-221-1212; www.delta.com
- Hawaiian Airlines: 800-367-5320; www.hawaiianair.com
- Icelandair: 800-223-5500; www.icelandair.com
- JetBlue: 800-538-2583; www.jetblue.com
- Lufthansa: 800-645-3880; www.lufthansa.com
- Mexicana Airlines: 800-531-7921; www.mexicana.com
- Northwest: 800-225-2525; www.nwa.com
- Qantas Airways: 800-227-4500; www.qantas.com.au
- Southwest: 800-435-9792; www.southwest.com
- United Airlines: 800-241-6522; www.united.com
- U.S. Airways: 800-428-4322; www.usairways.com

On-Board Essentials

Plan to carry the following items with you until you reach your destination:

- ☐ Passports
- ☐ Marriage license (if obtained at home)
- ☐ Birth certificates
- ☐ Plane tickets
- ☐ Cash, traveler's checks, credit cards
- ☐ Bride and groom's wedding wear (including shoes)

- ☐ Wedding rings and other jewelry
- ☐ Contact info and emergency numbers (including guests)
- ☐ Updated planning file and copies of contracts
- ☐ Eyeglasses and medications
- ☐ Digital camera

For Dummies: Bestselling Book Series for Beginners

BESTSELLING BOOK SERIES

Destination Weddings For Dummies®

Cheat Sheet

Speaking the Online Language of Brides and Grooms

You can discover a lot about destination weddings from perusing and using the community bulletin boards at `www.brides.com`, `www.theknot.com`, and `weddings.about.com`. Yet the abbreviations many people use on these message boards can be confusing at first. Some common ones you're likely to encounter and can start to use in your own posts (after you register, of course) include the terms in the following table.

Destination Wedding Lingo

Abbreviation	Actual Term	Abbreviation	Actual Term
AHR	at-home reception	H2B	husband-to-be
BFF	best friend forever	MIL, FMIL	mother-in-law, future mother-in-law
BIL, FBIL	brother-in-law, future brother-in-law	MOB	mother of the bride
BM	best man, bridesmaid	MOH	maid of honor, matron of honor
DH	dear husband, darling husband	OOT bags	out of town bags, welcome bags
FH	future husband	OTT	over the top
FI	fiancé	PPL	people
FIL, FFIL	father-in-law, future father-in-law	SIL, FSIL	sister-in-law, future sister-in-law
FNF	friends and family, guests	SO	significant other
FOB	father of the bride, friend of bride	STBMrs	soon-to-be Mrs.
FOG	father of the groom, friend of groom	STD	save the date
FW	future wife	TA	travel agent
GBF	gay best friend	WP	wedding planner
GM	groomsman	XW, XH	ex-wife, ex-husband

For Dummies: Bestselling Book Series for Beginners

Destination Weddings

FOR

DUMMIES®

by Susan Breslow Sardone

Romantic travel expert and creator
of New York Magazine's Weddings section

BICENTENNIAL
1807
WILEY
2007
BICENTENNIAL

Wiley Publishing, Inc.

Destination Weddings For Dummies®

Published by
Wiley Publishing, Inc.
111 River St.
Hoboken, NJ 07030-5774
www.wiley.com

WILEY

About the Author

Susan Breslow Sardone is the Web's leading authority on romantic travel. She has been the About.com Guide to Honeymoons and Romantic Getaways for a decade, and Forbes.com calls her site "Best of the Web in Romantic Travel."

A widely published travel journalist, Susan's assignments have led her from Alaska to Zimbabwe. Her work has appeared in print in *The New Yorker, Condé Nast Traveler, Modern Bride,* and other mass-circulation magazines. She has also served as a consultant to Expedia and American Express Travel.

Susan holds a master's degree in journalism and a bachelor's of arts degree in English. More recently, she studied Multimedia Technology at New York University, where she also taught writing classes. Susan and her husband, Vincent, live in New York.

Dedication

To Vincent J. Sardone: Marrying you in Las Vegas turned out to be the smartest bet I ever made.

Author's Acknowledgments

A tip of the hat to Barb Doyen, the agent who recruited me for this project, and the team at Wiley for midwifing this baby. Hugs to Dana and Yuri Daiter for the honor of including me in their ultimate destination wedding. Props to Scott Kurnit for coming up with the brilliant idea for About.com — and a shout-out to the many editors and other staff members I've had the privilege of working with since the beginning. You've given me the opportunity to guide a worldwide audience to the most wonderful places for couples to experience.

Mille grazie to Mara Urshel of Kleinfeld Bridal and Steve Davis of Jim's Formal Wear, who informed me what the well-dressed destination bride and groom are wearing. Merci to Stephannie Barba for her charming map. Appreciation also goes to cruise-wedding guru Valerie Brizuela at The Wedding Experience and master bridal consultant Sue Winner. Representatives of the many land-based destinations and properties mentioned herein also have my gratitude.

But most of all, I would like to thank my husband, Vincent, for the loving kindness, the laughter, and carrying the luggage. Without you, I might be a spinster with an unstamped passport. With you, I soar.

Publisher's Acknowledgments

We're proud of this book; please send us your comments through our Dummies online registration form located at www.dummies.com/register/.

Some of the people who helped bring this book to market include the following:

*Acquisitions, Editorial, and Media
Development*

Project Editor: Chad R. Sievers

Acquisitions Editor: Tracy Boggier

Copy Editor: Sarah Westfall

Technical Editor: Karen Emery

Editorial Manager: Michelle Hacker

Editorial Assistant: Erin Calligan Mooney,
Joe Niesen, Leeann Harney

Cover Photos: ©Stockbyte/Getty Images

Cartoons: Rich Tennant
(www.the5thwave.com)

Composition Services

Project Coordinator: Jennifer Theriot

Layout and Graphics: Stephanie D. Jumper,
Alicia B. South

Anniversary Logo Design: Richard Pacifico

Proofreaders: Aptara, Jessica Kramer,
Susan Mortiz

Indexer: Aptara

Publishing and Editorial for Consumer Dummies

    Diane Graves Steele, Vice President and Publisher, Consumer Dummies

    Joyce Pepple, Acquisitions Director, Consumer Dummies

    Kristin A. Cocks, Product Development Director, Consumer Dummies

    Michael Spring, Vice President and Publisher, Travel

    Kelly Regan, Editorial Director, Travel

Publishing for Technology Dummies

    Andy Cummings, Vice President and Publisher, Dummies Technology/General User

Composition Services

    Gerry Fahey, Vice President of Production Services

    Debbie Stailey, Director of Composition Services

Contents at a Glance

Table of Contents

Part V: The Part of Tens.............................281

Chapter 19: Ten Emergencies You May Face and How to Handle 'Em.........................283

Chapter 20: Ten Ways to Save Money on Your Destination Wedding 287

Index 291

Introduction

....

Aah . . . an old-fashioned wedding — the bride in a stiff white gown, the groom in an equally rigid tuxedo, the attendants decked out in identical outfits like Motown backup singers, the strict rules about how invitations must read and who sits where, the *seriousness* of it all! Plus don't forget about the huge price tag for an event that only lasts four hours. Does it make you wonder whether a better way to get married is out there? One that's more fun, more exciting, and less expensive?

The answer is *yes:* It's called a destination wedding. This enlightened style of wedding has convinced millions of smart couples to run away from home with their nearest and dearest to marry in a place where they can celebrate for days.

Having planned my own destination wedding without professional help, been to both plain and fancy weddings away, and traveled around the world, I saw a need for a book that could take a couple through the process without making it any more complicated or costly than it has to be. So if you're ready for the ultimate wedding experience, you've come to the right place.

About This Book

Unlike other wedding guides that may stress you out with all the details you're "supposed" to concern yourself with, this book shows you how really easy — and how much more affordable — a destination wedding can be. You can't find a timeline anywhere in this book because destination weddings aren't cookie-cutter affairs.

Instead, I created this book to be a tool — full of Web sites to check out, destinations to consider, and fun activities to try — to use at your leisure and on *your* timetable. You may choose to dip into only the chapters you need, but if you want to read the book from cover to cover, go for it. You can come back to any part when you need it.

When I started researching this book and read critiques of competing ones that complained, "I could find most of this information online," I knew that this book had to be different. I acknowledge you're more than likely to use the Web, and I encourage you to do so. Figures say that 77 percent of couples turn to the Net to plan their wedding; I think that number is even higher.

Conventions Used in This Book

When writing this book, I included some general conventions that all *For Dummies* books use. I use the following:

- I *italicize* any words you may not be familiar with and provide a definition.
- I **bold** all keywords in bulleted lists and the actual steps in numbered lists.
- All Web sites and e-mail addresses appear in `monofont`.

Foolish Assumptions

Destination Weddings For Dummies is for brides- and grooms-to-be, moms and dads, wedding planners interested in extending their range, and people who want to know more about this trend. In fact, I carried a picture of you in my head. Here's what I imagined:

- The two of you have recently decided you want to get married (congratulations, by the way).
- You're looking for a way to put your unique stamp on your wedding or a wedding you're helping to plan.
- You're wondering how you can have a great event without spending a fortune.
- You're the parents of an engaged couple — and you want to suggest a way for them to marry that won't crack your nest egg.
- You're not too experienced about this destination-wedding business, but you're smart.
- You're not *quite* engaged yet, but you like to be prepared for the future.
- You want a book that can explain the basics, and you can take it from there, using a computer and Internet access.

I can't tell you whether a destination wedding can meet your requirements and prevent an insurrection at home. But I can tell you how to make one as good as it can be — an event that you and your guests will remember with fondness for years to come.

How This Book Is Organized

This book is divided into five sections, each with several chapters that illuminate the main topic and assist you in making decisions and planning your destination wedding.

Part 1: Marrying Your Way: Away You Go

In this part, you discover why destination weddings appeal to so many couples. Chapter 1 gives you the facts. Chapter 2 helps you decide whether to go through with one yourselves. Chapter 3 helps tech-savvy and paper-loyal couples get organized. And if you want to figure out how to optimize your budget and deal with vendors, Chapter 4 has answers. And in Chapter 5, I show you how to productively involve friends, family, and wedding professionals.

Part 11: Picking a Destination for Your Wedding

Don't have a clue where to get married? Think of me as your detective. Chapter 6 starts you on the journey. The rest of this part highlights specific locations: Chapter 7 focuses on the United States and Canada; Chapter 8 features warm-weather spots and tropical islands; Chapter 9 is your guide to Europe, from cities to castles; and Chapter 10 looks at cruise-ship weddings.

Part 111: Getting the Destination Wedding You Want

Whether you work with a pro or do it on your own, this section gives you the 4-1-1 on how to pull together all the details. Chapter 11 proves you don't need to be a travel agent to get good deals for yourselves and your guests, and Chapter 12 is party-planning central. You can discover how to set up an altar in Chapter 13 and get tips on the range of acceptable outfits in Chapter 14.

Part 1V: Sharing the Joy at Your Wedding, Now and Later

You can hit the ground running when you arrive at your destination. Chapter 15 helps you stay on top of things after you settle in. Chapter 16 offers etiquette advice specific to destination weddings. And if you're disappointed that not everyone can attend your wedding away, Chapter 17 helps you find ways to include people at home. And, Chapter 18 helps you plan your honeymoon.

Part V: The Part of Tens

A catchall of useful information, this part deals with destination wedding emergencies in Chapter 19 (what event would be complete without at least one?) and how to save money in Chapter 20.

Icons Used in This Book

Small illustrations in the margin, *icons* clue you into extra info that can save you time, money, or aggravation. Here are the icons I use:

Find insider tips or tricks of the trade wherever you see this icon.

The equivalent of a piece of string on your finger, this icon calls out an essential piece of info or step you need to take to accomplish the task at hand.

This icon highlights my recommendations of the best places and services for your destination wedding.

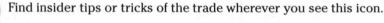

When I want you to avoid pitfalls or potential troubles, I use this icon to identify them so you can steer clear.

Where to Go from Here

If you're at the very beginning of planning a wedding away, or aren't sure yet whether one is right for the two of you, I suggest you start at the front. Otherwise, dive in wherever you find chapters that apply to the stage you're in. If you're not quite sure where to start, check out the table of contents or index and find a subject that piques your interest, and then start reading on any page. If you want to take a mental vacation, go straight to Chapter 6. I also recommend that you read Part IV early on, so you can begin to picture yourselves arriving at the destination before your guests do.

The last thing I want to tell you before you start the book is this: I've been there, and you have my word of honor that nothing is better than a destination wedding for an out-of-this-world experience. So hang in there, enjoy the journey, and let this book be your guide.

Part I
Marrying Your Way: Away You Go

The 5th Wave   By Rich Tennant

"What about the islands or the mountains, Peter?
I'm just a little nervous about getting married
in a place called 'Never Never Land.'"

In this part . . .

Welcome to the world of destination weddings, which truly span the globe. This part shows you how a destination wedding differs from an at-home one, whether a wedding away is right for you, how to organize a destination wedding, what you can expect to spend, and who to turn to for help.

Chapter 1 explains why destination weddings have become so popular. In Chapter 2, I help you weigh the pros and cons of choosing this type of wedding and prepare you to deal with possible obstacles if you proceed. Chapter 3, unique among wedding-planning books, provides specific advice on how to organize a destination wedding by using your computer and the Internet (you can also find tips to keep a paper trail). Chapter 4 delves into budgeting and negotiating to fund the wedding you want. And Chapter 5 discusses where to turn for help and how friends, family, wedding professionals, and specialized vendors can contribute to your day.

Chapter 1

Destination Weddings 101

In This Chapter

▶ Understanding what a destination wedding is (and what it isn't)

▶ Making sure your marriage is legal — wherever you wed

▶ Discovering the most popular places for destination weddings

▶ Finding answers to your destination wedding FAQs

▶ Taking your destination wedding one step at a time

*E*very marriage begins with a unique love story. If yours also includes a taste for travel, a passion for adventure, and the commitment to celebrate in your own way, yours can lead to extraordinary places in your journey to marry at a destination wedding.

Today, as many as one in four engaged couples has a destination wedding. Do you and your fiancé envision yourselves as one of those couples? If so, this chapter can help you begin, serving as your jumping-off point into the world of destination weddings — what they mean, whether a wedding away is right for you, and how to plan one as the next chapter in your love story.

Defining Destination Weddings and Why They're So Popular

A *destination wedding* is a wedding ceremony and celebration held in a location away from where the bride or groom live. Basically it's your wedding, your way . . . just away. Because a destination wedding always involves travel, more time is allotted for the occasion, and the wedding becomes a multiday event.

Laid-back beach hotels, mountaintop ski resorts, lush vineyards, glitzy casino hotels, full-service cruise ships, exotic islands, and European castles and villas are among the top venues couples choose because the "destination" part of the equation is as important as the "wedding" one.

You may hear a destination wedding referred to as a *wedding away* or a *weddingmoon*. Although most couples do segue from their destination wedding right into the honeymoon, it's not necessarily part of the overall plan. Whether you take your honeymoon before, immediately after, or sometime in the future, Chapter 18 discusses the advantage of each choice and having the honeymoon you want.

This section gives you a quick overview of destination weddings, including the main advantages of weddings away and why they're becoming the fastest-growing segment of the bridal industry. Chapter 2 helps you determine whether one is right for you.

Simplifying your wedding

Destination weddings allow you, the couple, to make your own rules. At hometown weddings, the reception always follows the ceremony. And a young bride and groom who are heavily influenced by their parents' taste and budget may be pressured into having a more traditional or complex wedding than they really want.

When more-independent couples wed, they're likely to make choices that are personally important to them, rather than following what others say they "should" have or "should" do at their wedding. Overall, destination weddings tend to be modest and casual. The emphasis is on relaxation and shared experiences. Your ceremony could be followed by guests mounting waiting horses to take off on a trail ride, or boarding a catamaran for an afternoon of snorkeling. And in place of a stuffy, old-fashioned reception, you can have a beach barbecue capped by fireworks.

The fun, ease, convenience, and simplicity of a wedding away are especially appealing to certain types of couples, especially more-mature ones. They may have busy careers but a fondness for travel. Perhaps one or both of them are getting married for the second or third time, and they want to do something in a completely different way from an earlier wedding. Or they may not have the time, taste, or funds for a big, complicated affair.

Paying the price

The expense of a hometown wedding is a strong incentive to make couples scan the horizon for a cheaper place to tie the knot. On average, weddings away cost about 40 percent less than traditional at-home weddings. The price of a nice ceremony in the Caribbean or Mexico rarely exceeds $10,000 — and many come in at half that amount or less.

The rationale for my wedding away

When I was planning to get married, I interviewed several people in the wedding industry in New York City. At one hotel, the banquet manager painted this picture:

"Imagine yourself gliding down our 60-foot aisle wearing a long satin gown and train dotted with rhinestones. Everyone you know (we can fit 400 in our space!) is gazing up at you. In one corner of the room, a string quartet serenades you with a work by Beethoven, and the entire space is decorated to resemble a winter palace, complete with faux hanging icicles."

Knowing I'd feel dressed for Halloween in that fashion, hating the idea that people would be staring at me, loathing classical music, and imagining that the budget for an event decorated that way would approximate the Gross National Product of a small country, I gulped, ran home as fast as I could, and said, "Honey, we're going to Vegas. . . "

The average American wedding now runs $27,852, according to a recent *Condé Nast Bridal Group* study. And with wedding costs rising about 8 percent annually, by 2010 the average wedding tab is likely to approach $35,000. In urban areas that include New York City; Washington, D.C.; and Los Angeles, that's already the price tag for a modest affair.

How much sense does it make to spend money on a wedding that you could otherwise use to buy a new car, put a down payment on a house, or take the honeymoon trip of a lifetime? That's something you have to decide for yourselves — although many destination wedding couples already know they would rather put the cash in their pockets than in a conventional wedding's coffers.

Choosing quality over quantity

Transporting friends and family to a dream destination to see you marry can feel like stepping into a fairytale or an adventure film. Lifting people out of their everyday lives and bringing them to a place that's beautiful and exciting has a magical quality to it — a definite destination wedding appeal.

Weddings away are also popular because you get to invite only the people you truly want to come. Because not everyone can afford to travel, guest lists are smaller than those of hometown weddings. Fewer guests means a more intimate event in an ideal setting to reunite with those who mean the most to you. (You can find advice on who to invite in Chapter 12.)

The size of a guest list for a destination wedding can range from zero into the hundreds, but most lists usually don't exceed 100. A typical wedding away involves just 15 to 20 guests, although that number is expanding as more and more couples get wise to the advantages of affordable out-of-town weddings.

Although couples can ease their financial burden by having a destination wedding, guests don't get off as easily. Their costs of transportation, lodging, and food and activities not covered by the hosts can easily top $1,000 over the course of a long weekend (not to mention a wedding gift). Attendants who are asked to wear special dresses and accessories or rent tuxedoes have to shell out even more. Fortunately, the prospect of combining a vacation with a celebration in a wonderful place helps most guests and wedding-party members justify the expense.

When it comes down to it, though, all it takes is two to marry — plus an officiant and witnesses, as required. So if you don't care to have guests at all, that's your prerogative. Plenty of couples who don't want any fuss build a wedding into a vacation and comfortably marry without fanfare.

The Differences between Getting Married Away and at Home

Being aware of the differences between a destination wedding and an at-home wedding can make it easier to decide which is right for you. Chapter 2 goes into detail, but you need to know the following essential points if you're considering a destination wedding:

- **Location, location, location:** Destination weddings involve overnight travel to another place, often selected for its scenic appeal. If the setting is particularly beautiful, the wedding couple may be able to save money on certain aspects of the wedding, such as flowers and decorations.

- **More time to celebrate:** A conventional hometown wedding lasts between three and five hours, longer if you have a break between the ceremony and reception. In general, a destination wedding takes place over three days or more.

- **Lower cost:** Despite the longer amount of time involved, destination weddings are usually cheaper than at-home ones. Find out about budgeting in Chapter 4 and see the "Paying the price" section earlier in this chapter for more info.

Understanding how eloping differs from a destination wedding

In the past, marrying away from home was synonymous with eloping. That was usually the only option for young couples who needed parental consent for marriage but couldn't obtain it. They'd quietly leave home — often concealed under the cover of night's darkness — bound for a place where the legal age for marriage was lower, and no one would appear to challenge their intent to wed. (Read about Gretna Green, Scotland — a refuge for lovers for centuries — in Chapter 9.)

When couples of legal age eloped, they often did so to avoid familial conflict over differences in color or creed. Sometimes, though, couples simply eloped because it was fast, easy, private, and cheap.

Today the definition of *eloping* refers to any couple who secretly heads off to another place to marry. Sometimes the decision is impromptu, but other times, their intentions are planned far in advance. Either way, guests are rarely involved and vows typically aren't followed by a reception. The couple either continues on to a honeymoon or returns to their normal lives right away, announcing the marriage at a time when they see fit.

✔ **Casual versus traditional celebration:** Hometown weddings are normally traditional affairs, sometimes stodgy and often predictable due to formulaic agendas. At a destination wedding, you can toss out conventions you don't like and make the event as laid back or as formal as you like. Most couples opt for casual ease.

✔ **Making your own rules:** Beyond the necessity of obtaining a wedding license and being married by a licensed officiant, destination weddings don't have any hard-and-fast rules. For example, you know that one about the groom not seeing the bride in her dress before the wedding? At a destination wedding, the couple may have checked into their room a couple of days before the event — and he's the one to zip up her dress and tell her she looks beautiful before they head off together to say their vows at an oceanside gazebo.

✔ **Say good-bye to the home team:** Because a destination wedding usually takes place a significant distance from home, anyone you can't do without — from your pastor to your pedicurist — you have to invite to the wedding and pay for their time, travel, and services. Otherwise, expect to use a local officiant and vendors. (For more on gathering your destination wedding team, see Chapter 5.)

Making Your Wedding Legal: What You Need to Know

In order to become legally married, you need to apply for and obtain a marriage license and have your vows formalized by an authorized officiant within a designated time period. When you're getting married in a location other than your hometown, you must follow its laws to ensure that your marriage there is legal. This section briefly looks at various locations within the United States and elsewhere to help you be aware of laws in different destinations.

Marrying in the United States

Marriage license laws and requirements differ from state to state and locality to locality in the United States. All have a minimum age requirement, but that varies as well. If you're getting married in the U.S., prepare ahead of time by finding out what the laws and requirements are where you intend to marry. To do so, contact the town or county clerk in your chosen destination and ask how to apply for a license.

Different U.S. states permit a wide range of officiants to perform civil and religious ceremonies. Find a state-by-state list at `marriage.about.com/cs/marriagelicenses/a/officiants.htm`. To have a religious ceremony in a U.S. church, synagogue, mosque, or other house of worship, contact the local cleric for information.

Getting hitched in another country

A legal overseas marriage license is also legal in the United States, as long as it doesn't break any state laws. Exceptions include same-sex marriages, which are legal in Canada, Belgium, the Netherlands, South Africa, and Spain, but not in the United States. Only in Massachusetts can same-sex residents legally marry.

For all couples, countries outside the U.S. have strict guidelines before issuing a license. These can include residency requirements and the expense of translating relevant documents into the country's official language. To find out more about the legality of an overseas wedding, check out Chapter 6. You can also find the official link to marriage license information for all the locales mentioned in this book in Chapters 7, 8, and 9.

To avoid delay and complications when marrying abroad, many couples opt to first have a private civil ceremony where they live.

The event that takes place during the destination wedding then becomes a symbolic ceremony. You can read more about these in Chapter 6.

If you want to have a religious ceremony abroad, set the wheels in motion by requesting a meeting with your rabbi, minister, or parish priest. He can put you in touch with regional headquarters, which can help you contact overseas prelates.

 Don't allow yourselves to fall in love with the idea of marrying in a foreign church simply because its stained-glass windows are amazing or the architecture is majestic. Some churches and synagogues don't accommodate the wishes of couples who aren't long-standing congregation members.

Looking at the Most Popular Locations

When a particular destination is favored by a large number of couples, you can usually find a good reason for it. (Convenience and ease of travel are major ones; that's why, according to statistics, two-thirds of couples choose the United States.)

Part II helps you explore all the best places for a destination wedding in depth. However, if you can't wait to find out what they are, here are the top spots, year after year:

- ✔ **Las Vegas:** Vegas weddings are fast, fun, and can be very affordable (as long as you don't blow your stash at the casinos or opt for an over-the-top affair). And nowhere else does a marriage license bureau stay open until midnight every day. Chapter 7 helps you plan a Vegas ceremony where the odds are in your favor.

- ✔ **Hawaii:** Heavenly beaches and resorts dedicated to the pursuit of pleasure make these islands (especially Maui) a popular choice. Explore them in Chapter 7.

- ✔ **Disneyland and Disney World:** Having recently introduced opulent couture weddings, Disney's Fairy Tale Weddings keep spreading pixie dust on loving couples. For more, see Chapter 7.

- ✔ **The Caribbean and Mexico:** Quintessential beach getaways, the islands of the Caribbean, the coasts of Mexico — and the all-inclusive resorts they harbor — have perfected the art of providing couples with *turnkey* weddings (where all the elements are bundled together for your convenience). Dig up the details in Chapter 8.

✔ **Canada:** As charming as France in the east and as scenic as the Alps in the west, Canada speaks your language. With an advantageous exchange rate and legal same-sex marriages, Canada provides ample reasons to head north of the border. Find out more in Chapter 7.

✔ **Fiji:** This bit of heaven on earth is a long way to go to get married (and paradise doesn't come cheap), but that doesn't discourage couples who want an uncommon ceremony in a lush setting. Refer to Chapter 8.

✔ **Europe:** History, romance, scenic beauty, and sophisticated culture draw couples here. Complex marriage requirements erect obstacles in some countries such as France, although others, like Scotland, are more welcoming. See Chapter 9 for specifics.

✔ **Cruise ships:** The price is right, and so is the strategy: Marry in port, and then sail off on your honeymoon. You can discover the ceremony, reception, and sail-away options offered by different cruise lines in Chapter 10.

Answering Some Questions You May Have

If you're seriously considering a destination wedding, you already may have dozens of questions in mind. This book can answer many of them and help make your destination wedding a once-in-a-lifetime experience. The following addresses some of the bigger-picture questions you may be wondering about:

✔ **With so many amazing places to choose from, how do we decide where to have the wedding?** The short answer is to find a place that's in some way meaningful to the two of you. Chapter 6 can help you blue-sky the possibilities, and the rest of Part II offers specific recommendations.

✔ **How long should we wait to book the wedding?** The sooner, the better. If you have your hearts set on Santorini in Greece, you may have to wait two years or longer to nail down a date at a preferred place. Saturday nights everywhere book up fastest. But you can always get married tomorrow in Las Vegas.

✔ **Is it wrong to e-mail save-the-dates?** If everyone on your guest list has e-mail and checks it regularly, go ahead, but that means forgoing tangible ones that provide a lasting remembrance. See Chapter 12 for more info on save-the-dates.

✔ **How do we handle friends and family with kids if we want to keep the wedding adults-only? And what do we tell people who expect to be invited — but aren't?** One of the advantages of destination weddings is that people expect them to be smaller than at-home ones, so they usually understand. Read about who to invite and who to leave at home in Chapter 12 — and how to communicate those decisions gracefully in Chapter 16.

✔ **Which last name should be on the bride's first passport: maiden or married?** You can't legally change your name until after you're married (unless you go to court to do so beforehand). To avoid confusion, I advise you to keep all ID and travel documents in the same name until you return. Find out how to get a passport in Chapter 11.

✔ **Is it tacky to get married in Las Vegas?** At the AAA Five-Diamond Award-winning Bellagio hotel, wedding packages range in price from $1,500 to $15,000. They're definitely not tacky, nor are chapels inside Las Vegas's other top casino hotels. Discover the real deal on Vegas weddings in Chapter 7.

✔ **Do we need a wedding planner?** If you're having a small wedding at a hotel or chapel that provides its own wedding coordinator, absolutely not. However, bigger events and ones in more-remote locations where weddings aren't an everyday occurrence require local assistance. See Chapter 5 on assembling your wedding team.

✔ **How important is visiting the destination before the wedding?** Checking out your location prior to the festivities can help set your mind at ease. But as long as you have someone in the location working on the wedding on your behalf, you plan to get there ahead of time, and you're not a control freak, visiting isn't essential. Again, the bigger the wedding, the more advance planning is required, which argues in favor of having your feet on the ground well before your event.

✔ **How long do we have to entertain wedding guests after the ceremony?** Typically, the reception follows the ceremony and then a farewell brunch takes place on the last official day of the wedding. After that, they're on their own (and so are the two of you!). Chapter 15 offers tips on entertaining guests throughout their stay.

✔ **Who pays for what?** Couples usually pay for their own destination weddings, sometimes with assistance from family. Guests pick up the tab for their travel and lodging. Chapter 4 is dedicated to budgeting, so you can find more answers to financial questions there.

Seeing stars: Celebrity destination weddings

Nearly ten years ago model Cindy Crawford and nightclub impresario Rande Gerber had a barefoot wedding at a beach resort in the Bahamas. She wore a short white gown, and he stood up in a white shirt and Armani pants. Photographs of their happy day attended by a few close friends and family members circulated around the world, inspiring thousands of other couples to choose an easy, breezy destination wedding for themselves.

Crawford and Gerber weren't the first stars to get married away, and they certainly won't be the last. But they're in good company. The following couples also said their vows far from home:

- Ashley Judd and Dario Franchetti: Skibo Castle, Scotland
- Avril Lavigne and Deryck Whibley: Montecito, California
- Ben Affleck and Jennifer Garner: Parrot Cay Resort, Turks & Caicos
- Bill Gates and Melinda French: Four Seasons Lanai, Hawaii
- Brett Hull and Darcie Schollmeyer: Esperanza Resort, Los Cabos, Mexico
- Christiane Amanpour and Jamie Rubin: Odescalchi Castle, Bracciano,Italy
- Christina Aguilera and Jordan Bratman: Staglin Family Vineyards, Napa Valley, California
- Duke and Duchess of Windsor: Château de Candé, Loire Valley, France
- Eva Longoria and Tony Parker: Paris, France
- Gwen Stefani and Gavin Rossdale: St. Paul's Church, Covent Garden, England
- Heidi Klum and Seal: Puerto Vallarta, Mexico
- John Lennon and Yoko Ono: Gibraltar
- Liv Tyler and Royston Langdon: private villa, Barbados
- Madonna and Guy Ritchie: Skibo Castle, Scotland
- Pink and Carey Hart: Costa Rica
- Tiger Woods and Elin Nordegren: Sandy Lane Resort, Barbados
- Tom Cruise and Katie Holmes: Odescalchi Castle, Bracciano, Italy
- Tori Spelling and Dean McDermott: Wakaya Island Resort, Fiji
- Reba McEntire and Narbel Blackstock: Lake Tahoe, Nevada
- Sarah Michelle Gellar and Freddie Prinze Jr.: Jalisco, Mexico
- Sylvester Stallone and Jennifer Flavin: Oxfordshire, England

Las Vegas chapels attract more celebrities and civilians than anywhere else. Although not all star weddings have stood the test of time, they certainly seemed like a good idea at the moment. Vegas wedding alumni include:

✔ Angelina Jolie and Billy Bob Thornton (divorced)

✔ Britney Spears and Jason Alexander (annulled after 55 hours)

✔ Demi Moore and Bruce Willis (divorced)

✔ Elvis Presley and Priscilla Beaulieu

✔ Jon Bon Jovi and Dorothea Hurley

✔ Kelly Ripa and Mark Consuelos

✔ Natalie Maines and Adrian Pasdar

✔ Paul Newman and Joann Woodward (50 years and still going strong).

✔ **How can we transport a wedding gown without it getting completely wrinkled?** Tissue paper, tissue paper, and more tissue paper. Turn to Chapter 14, devoted to wedding wear, for tips from the pros and selecting a dress that travels well.

✔ **Can the groom still wear shorts if the bride wants to wear a long gown?** Yes — if he's man enough to bear the scorn and ridicule of his yet-unborn children when they're old enough to view mom and dad's wedding pictures. For specific advice on what guys can wear, head for Chapter 14.

✔ **Does the captain marry couples on a cruise ship?** Only captains of Princess ships are permitted to do so. On other cruise lines, couples are married by a regular officiant when the ship is in port. Chapter 10 goes into detail on cruise weddings.

✔ **Will we feel as if we've missed out on something if we don't get married at home?** If you define *home* as the place where the most important people in the world are, then anywhere you bring them together will feel like home. Lots of couples also plan at-home receptions afterwards. Get ideas for those in Chapter 17, plus ways to include guests who couldn't attend.

Getting Going: 20 Steps to a Destination Wedding

Even the simplest destination weddings require a degree of planning. If you follow a logical order in doing things, you can feel less stressed, work more efficiently, and accomplish all the necessary tasks on schedule. How much time do you need to set everything up? That depends entirely on you and how complex the wedding you have in mind is.

Breaking down the process to 20 steps, these are the major milestones:

1. **Decide that a destination wedding is right for you.**
2. **Choose possible dates.**
3. **Consider where to go.**
4. **Select a destination.**
5. **Draw up a guest list.**
6. **Pick a place to wed and a place to stay.**
7. **Alert friends and family.**
8. **Make travel arrangements.**
9. **Decide whether or not you need to hire a planner.**
10. **Shop for wedding wear.**
11. **Focus on the type of ceremony you want and the spot.**
12. **Decide on the type of reception you want.**
13. **Pick a reception location, caterer, and menu.**
14. **Select flowers, decorations, and music.**
15. **Opt for photography, videography, and/or a Web cast.**
16. **Arrange all group activities for the wedding weekend.**
17. **Pack all the necessities (from wedding attire to important documents); you can ship remaining items, such as guest welcome bags, to your location.**
18. **Arrive early to check on the details.**
19. **Savor every moment of the occasion.**
20. **Continue onto the honeymoon or head directly home to start the next chapter of your life together.**

Fortunately, I've detailed every one of these steps in this book, so you needn't feel overwhelmed. (And if I, a destination bride whose party-organization skills previously were limited to throwing my dirty clothes in the closet and opening up a jumbo bag of M&Ms before guests arrived could pull off an event of this magnitude, so can you.) By referring to this book's table of contents, you can find what you need to know, when you need to know it, and how to make it all work for you.

Chapter 2

Is a Destination Wedding Right for You?

*A*lthough a destination wedding can be a wonderful occasion, not every couple planning to get married is cut out for one: The bride-to-be who dreamed since she was a little girl of having a wedding in the family church and the groom who figures he only needs to walk around the corner, utter "I do," and can be back in time to catch the end of the game aren't prime prospects for this kind of affair. But if the idea of having a destination wedding appeals to you, this chapter explains how an out-of-the-ordinary may suit the two of you.

Why a Wedding Away May Work Best for You: The 3F's

Reasons to have a destination wedding abound. Perhaps you don't have the time or inclination to spend the better part of a year planning a wedding. Or although your budget is small, you want a wedding with style. Or you have family issues that can be eased by locating the wedding in a neutral place — that just happens to have a climate you love.

If you're less concerned with doing what's conventional and more with doing what feels right to you personally, being a "runaway" bride and groom may be as practical a decision for you as it is a romantic one.

The "3F's" — freedom, flexibility, and fun — are the greatest incentives to choose a destination wedding. This section takes a closer look at each of them.

Freedom (from convention)

Whether small or large, casual or less so, a destination wedding provides you with the freedom to be yourselves and shape your wedding, your way. How do you know whether a destination wedding is right for you? They're popular with and ideal for:

✓ **Couples who are slightly older:** As maturity increases, so does the desire to have an event that is more a reflection of your own taste and lifestyle than your parents'. And that's a cornerstone of weddings away.

✓ **Couples who have been married before and don't want to replicate the white-dress, dad-walks-the-bride-down-the-aisle, and we-all-eat-rubber-chicken-afterward routine:** Anyone who's been there and done that may be excited by the prospect of going someplace new and marrying in a different way.

✓ **Couples with children:** Relocating everyone to the neutral territory of a family-friendly, all-inclusive resort or cruise for the wedding is an excellent way to help a blended family bond.

✓ **Couples who value privacy and simplicity above all:** Many who choose a destination wedding invite no guests at all yet experience a beautiful and meaningful ceremony with simply the officiant and local witnesses present.

Flexibility (to do it your way)

The most beautiful thing about destination weddings (besides the surroundings) is that you don't have to follow hard-and-fast rules regarding how the wedding looks or feels or how long it lasts.

Simply by inviting guests to a faraway place, they expect something different. That also means elements you've witnessed at other weddings and don't particularly like can be tossed away like the traditional bride's garter. Instead, you can create your own traditions. And no one will ever be able to say your wedding was a cookie-cutter affair. Thanks to a destination wedding's flexibility, you aren't tied down to the old rules. Consider some examples:

✓ **The dress code:** Find the idea of wearing Vera Wang or wingtips too constricting? Nowhere does it say you can't don island gear and flip flops (or go barefoot altogether) to pledge your love. Chapter 14 looks at stylish options.

> ✔ **The convenience of having the ceremony and reception in the same place, if that appeals to you:** Destination weddings that take place at beach or mountaintop resorts, for example, usually have an altar or other area dedicated to ceremony space. At adjacent restaurants, terraces, and elsewhere on the premises, the entire group can celebrate afterward. Alternatively, if you want to separate the two events by miles, hours, or even days, all you need to do is plan it that way. (Check out Chapter 12.)

> ✔ **The ease of planning:** Many hotels in resort areas are experts in orchestrating the entire event for you — right down to the food, music, flowers, and decorations. Some offer a free weekend stay so couples can come and discuss how to customize the wedding.

Fun (that's the key)

Although the word *wedding* may bring a sparkle to your eyes, the word *vacation* makes everyone perk up. And that's basically what a destination wedding is: The best vacation you can imagine in a place you've hand-picked, in the company of your favorite people, filled with events you select and activities you enjoy, and capped by a party that suits your taste, style, and interests.

Pinpointing Destination Wedding Delights

If the 3F's in the previous section don't convince you to apply for a passport (find the lowdown on that in Chapter 11) and start packing, consider the following advantages of having a destination wedding may.

Arousing your adventurous side

Do the two of you like the beach? If you haven't yet tried surfing, water-skiing, or snorkeling, would you like to? Do you strap on ski boots and head for the hills as soon as the first snowflakes drop? Would you relish the idea of horseback riding across rugged terrain? If so, you may want to combine your destination wedding with a fun-packed weekend of adventure.

Couples who welcome new experiences find destination weddings to their liking. The adventure can extend from the location you choose to the places where you hold your ceremony and reception to the activities you select for yourselves and your guests.

Planning an active wedding includes organizing activities, so be sure to choose a destination that offers a lot to do. (You can find location inspiration in Chapter 6.) If you love the outdoors, lead your family and friends down to the beach, aboard a sailing ship, or aloft in a hot-air balloon. Just imagine how extraordinary the photos will be!

Most beach resorts offer instruction and equipment that enable guests to try water sports such as windsurfing, paragliding, and water-skiing as well as snorkeling, scuba diving, canoeing, and kayaking. Depending on the destination and season, on-land adventurers may want to choose a destination that includes horseback riding, hang gliding, zip lining, mountain hiking, biking, golf, tennis, or skiing. And with today's emphasis on wellness, locating a place that offers power walks, yoga, Pilates instruction, and spa treatments isn't difficult.

Combining your wedding and honeymoon

When time and money are important considerations (and when aren't they?), having a destination wedding as a prelude to a honeymoon is one of the most cost-effective planning choices a couple can make.

Whether you're so in love with your destination that you intend to remain there after your guests clear out, or it's the first of one (or multiple) locations you plan to visit on your honeymoon, as Mr. and Mrs. you're already packed and in travel mode. Chapter 18 has specific honeymoon-planning advice.

Sharing the fun with your friends and family

When was the last time you spent a long weekend — not just a quick cup of coffee or a dinner meal — catching up with the people you love most? If the answer is "too long ago" or "I don't remember," a wedding away presents the perfect time to rendezvous.

Combining your wedding with a gathering of family or close college friends in a setting where people are at ease and in a celebratory frame of mind is an event both you and your guests will cherish. And after everyone arrives, group events — picnics, beach parties, hot tubbing, and simply banding together to watch the sunset or the stars come out — make indelible memories.

Earning perks and upgrades because you're in love

If you're planning a wedding or honeymoon, announce it to the world — not simply because everyone loves a lover, but because you're entitled to benefits you may not even know about. These benefits can include VIP treatment at hotels, especially when you can reserve a block of rooms for your guests. In fact, hotels offer perks and upgrades for one smart reason: to build customer loyalty. They want you to come back again for your anniversary, with your kids, and on your next vacation.

Perks start becoming valuable when the length of your stay or the size of your guest list grows. If you can gather ten people or more to take the same flight together, most airlines extend a discounted rate to all. In some cases, they upgrade you from coach to business or first class. Each airline has its own rules. Although you may be able to find the benefits listed on an airline's Web site, you normally have to phone a representative to activate the offer. Turn to Chapter 11 for more about planning group travel and taking advantage of these perks.

Hotels operate in much the same way as airlines when it comes to discounts. If your guests can occupy a minimum of ten rooms, inform the property. Ask for a volume discount so that guests in each room pay less than if they would have booked individually. This price difference could be the deciding factor between a trip that's affordable for a guest and one that isn't.

In addition to a hotel offering a group discount, the management may also be willing to upgrade your quarters to larger ones, throw in a complimentary hospitality suite, or waive the fee for your ceremony space — even if the two of you are traveling alone. In all instances, asking nicely for the added value never hurts.

To receive special treatment, ask about romance packages when you book your room. A hotel that's really on the ball delivers a fruit basket, perhaps sparkling wine, or even strawberries dipped in chocolate to rooms of wedding and honeymoon couples without asking them in advance or charging extra. Some hotels may even surprise you with rose petals on your bed when you return from dinner. To ensure you receive such amenities, you may have to request them in advance and pay an additional fee, though.

Other advantages

In addition to the preceding benefits of a having a wedding away, you can also consider these selling points:

✔ **Saves time:** Many destination weddings are turnkey affairs: You pick a hotel or resort, you connect with the property's free on-site wedding coordinator, and you can set up your entire ceremony, reception, and accommodations via phone or e-mail.

✔ **Obsessive planning not required:** You can pull together a small wedding quickly in plenty of places (including Las Vegas, Hawaii, and the Bahamas).

✔ **Less stress:** If the idea of going from place to place to sample menus and listen to musicians and meet with photographers drives you mad, avoid it by opting for a wedding package where choices are limited and everything is provided.

✔ **Money goes further:** Even after factoring in the cost of airfare and lodging, a destination wedding can be cheaper than one at home.

✔ **Choose your climate:** You can have a sizzling ceremony in January or chill in August; having a perfect wedding is just a matter of picking a place where the weather's fine (turn to Chapter 6 for help on selecting a location).

✔ **Nature does the decorating:** No need to splurge on flowers or other decorations in a gloriously scenic setting.

✔ **Cultural exchange:** A wedding in a different country enables you to integrate local foods, flowers, and customs.

✔ **Mixed-marriage solution:** A civil marriage away from home provides an ideal solution for interfaith couples.

What a Destination Wedding Isn't: The Downsides

Yes, you can find many wonderful reasons to plan a wedding away. But be aware there are negatives, too. Understand both sides before you arrive at a decision. This list includes many of the downsides. Be aware of them before you make your decision about whether a destination wedding is right for you.

✔ **Few familiar touchstones:** Those who've always imagined marrying in their hometown, or carrying flowers from a friend's garden, or even having their hair done by the one stylist who knows how to manage it forfeit the comforts of home.

✔ **Guest expenses:** Weddings away are more costly for wedding-party members and guests to attend than a wedding at home.

✔ **Requires crowd control:** To stay within budget, you may have to trim the size of your guest list (although for some couples, this is a major plus). Guests usually assume the costs of their travel and lodging, but you'll be expected to pick up other expenses — including paying for them at the reception (caterers charge a per-person rate), excursions you organize, and perhaps their rehearsal dinner meal and bar tabs.

✔ **Inconvenience:** Not everyone you want to celebrate with will be willing and able to travel during the time your event is scheduled. A wedding away requires guests to spend more time away from home and work and may conflict with planned vacations or business meetings.

✔ **Long-distance planning:** Even if you make one or more trips to the destination before the wedding, you still need to do a fair amount of planning from home, which can lead to misunderstandings.

✔ **Local marriage laws:** Some municipalities make it simple for nonresident couples to marry. Others require a long residency period or only allow marriages between citizens. Symbolic weddings (see Chapter 6) are one way to overcome this challenge.

Are You a Destination Wedding Kind of Couple? A Checklist

If you haven't already decided whether a destination wedding is right for you, see how many of the following describe you. Answer "yes" to a majority, and you most likely will be happy with a wedding away.

❑ We're on a tight budget.

❑ We like to travel.

❑ We hope to keep our wedding intimate.

❑ We want our wedding to take place in an unusual setting.

❑ We think of ourselves as more casual than formal.

❑ We have friends and family scattered across the country.

❑ We believe that our closest friends and family want to celebrate with us wherever we hold the wedding.

❑ We're willing to have a wedding in a place we haven't visited before or have only seen once or twice.

❏ We aren't control freaks: We realize that we may not be able to manage all the details of a destination wedding as hands-on as we would at one at home.

❏ We appreciate cultural differences.

❏ We want a wedding that enables us to combine our wedding and honeymoon trips or simply start our honeymoon sooner.

❏ We aren't sentimental about the past; we want to create new traditions.

If this checklist clarifies that you're cut out to be a destination wedding type of couple, now the fun really begins. Chapter 6 can help you determine a destination that's right for you.

Dealing with Doubts and Doubters

Even when you're 100 percent convinced that a destination wedding is right, your other half may still be on the fence. He may have a preconceived notion about a destination wedding, or she may not like the idea of getting married in a strange place. Forcing an opinion on someone else is never a good idea, but by understanding the obstacles, you may be able to reach an accord. This section helps you handle a doubter.

When your partner still isn't certain

As couples begin talking about the kind of wedding they want, differences of opinion emerge. That's natural, so don't be surprised if you both don't automatically agree on having a destination wedding. Ultimately, though, both of you must be in agreement about having a wedding away before taking further steps.

If your other half is teetering and not quite sure, discuss both sides and see what elements of a wedding away you can agree upon — consider it good practice for marriage. Another suggestion — which may sound crazy at first — is to switch roles. Have the one who doesn't want the destination wedding provide reasons to do it, and have the destination wedding fan voice all the objections. By articulating one another's concerns, you may both become more aware and more comfortable with whether or not you should embark on a wedding away.

Flying — and those who fear it

You may hear the strongest objections to having a destination wedding from people who resist boarding an airplane. Some may have never flown, while others may have flown and had a bad experience either in the air or delayed at an airport.

Whatever the reason for such feelings, respect them. Travel, even the prospect of it, stresses some people out. Nonetheless, other people's travel trepidations shouldn't deter you from planning a wedding away. When you or your guests truly want to celebrate your marriage away from home, but need some encouragement, these suggestions may help ease the journey:

- ✔ If the bride or groom is afraid, don't select a destination you can only get to by flying — that location isn't for you.

- ✔ Pick a destination that can be reached multiple ways (such as by car, train, private rented van or motor coach, and so on).

- ✔ Call the local airport and ask for a referral to a fear-of-flying desensitization course.

- ✔ Ask a physician to prescribe anti-anxiety medication to take before boarding.

- ✔ Have a drink to relax you before boarding the plane (unless on medication).

- ✔ Choose direct flights whenever possible, so that you'll spend less time in the air and avoid the confusion of switching planes.

- ✔ Fly at off times, including midweek and very early in the day; those times are known to have fewer delays to stress out nervous travelers.

- ✔ Buy a business- or first-class ticket or ask a frequent flyer you know to sell or donate mileage to you in order to get an upgrade. A better seat and more attention from the flight crew can ease your mind.

Is your other half dead set against a destination wedding? Then don't force it. Or if making a nontraditional choice makes either of you uncomfortable, get married at home. Nothing is worse than traveling to a place where you don't want to be — or feeling as if you've dragged the person you love there unwillingly.

Preparing for pushback

Although every couple hopes people will be supportive of their decision to have a wedding away, the idea of traveling a considerable distance for a wedding may alarm some guests. So you may be in for a surprise when you start sharing your intentions with your nearest and dearest.

Will they say you're running away? Maybe. But look at it more like you're running toward something — the start of a life together, doing things your way. In the event you encounter resistance from family and friends and feel you need to defend your decision, Table 2-1 offers guidance and possible solutions.

Table 2-1:	How to Handle Objections
Objection	*Solution*
It will cost too much.	Clue them in: The average hometown wedding costs $25,000+. Modest destination weddings are cheaper. And although the wedding may be inexpensive, the experience will be priceless!
You should get married at home.	Explain that "home" to you is wherever your loved ones gather.
It's too far to go for a wedding! It will be too difficult for some older and physically challenged guests. The wedding date is inconvenient.	Plan a post-wedding celebration at home for those individuals who can't or won't attend.
It's going to cost too much for some people to attend.	Not everyone can make the wedding; if you can afford it, discretely offer to subsidize essential guests.
You can't have a religious ceremony.	Having a religious ceremony may be difficult, but not impossible. Ask local clergy for guidance.
You'll have no privacy with everyone around.	Plan to arrive a few days before guests and then leave for your honeymoon soon after the wedding.
Fewer guests mean fewer gifts.	Politely explain that you aren't getting married for the gifts.
People who aren't invited will be upset.	This problem is the same everywhere; at destination weddings, you can easily justify a smaller guest list. If you like, you can extend an invitation to them to attend your at-home celebration after the real wedding.

Chapter 3

Organizing Your Wedding Away: With and Without a Computer

In This Chapter

▶ Understanding why organization is important

▶ Organizing your destination wedding planning digitally

▶ Working with plans you can hold in your hands

*W*hen you enter the planning stage of a destination wedding, a funny thing happens: The possibility that you actually can pull off this incredible event starts to feel real. It's exciting. Intoxicating. And it can also seem overwhelming.

In addition to all the major decisions an engaged couple needs to make — when to have the wedding, who to invite, what to wear, and so on — you also need to research locations and work out travel plans. That adds a level of complication.

Does that mean you require the global knowledge of a geography teacher, the booking ability of a travel agent, the negotiating skills of a lawyer, and the organizational expertise of an executive assistant to successfully plan an out-of-town wedding? Absolutely not! But it does mean that you need to solicit information, categorize it, and be willing to devote time to evaluating the different options.

Despite the decisions awaiting you, you *can* pull this off — especially if you start by getting organized. The reward will be an event that is beautiful, well-coordinated, and to your taste. This chapter covers the importance of being organized and options to get you there to make your destination wedding everything you wish.

The Importance of Being Organized and Where to Start

Every wedding is the result of hundreds of details and decisions large and small, which can at times challenge the brightest bride's wits and the most buttoned-down groom's memory.

Which place offers a free wedding when you pay for a weeklong honeymoon: Is it in Jamaica . . . or Antigua? Where did I see the ad for those shell-embossed invitations? How much did the musicians say they would charge if we book them for both the rehearsal dinner and the reception?

Questions like these can keep a bride- and groom-to-be awake at nights. But if you get organized at the beginning of the destination wedding planning process, you can access the information when you need it — and sleep more peacefully.

What's the danger of throwing everything you receive into a manila folder or keeping it stacked somewhere at home? Doing so wastes your valuable time when you have to rifle through the same material every instance you need to find something. Worse, data can get misplaced or lost.

To keep your pre-wedding stress to a minimum, commit to keeping all the info you solicit organized. Not only can you find it when you need it, but you also show your spouse-to-be that you're someone who can be counted on to come through with the goods. This section can help you get started.

Leading with your strengths: The division of labor

Which of you should be responsible for doing most of the planning for the destination wedding? Although couples often make the big decisions mutually, someone still has to "keep the books."

One of you may be a natural event planner and know right away how to start organizing your destination wedding. If that's you, go for it. If you're both novice party planners, decide which of you has the most available time, the better organizational ability, and the greatest affinity for the task.

Doing all the organizing yourself or strictly relying on a pro

Invitations! Food! Music! Overnight hotels! Rehearsals! Contracts! Logistics! If the thought of organizing all the details for your destination wedding seems too much to handle, you may want to hire a professional wedding planner. Although you're the ultimate organizer for your wedding, a wedding planner can coordinate the various elements that you want and ensure they operate in harmony.

These individuals, who are experienced in organizing parties, wedding ceremonies, receptions, and travel arrangements, can be found locally where you live, online, and on the ground in the place where you want to hold the wedding. One online resource is www. theweddingexperience.com, a company that specializes in destination weddings and offers a free consultation.

Another option to consider is calling upon a wedding coordinator at a hotel or resort where you'd like to host your event. Services provided by these women (and 99 percent are female) are typically free to customers and extend from the initial planning stage through the expediting of marriage documents all the way to the reception. You can expect a staff planner at these places to present a ready-made menu of choices you can make to personalize your event.

If you do hire a planner, make sure that you feel comfortable with her at your initial meeting and understand the terms of her fee upfront. Part of having a good working relationship includes trusting a planner to understand your taste and the level of involvement you want to have in the decision-making process. (Check out Chapter 5 for how to hire a planner.)

Choosing an organizational system that works for you

Are you someone whose laptop is never far away, and you keep the most important details of your life on it? Or are you more of an I-need-to-see-it-to-believe-it, hold-it-in-my-hands type of info gatherer? Perhaps you're a bit of both. Either way, you need to figure out a method to stay organized that is best for the two of you.

You basically have the following two choices of how to organize your destination wedding:

- ✔ **The digital route:** This method depends on computer-based record-keeping. A digital planner is best if

- You both have personal computers and fast and reliable Internet access.

- You can easily create folders and file documents on a computer.

- You're familiar with and can open common types of files, including documents (.doc), spreadsheets (.xls), music (.mp3), and pictures (.jpg).

✔ **The hard-copy, paper route:** This approach uses an old-fashioned filing system. A paper organizer is best if

- You're both tactile, and you like to see and touch everything, from contracts to invitation copy.

- You don't mind regularly updating a three-ring binder or accordion folder.

- You want to circulate brochures and other documents to family members who aren't computer savvy.

- You like to use a large piece of paper to work out elements like seating charts; it helps you to visualize things.

- You plan to hold on to pieces you receive to create a wedding scrapbook in the future.

Regardless of what route you take, you may still need to use a combination of each. For example, the hotel may e-mail you an invoice, but a local vendor may give you a hard-copy written receipt. You need to organize some info in your computer and some in a paper organizer. Just remember to cross-reference when you file something in each format.

Decide early on in what format you primarily want to collect destination wedding information. That way you have time to establish a system before the flow of info turns into a deluge — and you know just where to file it after it starts to spill into your real or electronic mailbox.

To determine whether you ought to rely more heavily on digital or manual organizing, ask yourself the following questions:

✔ **What will be the easiest way to share info with my partner and provide a way for him or her to add to and comment on it?** Make this decision together. It's good practice for marriage!

✔ **Do we see each other almost every day?** If so, then either system will work for you. If not, and you're both online, go the digital route.

✔ **Are my partner and I most likely to call, e-mail, text, or send an instant message when we have something to tell each**

other? If you prefer the electronic methods of communication, go digital. Otherwise you'll be more comfortable establishing a paper trail.

The bottom line: Whether you decide to coordinate your wedding primarily on your computer or in a paper planner, stay organized. The rest of this chapter looks more specifically at these two options to help you keep track of your destination wedding.

Love in the Computer Age: Digitally Organizing

According to a recent statistic, more than three-quarters of couples research their wedding online. So if you're a tech-savvy duo about to plan a destination wedding, you already know that a personal computer can be your best tool and the Internet your best resource. This section focuses on steps to organize your wedding digitally, including setting up and keeping track of all the details on your personal computer and using the Web to research your wedding.

If you're not ready to go digital, don't despair. You have ways to get around that and still harness the power of the Web to help you find potential vendors and locations. Check out "Organizing Your Wedding with a Paper Trail," later in this chapter for more info.

Create a destination wedding folder

To begin digitally organizing, you must first designate a central place where you can keep all the important info. The best place for you to keep any wedding info is in a new destination wedding folder that you create on your (or your partner's) computer or online.

One program that helps you manage your info is Microsoft Excel. This powerful spreadsheet program can help you to organize wedding planning, maintain your budget, keep an eye on your invitation list and record RSVPs, and compare offerings from a variety of vendors. (Check out Chapter 4 for more on how you can use Excel to track key info, including your budget.) If you're somewhat familiar with Excel but just need a refresher, check out http://spreadsheets.about.com, which offers free tutorials and inspiration for different ways to slice and dice your data. These sections outline where and how to set up your wedding folder.

Getting an e-mail account just for wedding details

Changing your e-mail address before the wedding — at least when using it for wedding-related communications — is a good idea. As an engaged couple, you're a prime target for vendors eager to sell you everything from attendants' gifts to xylophone rentals. Every time you sign up for something or request information, your e-mail address may be compiled on a list, sold to others, and soon you may be deluged with unsolicited pitches.

So instead of cluttering up your regular e-mail address, get a new one. Free e-mail accounts are available from Yahoo!, MSN (Hotmail), Google, and AOL. Just remember to check yours regularly after you set it up and save important e-mails in the proper folder (see the section "Create a destination wedding folder"). After the wedding, you can decide to keep or abandon the account, depending on whether or not spammers are targeting it.

Keep your info on your personal computer

If you each have your own computer, you can store and send files online (see the next section). If you're not comfortable doing that, get a *portable flash drive* (a small, inexpensive extra storage device you can plug into any computer's USB port). You can copy the entire destination wedding folder or just selected folders onto it, and pass the drive back and forth.

Don't risk losing hours of research and important contacts. Back up your destination wedding folder to a CD or a portable flash drive on a regular basis; don't depend on a backup copy on the personal computer where the original folder lives. The only crashing you want to do is when the wedding is over!

Store files online

You can share files by storing them online so that they're accessible at any time by either one of you. Here are some ways that your entire wedding folder can live in cyberspace and you can jointly access it from any location:

- ✔ If you have an Apple computer, you can sign up and pay for a Mac account (www.apple.com/dotmac). You can use this account to transfer, open, work on, and retrieve files online.

- ✔ PC users can take advantage of www.youos.com, which is a free file-sharing site.

✔ On www.foldershare.com, users of both Mac and PC operating systems can view the same personal info from two different online locations.

Organize your folders and files

Even before you have information to file away, you ought to set up subcategories within your destination wedding folder. That way, you can house all your information logically and thematically. For example, you can place all your top picks for wedding ceremony sites in a Potential Destinations folder, put spreadsheets in a Budget folder, and so on.

Create as many folders as you like. Figure 3-1 shows what your folders and files can look like after you label them.

Folders can hold every kind of file you receive. In this multimedia world, you can view JPEGs of locations, choose music based on MP3s, and watch a digital video of another couple's wedding. You can then save and store these files in folders along with important e-mails, Web pages, Word documents, and other digital files.

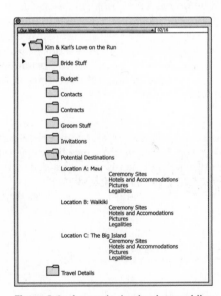

Figure 3-1: A sample destination wedding folder setup.

At any point, add new folders and subfolders as needed. Just don't throw anything important out. Instead, create a new folder for it — call it *Discards* — and store unwanted files there instead. You never know when you're going to want to go back and re-examine something you found weeks earlier.

Surfer beware

When you're using the Web to organize your wedding, approach what you find with a degree of healthy skepticism. Commercial Web sites that promote wedding locations and services are designed to appear tantalizing and generate sales. You mean big business to them!

One of the best ways to find out what a place is really like is by reading up on it at an opinions Web site. For hotel-related information, www.tripadvisor.com is my favorite because previous guests post firsthand reviews, positive and negative. By skimming a variety of posts, you can get a more accurate picture of a property than you would in a brochure prepared by the hotel.

Use the Web to your advantage

Connecting to the Internet is one of the best things about having a computer at your fingertips. For a couple who has decided to wed far from home, you have no easier means than Web-surfing to locate potential vendors and places for your event.

By being as specific as possible, you can get to information you want more quickly, and you aren't plagued by the prospect of having to choose from millions of potential Web sites whose legitimacy can't be proven until verified. (Check out the nearby sidebar, "Surfer beware," for more info.)

For example, searches on Google and Yahoo! can bring a world of possibilities to your desktop. When you're searching, try to narrow down the search by adding specific keywords. For example, if I searched with the keywords *sarasota florida wedding,* Google reduced the possibilities to a still-overwhelming 1,290,000 pages. But *sarasota florida wedding florist affordable boutonnière* found only 126 pages.

Bookmark Web pages

Whenever you come across a Web site that has info you think you can use, bookmark it. Perhaps you find the homepage of a destination wedding planner, or the specific marriage requirements of a country you hope to marry in, or a bridesmaid gown you want your attendants to view. When you have the Web page stored, you can access it at will.

You can bookmark a Web page in the following ways:

✔ **Use your browser.** Make a new bookmark folder called *Wedding*. If you don't know how to do this, use the Help menu in Internet Explorer, Safari, Firefox, or whichever browser you use and search for "add bookmark folder" to get instructions. File the bookmarked page in a Wedding folder in your browser. You can make subfolders for additional topics within the Wedding folder as needed.

Bookmarks only exist on the computer where they're created. You can't access your bookmarks from your partner's computer if the bookmarked site is only on your computer. But copying the URL and e-mailing it to your partner is easy enough.

✔ **Save the Web page in your desktop Wedding folder.** Doing so allows you to download the full contents of a page. However, a URL may disappear or become garbled, and the Web page only exists on the computer where it's saved.

To save a Web page into your folder, Go to File ➪ Save As, navigate to your Wedding folder, and send to the appropriate subfolder.

✔ **Use a social bookmarking site.** A social bookmarking site, which is a free service for storing, sharing, and discovering Web bookmarks online, is what I recommend because it lets you view pages from any computer. By using the search box on the bookmarking site, you also have the opportunity to discover related Web sites real people find valuable.

The most popular social bookmarking site is del.icio.us, (pronounced "delicious"). To use this site, do the following:

1. **Go to `http://del.icio.us` and use the prompts to set up a free account.**

2. **Follow directions to install the Post to Delicious and My Delicious buttons on your browser.**

3. **When you find a Web page worth saving, click on Post to Delicious.**

4. **Use the tags Delicious recommends or tag the page with your own keywords, such as *Wedding Invitations Themes*.**

Del.icio.us stores all your bookmarked URLs. You can access your bookmarks from any computer, anywhere. Just be sure to share your username and password with your partner. Also, save newspaper articles, which tend to expire, as Web-page files rather than on del.icio.us. (I learned this the hard way.)

Establish your own destination wedding Web site

One of the most creative and memorable ways to start things off with a splash — to say to family and friends "this is going to be a wedding you won't want to miss!" is to create your own destination wedding Web site (also known as a *wedsite*).

Having your own wedsite is an efficient way to communicate information about the event to friends and family. They may have a million questions — when and where is it taking place? Who else is coming? How do we get there? What should we pack?

You can anticipate those questions and answer them for one and all on your own wedsite that reflects your personalities. After your site is live, you can send a mass e-mail to notify family and friends to visit and then again when you post important updates. If you're interested in a destination wedding Web site, this section looks at the three ways to create one.

Buy a domain

You can actually buy a specific *domain name,* a Web address or URL, such as susanandvince.com. Having your own domain allows you to emphasize your identity as a couple and show off your personal style. The site can be as simple or as complex as you want. You can also restrict access to the site to people you know by requiring a password to enter.

Buying the domain does have its disadvantages. It can be expensive and the setup can be time consuming. Furthermore, you need some knowledge of Web design and HTML coding.

However, if you're interested in purchasing a domain and setting up your own destination wedsite, you can do the following:

1. **Choose a unique name (URL) for your site (sorry, "ourdestinationwedding.com" is already taken) and register it with an online registrar.**

   Although many online companies sell domain names, the most established place to register is www.network solutions.com. Any domain registrar can tell you whether the name you want is available and offer alternatives if it isn't. After you have a name for your Web site — and you find that it is available — you can buy it immediately.

Just for fun, Google your names — such as "jenandmike" or "lindaandpaul." Chances are some creative couple already has the URL, but you can always swipe ideas from them.

2. **Find a company to host your domain.**

   Your Web site will need a place to live online. That's its *domain.* Network Solutions offers that service, but I prefer www.earthlink.net because it has tools and templates that can make the site-building process simpler. Another popular low-cost hosting service is www.godaddy.com.

3. **Choose domain options that meet your destination wedsite needs.**

   Other services that you can choose include multiple e-mail accounts and design help.

Sign up with a wedding Web-site provider

Couples who don't want to devote time to Web-page design and all the techy stuff required to develop their own wedding domain can still have a great-looking wedsite. Numerous online companies allow you to use their tools and bandwidth to make a site.

Signing up with a wedding Web-site provider is easy. Just follow the directions on the site. Most provide thorough step-by-step directions to help you customize your own Web site. You can take advantage of different tools, including online RSVPs, e-mail newsletters, and registry links. To protect your privacy, most require that your guests use a password to access the site.

A wedding Web-site provider isn't for everyone, though. Pages from bridal sites tend to have a cookie-cutter look, so take time to personalize yours with rich details and photos. Also, expect to receive numerous upsell e-mails from the host. Some charge a fee.

The following are among the best-known and most-reliable companies where you can sign up for a wedding Web site:

✔ www.weddingwindow.com

✔ www.theknot.com

✔ www.brides.com

✔ www.blueskiesanddaisies.com

✔ www.ewedding.com

✔ www.weddingsolutions.com

Create a wedding blog

A *blog,* also known as a *web log,* is a personal online journal similar to a diary that you share with the world. You can create a blog with the specific objective of sharing your thoughts and plans about your upcoming destination wedding with friends and family. Keep in mind that a blog is only as good as you make it. If you don't have the time to regularly update it, your blog will appear stale.

To set up a blog, follow the directions on the blog setup site. Many blog setup sites are easy to use and allow you to embed links and RSS feeds to related sites. (An *RSS feed* is like a news bulletin from another Web site that automatically updates itself when new content is posted.)

My personal favorite site for creating a blog is `www.blogger.com` because the service is free and easy to use. And check out `www.weddingbee.com` and `http://manolobrides.com` as examples of wedding blogs to get a feel for what they look like and how they work.

What to include on your wedsite

Whether you set up a unique Web domain, use a wedding Web-site provider, or create a blog, provide your guests with the essential info they need. Use your wedding Web site to announce the good news and post details of the upcoming event. The following are some topics you may want to cover:

- ✔ Save the date
- ✔ How we met
- ✔ Photo gallery
- ✔ The proposal
- ✔ Our wedding
- ✔ Date and location
- ✔ Attendants' photos with IDs
- ✔ Guests' travel information
- ✔ Getting there
  - Maps and directions
  - Places to stay
  - Car rental info
  - What to see and do in. . .
- ✔ Destination wedding schedule (check out Figure 3-2 for an example of a schedule)

Schedule of Events   **Trish and Jon's Wedding**
                            Welcome to Puerto Rico

Thursday

	Trish & Jon arrive
	Best man, maid of honor arrive
	Parents arrive
	Early guests arrive
6:00	Meet on Su Casa terrace for drinks
7:00	Join us for the rehearsal dinner inside Su Casa

Friday

8:00	Optional: Morning yoga session on beach
noon - 5pm:	Guests arrive
2:00 - 4:00	Optional: Join us at watersports center for windsurfing lessons and practice
7:00	Meet for cocktails at the pool house
8:00	Dinner beach barbecue
9:30 - ?	Optional: Texas Hold'em lesson and game in casino

Saturday

8:00 - 10:00	Buffet breakfast
11:00 - 1:00	Optional choice of bridal spa or beach volleyball
2:00 - 4:00	Optional choice of van shopping tour of downtown or scuba excursion
5:30	Meet for cocktails on Reef Terrace
6:30	Sunset wedding ceremony at South Gazebo
7:15	Reception dinner at Redmond's

Sunday

8:00 - 10:00	Morning-after breakfast
11:00	Checkout
Noon	Complimentary airport van departs

Figure 3-2: A sample destination wedding schedule.

✔ RSVP (plus a confirmation thank-you message)

✔ Gift registry

✔ Guest comments

✔ The honeymoon

✔ Contact us

In addition to content you create on your own, include links to other sites that your guests may find useful, such as www.trip advisor.com to provide guests with a list of hotels rated by travelers. There are also many useful local sites, such as www.vegas.com, which provides Vegas-bound guests with information on shows and buying tickets online.

Join the conversation

As you start making wedding plans, many questions arise. Often there's nothing better than talking to another bride-to-be or groom-to-be — to get recommendations, to help you weigh the pros and cons of a decision, or simply to send some empathy your way. The following are different ways you can converse with others.

Meet destination couples online

One of the best places to go for answers, support, and ideas are free online forums. A *forum* is a bulletin board where you can ask and answer questions. You won't necessarily get a response the same day, but if the board is active, you will get feedback.

My two recommended forums are on www.brides.com and www.theknot.com because both have separate areas devoted to destination wedding discussions. You can also go outside those areas, of course, to get info on topics of interest to all couples ranging from food and drinks to honeymoon plans.

As with all forums, lurking for a while is smart. If you have a particular question, use the search box to see whether it's already been answered. If not, register for permission to post, and put your message up on the board.

Send group e-mails to friends and family

Are you having a big wedding with lots of attendants, or want to keep a certain circle in the loop? Then create a group in your e-mail account in order to (judiciously) send mass e-mails. (That way, you don't have to waste time typing in every single person's e-mail address every time you send an e-mail.)

For example, you can send a group e-mail that reads like this:

Hi everyone.

I never thought so many of our friends would agree to join us for our wedding in Mexico. Tom and I are so thrilled that we aren't going to be entering Mexico — or our marriage — alone. Because there are plenty of details involved and I know you'll need to work out your schedule to make celebrating with us possible, I'm starting this wedding e-mail group to keep you updated. Feel free to ask me any questions by just hitting "reply"; if it's something for the group to know or discuss, hit "reply all." And to prove that I'm not turning into a bridezilla, you can unsubscribe from this list at any time. You'll still be welcome at the wedding.

Love,

Stacy (and Tim)

To set up a group, use the Help menu in your e-mail program. After you've created and named the group, drag or enter the e-mail addresses of everyone you want onto the list. Then save it. Whenever you want to contact the group, simply type in the group's name in the To: box and the e-mail goes to the entire group.

When you send your first e-mail to the group list, introduce it, tell your gang what to expect, and let people know how to unsubscribe if they wish. Encourage recipients to reply with questions and comments about the upcoming event.

Chat with friends and family

Don't save all the good news for the wedding day: On the Web, you can chat with those who enthusiastically want to anticipate and help plan the event along with you.

To schedule an online chat with Web-savvy guests, pick a mutually convenient day and time and invite list members to attend. During the chat, your guests can ask you any questions they have, and you can let everyone know the answers, all at one time.

AOL introduced instant messaging and anyone can register for a free account and use this service. Yahoo! Messenger offers similar functionality. Whichever you use, you can continue to e-mail during the chat, even sending images for everyone to see and comment on.

Using the Web When You Don't Have a Computer

The Web is a truly invaluable resource for planning a wedding in a distant location. Even if you don't have a computer of your own, you can still do online research and send e-mail by accessing a computer in the following locations:

✔ **Visit the library.** Just about every library has at least one public computer available. If you live in that municipality, you usually qualify for a library card, which allows you free access to the library's computers.

✔ **Log on at an Internet cafe.** Usage fees are typically calculated by the minute, but you often can buy a block of time to save money.

✔ **Borrow a buddy's computer.** Your friend may be willing to let you surf the Web when he or she isn't using the computer.

✔ **Go to a 24-hour FedExKinko's.** Locations that are open around the clock have Windows and Macintosh workstations with Internet access that you can rent and use on the premises.

✔ **Use your work computer.** Many companies may frown upon using your work computer for personal use, but face it, most people do it. Web-surfing a few minutes a day during your break time usually isn't a problem. (Ask your boss if you're concerned.)

Because you can't bookmark important sites on someone else's computer, print out Web pages you need when you come across them and file them later in your paper organizer.

Organizing Your Wedding with a Paper Trail

Something about using the old-fashioned method of keeping wedding materials in a paper file is still satisfying. Whenever you want, you can pull out what you need and compare photographs, contracts, and other printed material side by side.

In every bookstore's Weddings section, you can find a shelf filled with a variety of organizers you can buy. Some are elaborate, ribbon-tied affairs as thick as the Manhattan phone book. Some open to a giant tabbed accordion folder. Others are notebooks where you can write in information. Still others are three-ring binders that you can add to as your data pile grows. This section can help you organize with a paper trail.

Customizing a paper wedding planner

Because your wedding isn't that different from a hometown wedding in that you still need to choose a dress, invitations, flowers, food, photography and all the other elements that differentiate a wedding from, say, a NASCAR race, I'll leave it to the paper wedding planner you select to help maintain organization in those areas.

Most store-bought wedding organizers are missing one critical category: Travel! Even those that allow a few pages for honeymoon details aren't built to accommodate the bulk of info a destination wedding couple is going to amass. So if you opt for a paper organizer, choose an expandable three-ring binder model. You can pick up extra dividers, tabs, and pages with pockets to insert in the book. And don't hesitate to throw away any preprinted topic you don't need; your book will fill up with necessary info soon enough.

To start, I suggest you add these main folders to a standard ring-binder wedding organizer to transform it into a unit that is destination wedding friendly:

✔ **Transportation:** Whether you and your guests travel by plane, train, or automobile, you need to keep schedules, tickets, and transportation resources together in this section.

✔ **Ceremony:** Use this folder to hold info that you gather on potential sites, officiants, and decorations.

✔ **Rentals:** If you're doing it yourself, or at least partly, keep tabs on where to get tables, chairs, tenting, and so on here.

✔ **Reception options:** You may end up having the ceremony and reception in the same place. If not, stash reception data — including locations, caterers, food and drink menus, and wedding cake ideas — in this section.

✔ **Accommodations:** Where will you, your wedding party, and your guests stay overnight? Keep all the possibilities under one roof here.

✔ **Weekend plans:** Setting the agenda is up to you. Do you need to arrange for a rehearsal, rehearsal dinner, and optional excursions from the destination? File ideas and plans here. You can also keep track of items you want to include in guests' welcome bags, make notes for a printed weekend agenda, and stash tearsheets from magazines that inspire you.

The larger your destination wedding, the more details you have to manage and coordinate. As each travel folder grows, subdivide it as needed so that you remain well organized.

Keep business cards you collect in one place: A vinyl pencil pouch in the front of your wedding organizer can be a safe place to save them; you can also buy dedicated business-card holders made for binders.

Making your own destination wedding organizer

Because you need to customize any store-bought wedding organizer to meet your destination wedding planning needs, does it make more sense to simply create your own? That's entirely up to you. Keep in mind that any money you save can go into creating an organizer better suited to your needs and style.

To do so, head to the office supply store, pick up a sturdy three-ring binder, a three-hole punch, a package of dividers, and manila folders slightly smaller than the binder. You can cut off the tops of those folders and hole-punch them to create usable pockets. Label each section accordingly and use the dividers for different sections.

To keep your homemade destination wedding organizer from looking like a high school notebook, do a little decorating at the start. Here are some fun and inexpensive ideas to dress it up:

- ✔ **Wrap it:** Buy some pretty wedding wrapping paper and cover the front and back of the binder with it. Laminate the paper with plastic film to keep it from getting dirty or fraying.

- ✔ **Decoupage it:** Soon enough, you'll be inundated with travel brochures. Instead of throwing out the ones you don't want, cut out pictures that appeal and decoupage them to the cover.

- ✔ **Scrapbook it:** Your local craft store is likely to have an aisle with scrapbook supplies that you can adapt to your planning needs. In addition to finding background sheets that you can use to staple receipts and other small pieces of paper onto, wedding-themed stickers, and even rubber stamps, you can purchase quality three-ring scrapbook binders that outclass standard ones. And after the wedding, you'll be ahead of the game in creating a book of memories.

If you go the all-paper route, you need to keep guests in the loop as your plans evolve. See Chapter 12 for info on creating timely save-the-dates, invitations, and wedding newsletters.

Chapter 4

Budgeting for a Destination Wedding

In This Chapter

▶ Considering why and how to construct a budget

▶ Knowing who pays and finding the funds you need

▶ Comparing prices and negotiating costs with vendors

▶ Staying within your means versus going for broke

*A*nyone who plans a wedding is bound to come across "The Number" sooner or later. In case you've started here, I provide it: The average cost of a wedding in the United States today is in excess of $25,000 dollars. That's a lot of money — especially for an event that's over before you have a chance to sit down, catch your breath, and savor a piece of your own wedding cake.

When you realize that you could have a destination wedding that lasts days rather than hours for less than that amount, the notion of getting on a plane and traveling to a gorgeous location becomes even more appealing. In fact, you may very likely save money by leaving home. If you marry at an all-inclusive resort or on a cruise, for example, you aren't charged for the ceremony location and you probably won't need rental equipment. And the bouquet, cake, and other extras may be included in one reasonably priced package.

Even though a destination wedding package may be less expensive than if you paid for a wedding and all the accoutrements at home, you still need to have a good grasp on how much you plan to spend. This chapter helps you develop a budget for your destination wedding and then stick to it.

Understanding Budgeting Basics (And Why They're Vital)

Unless you have unlimited funds or simply plan to charge everything and ignore the damages until your credit card bills come in (not a good idea!), having a budget number in mind for the maximum amount you can afford to spend on your wedding is wise. You don't want to be surprised — and you don't want to start your marriage off deeply in debt, either. This section discusses how budgeting can differ between the two types of weddings and what you need to do to budget.

How budgeting differs: A destination wedding versus a traditional one

Although no two weddings are alike and only you can decide what you can afford to spend based on your own current financial situation, the way you budget for a destination wedding does differ slightly from a traditional wedding. (To get a feel for what a typical wedding would cost where you live, type your zip code into the calculator at www.costofwedding.com.)

As with any wedding, you have certain basic and unavoidable costs: The marriage license, officiant's fee, and wedding rings are all necessary expenses. What a destination wedding adds to the mix is the cost of transportation and lodging. The good news is that most destination weddings still cost less than that daunting $25,000-or-more figure. So whether you opt for a turnkey event or one that's a more complex production, you can likely have a wedding you want, where you want, and at a price you can afford.

Knowing how much to budget

So how can you determine what you can afford and how much you want to budget for your destination wedding? These suggestions can help make the process easier:

- ✔ **Spend time researching real-world prices.** Doing so helps you to know how much to apportion to individual elements or in total. Make sure you take into consideration costs for items at your destination. (For example, a bunch of roses may cost only $20 at the local florist, but flying them to your destination and having them arranged can cost ten times as much.)

✔ **Discuss what's most important to you.** Is it having a drop-dead gorgeous designer wedding gown? As many friends and family as possible in attendance? A four- or five-star hotel for the reception and overnights? In advance of obtaining actual estimates, prioritize how you'll spend your budget.

Having a budget instills a kind of discipline that forces you to conserve funds in one area if you want to indulge in another. After you begin to get an idea of current prices, you can then decide what the most important elements are and look for ways to scale back on others.

✔ **Determine which costs are essential and where you can cut corners.** With a destination wedding, travel and lodging can take up a big chunk of your budget. As a result, you may need to rejigger what you spend on other aspects of the wedding. For example, in a hometown wedding, the reception itself typically eats up 50 percent of the budget. Then flowers, fashion, photography, and music each account for approximately 10 percent of the total, leaving the remainder for stationery and miscellaneous expenses.

You need to add a few more slices to the budget pie to account for what you spend on transportation, lodging, and perhaps the fee to rent and set up your ceremony space — and that means the existing slices will have to shrink as a percentage of your total budget.

Having a Wedding at Any Cost

The type of destination wedding you choose reflects not only your budget but also your taste. Throughout the process, keep sight of the fact that you control the purse strings and are the ones who can best decide whether you're most comfortable making modest choices or spending lavishly.

Whatever your final bill adds up to, the experience and memories of your wedding are likely to be priceless. If you find yourselves stuck and wondering how you can afford the wedding you want, consider contacting a financial planner or wedding consultant for advice. You can find out more about services in Chapter 5.

I believe that you can have a destination wedding just about anywhere you want that can still fit within your budget; it's just a matter of determining what your spending priorities are and pulling together resources at price points you're comfortable with. Table 4-1 shows you how costs can significantly vary, even at the same location (in this case, Las Vegas).

Table 4-1: **Low-Cost versus High-Roller Las Vegas Weddings**

Item	Low Cost	High Roller
Marriage license fee	$55	$55
Bride's dress	Rental gown from Loveland Wedding Chapel: $150	Lace gown by Monique Lhuillier from Kleinfeld: $4,620
Bride's shoes	Sequined flip-flops from eBay, with shipping: $16	Manolo Blahnik satin slingbacks from Neiman Marcus, Las Vegas Fashion Show Mall: $495
Groom's attire	Jerry's Tux Shop, Las Vegas: $50	Ermenegildo Zegna classic tuxedo from Neiman Marcus, Las Vegas Fashion Show Mall: $2,050
Wedding rings	His and her 14k gold Comfort Fit bands from Las Vegas Costco: $293	Two Lucida diamond band rings from Tiffany & Co.: $20,700
Airfare for two people	Nonstop roundtrip coach class from Chicago: $404	Nonstop roundtrip first class from Chicago: $2,496
Wedding package	All-inclusive package from A Las Vegas Wedding Chapel: $269	Cosa Bella Package: $15,000 (includes two nights in penthouse suite)
Three nights accommodations	Golden Nugget: $308	Bellagio: $700 (for third night in the penthouse suite)
Transportation to and from McCarran Airport	The Catride municipal bus for two: $5	Stretch limo: $92
Post-wedding excursion	Hoover Dam Bus Tour for two: $52	VIP Champagne Helicopter Flight over the Grand Canyon for two: $918
TOTAL:	$1,602	$47,864

All prices are approximate and were accurate at the time of writing. Meals, taxes, tips, incidentals, and gambling are additional.

Chipping In for a Destination Wedding

One of the earliest discussions to have regarding the wedding is about who's footing the bill. Unlike traditional at-home weddings, where parents typically play a large part, the couple usually picks up much, if not all, of the tab at destination weddings. And that's a good thing, because whoever controls the purse strings controls the wedding to a significant degree.

Figuring out who pays for what during a destination wedding can be a touchy issue, but it doesn't have to be. You may be wondering: How much money do you need upfront? Do guests pay their own way? This section helps you understand these financial issues without much discomfort.

Finding ways to cover costs

Not many couples have thousands of dollars lying around to fund a destination wedding. The money has to come from somewhere. If your lottery tickets don't pay off, expect to draw on these sources:

✔ **Savings:** After you get engaged, establish joint checking and savings accounts so you can both access them to pay upcoming wedding expenses.

If your wedding date is far enough away, consider having a set amount automatically deducted from your paychecks each month and diverted into a new joint account.

✔ **Loan:** No collateral is necessary for you to get an unsecured loan or line of credit from a bank. However, going into debt at a high rate of interest for the wedding isn't worth it if you anticipate struggling to pay the loan off.

✔ **Credit cards:** Get a set of credit cards you can both use to pay wedding expenses. When making payments, using credit cards is preferable to writing checks because cards provide a third party to take a dispute to should trouble arise with a vendor.

✔ **Parents:** A destination wedding is unlike an at-home one, where parents' friends and business associates are typically invited — so they may be less eager to fund your event. Depending on your relationship with them, though, it's worth having a conversation to ask them if they're willing to contribute or float you a loan.

Keeping tabs on guests

Regardless of who pays for the ceremony and reception, guests and attendants at a destination wedding are responsible for their own room and transportation expenses.

That doesn't leave you off the hook entirely, though. As soon as you look into the costs of a destination wedding, you find many more budget items than plane tickets, lodging, a ceremony, and a reception to consider. You, rather than your guests, are expected to pay for the extras, so be sure to factor them into your budget:

- ✔ **Adding on events or gifts:** Gracious touches that make a destination wedding more memorable for everyone involved can include a welcome or rehearsal dinner, a fun attendants' event, a generous welcome goody bag, group tours or activities, and a farewell brunch. But be prepared to cover the costs of these yourselves.

- ✔ **Lending a helping hand:** Another expense to consider is subsidized travel. Do you have a friend or family member you want at your wedding who can't swing the cost? If you can afford to pay their way, discreetly offer to do so. (See Chapter 18 for how to let your guests know who pays for what, so that any unapproved guest expenses don't appear on your bill.)

Knowing What to Include in Your Budget

During the budgeting process, you may start to wish you'd taken accounting courses in school (or paid more attention if you did). Actually, if your eyes glaze over at the sight of numbers, you ought to involve someone who's good with them to guide you through this part. This section helps you keep your budget info organized with a spreadsheet. It also discusses how you gather bids for different items and what you need to know when you price different elements.

You can create a spreadsheet in Excel (refer to Figure 4-1) to help identify potential costs. Because prices vary widely from place to taste, only you can determine the correct amount to allot.

When you make your own spreadsheet, feel free to use Figure 4-1 as an example to adapt for your own needs. To create and customize your own spreadsheet, follow these steps:

1. **Open a new spreadsheet.**

2. **Save your spreadsheet as "Wedding Budget" to your destination wedding file folder, but keep it open so you can set up your budget worksheet.**

3. **Add as many rows as you need with all the potential expenses.**

   In Figure 4-1, my list of expenses takes into account every major possible expense; don't let it overwhelm you because it's unlikely you'll need them all. The spreadsheet is simply a guide, and perhaps many of the items listed aren't necessary for your own wedding. So add and delete items as needed.

4. **Label the first column following each item "guesstimate."**

   A *guesstimate* is where you write down what you hope to spend. Coming up with these initial cost estimates can help to clarify where you want your dollars to go and what you imagine you can spend on the different elements — but don't count on the real costs matching. Until you start speaking to vendors and can insert actual estimates into the next column, you can't have a reliable idea of what the wedding will cost.

5. **Label the second column "vendor estimate."**

   Vendors' prices invariably exceed expectations. Even then, you may want to add a 10-percent cushion that allows for tax and overages.

   As you begin communicating with vendors and receiving bids, insert actual estimates into the second column. You can add additional columns to keep track of details such as your contact person for each item, when the contract is signed and mailed, the agreed-upon time for delivery or arrival, and so forth.

6. **Label the third column "actual cost."**

   This column is something you won't be able to total until after the wedding.

   After you return home, compare the real costs to the estimates. If it turns out that you're within 10 percent, congratulate yourselves for sticking to your budget.

You also may want to add or create a separate spreadsheet to track deposits that you make, balances, due dates for final payments, and other expenditures. If you don't like the spreadsheet format, use a table in Word, a blank budgeting book, or another record-keeping method that is more comfortable for you. The important thing is to watch the bottom line so you can avoid overstepping it.

Figure 4-1: Create a sample destination wedding spreadsheet in Excel.

Bidding and Buying

Requesting bids from at least three vendors before selecting one is a standard practice in the world of business and is a smart policy for a couple who is organizing a destination wedding without the help of a coordinator or consultant to assume this task.

So that you have a solid basis of comparison, send out the same request for a proposal to each vendor in a category. Provide as much information as you have, such as the time and location where you require delivery and make yourself available for follow-up questions (which are always a good sign that someone truly wants your business and is paying attention).

For example, suppose that you're requesting bids for a cake. Let potential vendors know what flavor, filling, and icing you want and how many people it will need to feed. Tell them whether there's a special theme or colors you have in mind and whether you want them to supply a topper and cake stand. Send a picture of a sample if you have one.

Pricing the elements

As bids come in, the range of prices you encounter may vary widely and the features may not be identical, so you need to closely examine and compare what each vendor offers. During your review, double-check what vendors offer. If a vendor offers something different than another vendor, ask why she's suggesting it.

Although you may not think that you need an element that a vendor recommends, the vendor knows the destination. And in the long run, it may enhance the day or weekend. For example, having chilled water bottles available for guests at your ceremony site in the Caribbean may not have occurred to you, but an experienced vendor knows thirsty guests will appreciate it.

If one vendor has added on extras that you simply don't want, ask her to reprice the bid without the frills. When you have everything in hand, compare bids side by side and weigh the options you do want. Be sure to check out the next section on negotiating.

Negotiating wisely

Negotiating during the bidding process is important because you don't want to pay more than you have to, and some vendors gross up their estimate because they assume you'll ask for a discount.

Keep a couple things in mind as you navigate the bidding and purchasing process:

✔ **You may have stars in your eyes, but vendors always see dollar signs.** In the United States alone, weddings represent a $50 billion annual for-profit industry. All those people whose talents come into play to help you pull off an extraordinary event expect to be paid — and the more, the better, as far as they're concerned. So no matter how much vendors feed your fantasy or pressure you, remember the bottom line and don't get suckered into paying for more than you want.

✔ **Everything is negotiable.** Because the wedding business is so lucrative, it's also very competitive. So consider the initial estimates you receive simply as starting points in negotiations. Don't be afraid to nicely ask early on, "Can you do a little bit better on the price?" More often than not, a vendor responds affirmatively.

✔ **Ask for everything in writing.** Be sure that every vendor writes down his offer, including refund and cancellation policies, because in a dispute you'll need to produce the specifics.

You can read more about dealing with vendors in Chapter 5.

Cutting costs

How much you spend on the individual parts of the wedding is entirely up to you. If you start to feel as if you can't negotiate or control costs, take a deep breath. Walk away from the situation briefly and gather your thoughts. Minor changes in plans can have a major effect on reducing the bottom line. (You can also check out Chapter 12 for more on all of these topics in this section.)

The cost of every element in a destination wedding can be adjusted up or down. For example, you may have to change vendors, or turn to family or friends to lend a hand, or forego an inessential, but never forget that you hold the power and the purse strings. The following shows how you can save money on major expenses.

Stationery

When you realize how many items accompany announcing, inviting, informing, and directing people to your wedding, you may feel as if you're about to generate more paper than an unabridged edition of *War and Peace.* Communications are essential, though, especially for a destination wedding. Yes, you can easily spend hundreds of dollars on an expensive printer to produce all your stationery. Or you can save lots of money and do much of the work on your own.

For example, if you're creative and have the time or a talented friend who's willing to help you out, make your own invitations. Many office supply stores sell blank wedding invitations that you can simply run through a computer printer. You can also create your own newsletter in a predesigned template in a word-processing program and print out hard copies or e-mail it to guests.

Flowers

Destination wedding couples have tons of options when buying flowers. Unfortunately, live flowers can be very expensive. If you're looking to save some money and stay within your floral budget while still having a beautiful and colorful ceremony, consider the following suggestions:

- ✔ **If your wedding is set in a scenic location, such as a gazebo overlooking the ocean, adding foliage is unnecessary.** Rely on the natural beauty around you to "decorate" your wedding.

- ✔ **Forego bouquets for the attendants or corsages for the mothers.** Although it's traditional for the bride to carry a bouquet (because it gives her something to do with nervous hands) and the groom to don a boutonniere, if you're looking to save money, ask yourself if these others really need flowers.

- ✔ **Choose in-season, locally grown live flowers.** These flowers are cheaper because you don't have to pay to import them.

Music

Before and after the ceremony and at the reception, music enhances the occasion. Whether you want to go all-out depends both on your budget and how important live sounds are to you. The following suggestions are inexpensive ways to surround yourselves in sound:

- ✔ Supply your own CDs and use the facility's sound system.

- ✔ Download a customized iTunes mix to your iPod, supply your own speakers, and ask a friend to be the DJ.

- ✔ Hire a group from a music conservatory, which is cheaper than hiring a band.

- ✔ Use the house band at a hotel, or perhaps just one or two players from it, rather than bringing in outside musicians.

Reception

Depending on how many guests attend your destination wedding, the cost of your reception may rival, if not exceed, that of your own travel and accommodations. There are mouths to feed! And if you're like most couples, you have definite tastes in food and you want to please and impress those guests, yet you don't want to spend a fortune on the meal. Some ways to accomplish that follow.

For example, the day and time when you schedule the party to take place and the type of meal you serve make a significant cost difference. Saturday night has always been the most desirable time to hold a destination wedding ceremony. But nothing keeps you from having a Friday night event or a Sunday brunch. Investigate to find out how much a difference a change of day can make.

Budgeting with foreign currency

If you travel to a place where U.S. dollars aren't the prevailing currency, you'll need to acquaint yourselves with the exchange rate. Use the Universal Currency Converter (www.xe.com/ucc) to quickly calculate conversions. A bank that deals in foreign currency can also tell you what the exchange rate is (these rates vary daily), and you can use a PDA or portable calculator to figure out what a particular amount is equal to in U.S. dollars. Big luggage stores also sell handheld currency convertors.

When dealing with foreign vendors, confirm whether their estimates are in local currency or U.S. dollars. To avoid price fluctuations, encourage them to deal in U.S. dollars. To get pocket cash that you will need for tips and incidentals, wait until you arrive at the airport to receive the best exchange rate. Pass up manned foreign currency desks and exchanges in favor of using an ATM; they have the best rates. Just make sure that your PIN number is only four digits; longer ones don't work in all overseas ATMs. And don't use your anniversary date; that's too easy to guess!

You may also want to consider changing the type of reception you have. A more formal reception means more dollar signs, but you can adjust the menu to meet your budget. For example, instead of having a seven-course, sit-down meal, you may opt for a festive dinner buffet. If the amount that you allot can't fund the event you envision, then you need to make some tough choices, such as dropping names from your guest list, scaling back your expectations, or increasing your budget.

Dealing with deposits

After you accept a bid from a provider, as a show of good faith, the vendor you select expects to receive a deposit by a certain date, which should be stipulated in the contract the two of you sign. Most vendors have a set percentage that they require as a deposit, such as 25 percent. Paying by credit card is preferable, in case a dispute arises. Whatever method of payment you use, get a detailed receipt and keep it in a safe place.

Most deposits are nonrefundable, but if you can convince your vendor to add a refund policy into the contract, you add a layer of protection. If not, try to make your deposit as small as possible and the due date for final payment as far away as you can. Don't be surprised if you're expected to pay in full before the wedding; that's typical of event providers.

Chapter 5

Gathering Your Destination Wedding Team

In This Chapter
▶ Recruiting help to plan and produce your destination wedding
▶ Involving friends and family versus hiring professionals
▶ Understanding what wedding pros can do for you
▶ Finding and negotiating with vendors at a distance

*B*ack when brides and grooms married at younger ages and weddings were simple affairs held at home or nearby, planning the wedding was traditionally the job of the bride's mother. Today unless Mom is a travel agent or wedding planner with available time, a couple typically organizes their wedding with help from friends, family, or professionals — or some combination of the three.

A destination wedding adds a layer of complexity to plans; distance and time changes can cause confusion, yet you have only one opportunity to get it all right. So don't hesitate to reach out for help and create a team that's on your side all the way.

To make the event and the months leading up to it less stressful, delegate as much as possible to qualified people you can trust. You're the bride and groom. *That's* your job. This chapter can help alleviate some of your angst about picking the right people for your destination wedding team.

Identifying the Wedding Services You May Need

Destination weddings can be simple one-stop affairs or elaborate productions. How much help you need depends on where you want to wed, the facilities, your budget, and how much hand-holding you require. After you know the answers to these details, you can then turn to the appropriate people for help.

The following list gives you an idea of the major elements involved in a destination wedding. Seeing this long list of services may drive home how time-consuming planning a destination wedding can be. As a result, you may want to consider a turnkey destination wedding package, where just about everything is taken care of for you. Or if you want certain people to help with specific details, this list can help you decide which areas you need help with:

- ✔ Establishing a budget
- ✔ Setting a timetable
- ✔ Shopping for and selecting the bride's and groom's clothing
- ✔ Searching for destinations and unique venues
- ✔ Learning and meeting your locale's marriage requirements
- ✔ Booking travel and hotel arrangements
- ✔ Deciding on a ceremony space
- ✔ Scouting reception sites
- ✔ Planning the honeymoon
- ✔ Wrangling the officiant and managing the processional
- ✔ Tracking invitations and RSVPs
- ✔ Conceiving decor, table-top, floral, and lighting design
- ✔ Knowing and following etiquette and traditions
- ✔ Hiring and supervising a photographer and videographer
- ✔ Finding a reception caterer and choosing a menu
- ✔ Organizing a rehearsal and rehearsal dinner
- ✔ Designing your seating plan
- ✔ Ordering a wedding cake
- ✔ Choosing musicians and music selections
- ✔ Locating on-site hair and makeup stylists
- ✔ Coordinating wedding-guest activities
- ✔ Organizing wedding-day and guest departure transportation
- ✔ Shipping supplies and favors

Determine which tasks are best left to someone else and those you would rather handle yourself. Whenever you assign one, try to make your wishes clearly known and your requests specific — and keep track of who you asked to do what.

Before you reach out to anyone to help organize your wedding, make sure you name your budget. Every professional you come in contact with wants to know this info immediately. If you haven't yet decided on a number, using descriptions such as *inexpensive, moderate,* or *luxurious* can start the conversation. (Check out Chapter 4 for info on establishing a budget.)

Exploring Your Dream Team Options

With so much hinging on having a great event, you need to know who you want helping to plan and execute your wedding away. Are you the type of couple who is more comfortable calling upon friends and family for help and support? Or are you most confident turning over the management of your wedding to a professional?

In many destination weddings, couples cull help from multiple sources to avoid making costly mistakes and etiquette *faux pas.* So your decision doesn't have to be either/or. But understanding the skills, advantages, and limitations of the human resources available to you is valuable.

Using friends and family

Couples naturally turn first to family and friends for help. Sharing the experience with someone close can make the journey more fun and less daunting. Anyone you consider asking to take part in the wedding should be a person you know to be 100 percent dependable and flexible enough to put your ideas first.

Before you consider asking friends and family to help, keep the following in mind. Using folks you're close to

- ✔ Provides a personal touch.
- ✔ Saves money and fees.
- ✔ Adds one-of-a-kind accents.
- ✔ Allows you to work with people who love you.
- ✔ Perpetuates family traditions.

Using friends and family does have drawbacks:

✔ Emotions run high, and you can't fire friends and family without repercussions.

✔ Your loved ones may lack the skill level of a pro.

✔ They may be more casual than you want about timing and details.

✔ Jobs and kids may prevent them from traveling with you on advance scouting trips to potential destinations.

✔ Compensation issues can get sticky. (Should you pay them? Yes — you should offer, and certainly pick up expenses.)

✔ You may be uncomfortable when you need to address them as vendors.

✔ Involving friends and family can curtail their enjoyment of the wedding as a guest.

✔ People who you don't ask to participate may feel left out.

Going with professional planners

You may not have friends or family members who are capable or available to help plan a wedding away. Or you may want to have complete control over your wedding and don't want those folks offering you their opinions. If so, a professional wedding planner can help you plan and execute your perfect destination wedding.

Going with professionals also has pros and cons. On the positive side, destination wedding pros

✔ Are experienced in producing weddings and comfortable handling multiple small details.

✔ Save you time.

✔ Can suggest different venues and products that conform to your ideas and budget.

✔ Have access to network of vendors and can find new ones easily.

✔ Assist in the selection of vendors and coordinate their activities.

✔ Are willing to travel to your destination on scouting trips and be present on your wedding day.

✔ Can save money by reviewing budget and contracts, making recommendations, and using negotiating skills.

✔ Adhere to a code of ethics if they're members of the Association of Bridal Consultants (www.bridalassn.com) or Association of Wedding Professionals (http://afwpi.com).

✔ Can act as a problem solver and a buffer between family members when necessary.

✔ Are dedicated to bringing your vision to life.

Disadvantages of using professionals include the following:

✔ Hiring pros can be expensive.

✔ They often have other clients to juggle.

✔ Efforts may be duplicated by a property's free on-site wedding coordinator.

✔ A pro's requests may make you feel as if you as a couple are late, underfunded, or otherwise inadequate.

Destination Wedding Pros: Who Are Your Choices?

Your wedding is (one hopes) a once-in-a-lifetime event; a pro has been involved with perhaps hundreds and applies her knowledge of travel, event management, and wedding protocol to help you make the right decisions.

When it comes to wedding help, there are four major types of providers who can consult, coordinate, and direct the event: wedding planners, travel agents, on-site coordinators, and event producers. To add to the confusion, you're likely to see the terms *bridal* and *wedding, planner* and *coordinator* used everywhere interchangeably. This section explains them.

Using a wedding planner

A *wedding* (or *bridal*) *planner* is intended to be your advocate. A wedding planner manages the details, the vendors, the event, and your expectations. When you find one you feel comfortable with, bring her in as early in the process as possible. These sections can help you know what to expect.

Discovering what a wedding planner can do for you

If you simply need someone to help you get started, ask for pre-wedding planning, which normally involves the development of a budget and referrals on destinations, sites, and vendors. Whether you meet with your planner once to get a crash course in organizing or hire her to coordinate the whole event, a planner should serve to put you on track and tell you how to stay within your means.

Avoid wedding planners who are paid a commission on the amount of your money they spend because they only push you to order more. The best bridal planners charge a fee and work hard to extract the most value from your budget.

Finding a reputable wedding planner

If you decide to use a wedding planner, the best way to find a good one is through word of mouth: Do you know a recent couple who had a destination wedding? Ask if they had a planner and were happy with her. You can also contact the Association of Bridal Consultants (www.bridalassn.com) or Association of Wedding Professionals (http://afwpi.com). If you want a wedding planner on the ground at your destination, contact the tourism bureau or local hotels for recommendations.

Before you hire anyone, ask for three recent recommendations, and check them, asking what were the planner's strengths and weaknesses and how close she stayed to their budget.

Share your vision in terms of decorations, cuisine, music, and so on with the wedding planner. This is your wedding. And it should be organized so that you get what you want, just the way you picture it. When you look back in 20 years, your fond memories should be of an event that reflects your taste, not someone else's.

Enlisting a travel agent

A *travel agent* has the broadest knowledge of destinations and resort facilities that can hold a wedding and accommodate guests. Travel agents are savvy about hotels and can help you and your entire guest list make the most direct air connections. They ought to know which beachfront resort is undergoing renovations and which one just switched from adults-only to family friendly. Agents may be more effective than you in negotiating prices and benefits.

For the greatest peace of mind, work with a travel agent who has professional credentials. Agents belonging to the American Society of Travel Agents (ASTA) follow a code of ethics. Agents who are experienced in planning destination weddings, such as the pros at

DestinationWeddings.com (`destinationweddings.com`), are also knowledgeable about marriage license and residency requirements in different places and can help you to navigate the process.

Advice from a professional destination wedding planner

Would you like to use a professional wedding planner to make your destination wedding run smoothly but are concerned about cost? Although the gold standard is having your own, full-service destination wedding planner, not every couple needs or can afford one for the duration. Hiring someone just for those parts of the wedding you don't want to handle and paying a day or hourly rate may work for you. Even if you can't afford to go all out with a full-time wedding planner, you can still use their sage advice.

According to master bridal consultant Sue Winner (`www.suewinnerweddings.com`), any couple considering a destination wedding needs to remember the following important points. Winner, who is based in Atlanta, has organized close to 700 weddings. She is a member of the Association of Bridal Consultants.

- **Find out what the marriage laws are where you want to have the wedding, and then determine whether you meet the criteria and can comply.** Check out Chapter 1 for more specific details about local criteria.

- **Visit your destination to meet with potential vendors — and do it during the week.** The best vendors are booked on weekends and may not be able to make time for you. If you can't visit your destination, send your planner.

- **Select the vendor who can provide the greatest value for your dollar.** Instead of making your first question to a vendor "What do you charge?", ask what you will receive for you money.

- **Have a backup plan.** An outdoor wedding on the beach sounds incredibly romantic, but you can't predict Mother Nature. Heat is as much an issue as rain.

- **Don't invite more guests than you can afford.** Expecting people to RSVP "not able to attend" is a dangerous game. You may be surprised by how many people want to attend.

- **Plan an activity for the groom and his wedding party the morning of the wedding.** The guys will have nervous energy to spare, so have them use that time for a quick round of golf or basketball game, but don't send them so far away that it makes the bride a nervous wreck.

- **If guests are booking their own hotel rooms, make sure they mention that they're members of your wedding party.** Many hotels provide a complimentary hospitality suite and bridal suite to parties that book a minimum of 20 rooms. However, if guests don't mention being a part of your wedding, you may not get the free suites.

Travel agents normally don't charge a fee; instead, they receive commissions from the airlines and hotels they book on your behalf. So you won't pay more; as industry members, they pay less when buying travel on your behalf. If a travel agent urges you to choose a resort that doesn't seem quite right for you, he may likely receive a higher commission from that place; don't feel pressured, and find another travel agent. (Refer to Chapter 11 for specific advice about making travel arrangements.)

Using an on-site coordinator

An *on-site coordinator* is based at a destination and is familiar with the local professionals. She has a working relationship with the hotel's staff and food and beverage manager as well as local florists, musicians, and others who regularly turn a wedding into a celebration at a facility.

Many hotels and resorts, especially in Las Vegas, the Caribbean, and Hawaii, have in-house wedding coordinators who are thoroughly familiar with the property. They have experience in helping couples choose the setting and menu and oversee the day at no extra cost. In the following sections, I provide advice for how to identify a good on-site coordinator and how best to work with one.

Working with an on-site coordinator

If you want to choose a hotel with an on-site coordinator, ask potential hotels what services its coordinator provides and meet with her, if only by phone or e-mail, before committing to having a wedding at that location. Your assessment is important, and it can be more of an impression than a battery of questions. You want someone with a good command of English, someone who responds to you quickly, someone who uses e-mail and checks it daily, and someone who doesn't sound like she's half alive. Make sure the on-site coordinator will be available to you and willing to propose a variety of settings around the resort to hold the ceremony and reception. She should also show enthusiasm for her job and interest in you as a couple.

If her hotel offers customizable wedding packages, ask the coordinator to present them to you and go over the options. Is she — and the property she represents — as flexible and responsive as you need them to be? If not, choose another hotel or hire your own coordinator.

What to remember when working with a coordinator

When you work with a resort's coordinator, yours may not be her only wedding taking place. If your hotel schedules multiple weddings on the same day, don't expect the same level of care as if yours were the only affair of the day or evening. To ensure that your needs can be met, book a specific time with the coordinator and get her assurance that you'll have her undivided attention during that period.

If you believe that your coordinator's time will be divided on the wedding day or you aren't confident in her vision for your wedding but still like the resort, consider bringing in a paid local event planner to tend specifically to your needs.

In an ideal situation, you introduce your new local planner to the on-site planner, and they work collaboratively. If you find that you can't work with the planner at all, her supervisor, or her supervisor's supervisor should know about it. You'll need to have the reception staff and other vendor information turned over to your own person. And if it were me, I would tell the highest-ranking person at the hotel that I expect to have the bill reduced because promised services weren't delivered.

Making use of an event planner

An *event planner* (also called an *event producer*) takes responsibility for orchestrating what takes place from the moment of arrival to the start of your honeymoon. His focus tends to be on the look, decor, and ambience of the event. The rehearsal dinner, ceremony, and reception plus all the vendors who contribute to those events are under his wing. Because his emphasis is on the visual and sensory aspects of a wedding, request evidence of previous events he planned. Ask for photos and references. And watch out for over-the-top prima donnas.

These artistic pros usually work independently or through companies. A tourism office can help you locate one who is experienced in working with couples who aren't from that location. For example, couples who want to rent an Italian villa for the ceremony and reception and who need everything from dishes to a dance floor need an event planner who speaks the language and can deal with local regulations and vendors.

Dealing with multiple vendors

Standing behind every destination wedding's bridal planner, travel agent, local on-site coordinator, and event planner is a troupe of specialized vendors who apply their skills to bring your event to life. By understanding their different functions, you can choose who to turn to if you want particular help.

Can you skip the middleman and work with them directly? Absolutely. The advantage is that you get to select those you like best, rather than working with someone else's preferred vendors. On the other hand, doing it on your own takes more of your time to recruit, interview, negotiate, and hire individual vendors. And unless boundaries and the hierarchy of decision makers are clear (you should always be at the top), it can create task overlap, a costly and unproductive duplication of efforts. Hopefully whatever team you assemble can work together harmoniously. Only the bride is allowed to play the part of the diva!

If you want to deal with individual vendors, the following sections are a few examples of typical vendors that couples need. As always, experience and quality count. Better providers function above and beyond their titles to coordinate all aspects of their area of expertise. If you want to know how to talk to a vendor, check out the section "Finding Good Help Far Away," later in this chapter, for more info. To find an actual vendor, check out Chapter 12.

Food service

If the hotel where you're holding the reception doesn't have an on-site coordinator, the banquet or catering manager is usually in charge of the food service. To plan a reception in a space that doesn't normally operate as a restaurant or hotel, you need a caterer.

A good banquet manager or caterer can help you with the following:

- ✔ **The menu:** If you don't already know what you want to serve at the wedding, the banquet or catering manager should be able to present you with a variety of options at different price points. And if you're serving wine with the meal, he should be able to recommend appropriate whites and reds within your budget.

- ✔ **Wait staff:** The banquet manager or caterer hires and directs the wait staff. Depending on how many guests and how elaborate your reception is, he may need to call in a maître d' and headwaiter as well. Often the bartender is included in the price of the package, but tax and gratuities are additional.

Officiant

People authorized to marry you legally fall into three categories:

- ✔ **Religious:** Priest, rabbi, or minister
- ✔ **Official:** Judges
- ✔ **Civic:** Notary publics or court clerks

A facility that holds weddings generally has a relationship with an officiant and calls upon him regularly.

Don't have time to meet the officiant in advance but still want to discuss the ceremony? You can audition an officiant over the phone (see Chapter 15 for more details). I asked ours, Reverend Judy, to tell us what she would say — and she recited the entire service over the phone. That turned me into a believer.

Some couples prefer to have a close friend or relative conduct the ceremony. Rose Ministries (www.openordination.org) provides nondenominational ordination to men and women by mail so they can legally officiate at weddings within many states of the United States. Check with the county clerk and the tourism bureau elsewhere to find out whether such officiants have legal status to marry you before booking one.

Finding Good Help Far Away

Locating reputable help for a destination wedding can be more difficult than gathering a team for an at-home wedding because oftentimes you're far away from your destination. However, this distance doesn't have to prevent you from finding the right people for your festivities.

If your wedding plans are fairly elaborate, either you or your wedding planner should make at least one trip well in advance of the wedding to schedule a site inspection. Traveling to your destination also gives you the opportunity to screen and hire local vendors in time to make adjustments, if necessary. And the best way to know whether vendors are right for you is by observing them in action.

Not all brides and grooms can take the time or afford to visit their site in advance. Couples who don't have an opportunity to meet vendors in person before the wedding needn't fret over it, though. This section helps you find reliable on-site vendors when you're far away, including how to verify references, what to ask potential vendors, and how to close the deal.

Hiring reliable local vendors

Despite the distance, hiring a vendor who you like and can trust is essential. You should feel that he not only understands your needs but also has your best interests at heart.

Fortunately, you have ways to locate good vendors from afar, discover what other clients have said about them, remain in contact with them, communicate what you expect at your wedding, and gain a thorough understanding of what they will deliver.

If you don't already have a local planner on the job and don't intend to hire one, the best way to locate skilled, reliable vendors is through referrals. Personal recommendations from friends and others who have experienced their services is always best. When that's not available, use the following:

- ✔ Ask the wedding venue to furnish a list of its top service providers.

- ✔ If you already have one vendor selected, such as the photographer, ask her to recommend colleagues.

- ✔ Call or e-mail the local tourist bureau.

- ✔ Search online. One price-competitive source for vendors in the United States is www.clienty.com. Post what you're looking for, and vendors submit bids for the job. Wedding Wire (www.weddingwire.com) has recommendations of U.S. vendors from real brides.

Verifying references

Before you hire any on-site vendor, make sure you check on the vendor's past work and whether previous clients were pleased. Keep the following points in mind when verifying references:

- ✔ **Ask potential vendors to supply names and contact information for at least three references.** Ideally, you want to speak to couples who are in the United States and whose wedding took place fairly recently.

- ✔ **Call references as soon as possible and ask as many questions as you can about the vendor's services.** Ask what the vendor's strong and weak points were, and whether they would have had the vendor handle anything differently. Also ask how closely the vendor's estimate and final bill matched.

- ✔ **To be on the safe side, do some other investigating.** If you're researching a U.S. vendor, check with the Better Business Bureau (www.bbb.com) to see whether any complaints are lodged against the vendor. For overseas vendors, get in touch with the tourism office and ask their advice in checking out the company or independent vendor.

Asking the right questions

Although just about every vendor vouches that he brings taste, style, and creativity to events, posing certain questions can give you an idea of who you're really dealing with. Good questions to ask potential vendors include

- ✓ What is your range of services?

- ✓ How many weddings have you done?

- ✓ When was the last one, and can you tell me about it?

- ✓ Can you show me photographs of prior work?

- ✓ Are you experienced handling a wedding of my size?

- ✓ Have you worked at my reception spot before?

- ✓ Are you the one who shows up on my wedding day, or will someone else from your company be there?

- ✓ What happens if you're ill or can't make it?

- ✓ Can you send me a sample contract?

- ✓ Do you understand my budget and can you work within it?

- ✓ Do you have any suggestions on how I can save money?

- ✓ How do you charge, and what is your fee? Do you accept payment in U.S. dollars or the local currency?

- ✓ When do you need a deposit, and how much is required?

- ✓ When is the balance due?

- ✓ When is the best time of day for me to reach you?

- ✓ Do you anticipate any problems?

Be wary of vendors who start out overpromising; they may proceed to underdeliver. Trusting your instincts and switching to another vendor early in the process is better than being yoked to one who will disappoint.

Communicating successfully with your team

When you can't be there in person, keeping in touch with your vendors is important. You want vendors who have voice mail or e-mail and who check it regularly. You'll have questions throughout the destination-wedding-planning process, and you want someone who provides prompt, clear answers.

When you work with a vendor who's e-mail savvy, you have the advantage of sending JPEGs and URLs for them to look at and understand your style. And if they can send back photo samples, that's helpful. When you're considering a faraway band, for instance, ask to have a DVD or CD mailed to you, or sample MP3 files e-mailed to you.

Closing the deal with distant vendors

Try to compare several vendors before selecting one. You don't necessarily have to be present to do so. For example, if you want to decide between several caterers, ask all of them to prepare and photograph the same three-course dinner (specify the appetizers and entrees you'd like). Then have them estimate what they would charge for the meal. It's only fair to offer to compensate them for the cost of ingredients when you ask them to go to such trouble.

The tricky part is that the vendor who bids lowest may not best be able to fulfill your expectations. Nor can the highest-priced one necessarily concoct the finest repast. That's why speaking to references can help you decide. After you've interviewed several vendors and selected the one you're confident is right for your wedding, you're almost ready to sign the contract and get things under way.

Negotiating 'til you sign on the dotted line

Before you take pen to paper, remember that almost everything is negotiable, even how a vendor structures his fee. Most vendors have a standard contract, but its provisions may be negotiable, too. Certainly cross out any sections that don't apply to your situation. You can read more about budgets and negotiating in Chapter 4.

Going to contract

Double-check to make sure that everything you asked for is in writing and there are no hidden costs added in before you sign anything. Read the fine print and ask questions if something looks fishy. If you're willing to bear the expense of having a lawyer review the contract, do so at this point.

If everything checks out, sign on the dotted line. If, on the other hand, you find something disturbing in the revised contract, question the vendor. If the answer is satisfactory, authorize the contract. If not, you haven't found the right vendor and don't sign.

Expect the vendor to ask for a good-faith deposit upfront, and don't overlook where the contract says nonrefundable (even that may be negotiable).

If you expect to be going to contract with several distant vendors, consider getting a fax machine if you don't already have one. Some still use this method rather than sending contracts via e-mails and PDF files.

Part II
Picking a Destination for Your Wedding

The 5th Wave   By Rich Tennant

"Well it's a real tussle for the bouquet down there, but it looks like cousin Judy's got it. No, now the shark has it...now Judy...now the shark...now Judy..."

In this part . . .

After picking the right partner, choosing the right location for your destination wedding is one of the most important decisions you make (and also one of the most fun). In this part, I help you brainstorm potential places that fit your needs, taste, and budget and help lead you to a decision. The rest of this part takes a closer look at specific locations worth considering — from places in the United States and Canada to exotic tropical islands to chic European cities. I even tell you what you can expect if you're thinking of sailing into matrimony on a cruise ship. So get ready for some globe-trotting armchair travel.

Chapter 6

Finding the Right Destination: There's a Place for You

*I*f you've decided to have a destination wedding, congratulations. You're embarking on an experience you won't ever forget. Now the big question looms: *Where?*

Before you start the decision-making process, understand that a destination wedding location consists of three parts, all of which you need to line up. Normally the process follows this order, drilling down from general to specific:

1. **Choose a destination.**

   Decide on the geographical location where your wedding will take place, such as Las Vegas, Mexico, Italy, or elsewhere.

2. **Select the property.**

   Finding the place that hosts your wedding — whether a resort, state park, private villa — is the essential next step.

3. **Pick the site.**

   The site is the physical space where you'll speak your vows, such as in a chapel, on the beach, or on a terrace.

This chapter presents ideas to help you identify settings appropriate to your taste and budget. After you decide on the type of location that suits you, Chapters 7, 8, 9, and 10 offer information and details about specific locales.

Exploring Where to Go

Weddings take place in every country and culture in the world. If you haven't yet settled on a particular destination, get ahold of a globe, atlas, or map to start. A visual aid stimulates the conversation about how far you're willing to travel from home and the types of places that are special to the two of you. When you're ready, start drawing up a list of potential destinations. To help you build that list, this section provides insights into the many different types of locations worth considering.

Pursuing places of the heart

When faced with a world of possibilities, narrowing down where to have your wedding can seem like a daunting task. Fortunately, you can use several ways to find suitable locations.

Discussing places that have been personally meaningful to you throughout your lives, and their viability as wedding locations, is a good way to come up with potential venues for your list. The following suggestions include more ways to help you identify your "happy place":

- **Revisit a childhood home.** According to the last United States Census, about one in six families moves every year. If you have lived in more than one place, which holds the best memories? Was it a place where you felt especially connected to friends, family, or the community? Can you see yourself returning to it for a celebration? Then add this location to your list.

- **Consider the land of your ancestors.** America is comprised of many different ethnic groups, and some couples have a yearning to return to the place their parents or grandparents came from. Whether an older relative passed on stories of a county in Ireland, a pueblo in Mexico, a city in Asia — or if you simply feel drawn to a place that echoes your family history — consider ancestral stomping grounds as a destination.

- **Remember vacation sensations.** Ever take a trip somewhere and promise yourself, "One day I will return"? Your wedding could be the right time to fulfill that promise.

✔ **Look at destinations you've always wanted to visit.** If you haven't traveled much, you can still come up with ideas. Have you ever watched a movie set in an appealing location and said to yourself, "That's where I want to go!"? Put it on your list.

✔ **Opt for romantic getaways.** People associate many places around the world with love and romance — Paris, of course, along with Provence and the French Riviera, and all of Italy, from golden Tuscany to Venice to the Amalfi coast. In the United States, the Hawaiian islands, Wine Country, and even Rocky Mountain retreats bring out starry-eyed smiles. Because these destinations all are well-established, they offer couples extensive properties in which to hold a wedding.

✔ **Do some research.** Every bookstore has a travel section, filled with guides and picture books that transport armchair travelers to appealing places. Other media — magazines, travel posters, the Internet, and even ads — can also provide destination inspiration that sets you on a path to your wedding spot. As you research, take note of the destinations that you linger over — one of those may prove to be your wedding wonderland.

About.com Travel (`about.com/travel`) has more than 50 guides, real people who are experts on different destinations. Not only can you research cities, countries, and entire continents on the site, but you can e-mail guides directly with a question.

Reveling in a climate you love

Weather can play a huge role in selecting potential locales for your destination wedding. What's your ideal outdoor temperature? Are you in your glory when the thermometer reads in the torrid 80s and sizzling 90s? Or do you prefer more temperate surroundings? Perhaps you think nothing is as invigorating as winter's chill, especially now that you have someone to cuddle with. Even if you intend to hold your wedding indoors, you'll be spending a significant portion of time outdoors during your stay. So deciding where you'll be most comfortable is important.

Everyone wants good weather on his or her wedding day; however, you can only gamble, but not depend, on Mother Nature. That's why scheduling your wedding during months when the weather is most likely to cooperate can help the odds. Table 6-1 features popular destinations and optimal times to hold a wedding in them.

Table 6-1:	Considering the Weather	
Destination Wedding Location	**Best Wedding Months**	**Weather-Wise Details**
Las Vegas	October–April	Summer months bring lowest rates but highest temps in the dry desert.
Florida	December–March	Most visitors prefer winter; heat and humidity occur any month.
Hawaii	All	Year-round, Hawaii's daytime temperatures deviate little from the mid-80s; spring and winter may bring rain.
Bermuda	May–October	Too chilly for swimming much of the year, Bermuda blossoms in summer.
Caribbean	December–May	Hurricane season stretches from June to November, but doesn't reach Aruba, Bonaire, and Curaçao.
Mexico	November–May	Summer, the rainy season, is extremely hot and humid country-wide.
Canada	June–October	Summers are warm and pleasant. Cold-weather fans can ski and attend festivals.
Europe	April–July and September–October	Service staffs are reduced in August — Europeans' vacation month.
South Pacific	May–October	With seasons reversed, December through April is the summer rainy season.
Cruise ports	All	Ships sail every month of the year. Alaskan cruises operate May–September. Caribbean cruises sail year-round.

Eyeing travel expenses

As you compose a list of potential destinations for your wedding, think about how much you want to spend and how much your guests can afford to pay to travel (for more on budgeting, see Chapter 4). As a general rule, the farther away you go, the more expensive transportation is and the longer it takes for people to reach the place, making it less likely that everyone you want to attend will be able to make the trip. Yet if you propose guests meet you in a warm destination in February or embark on a wedding cruise with you in August, you may find the enticement of travel makes distance no obstacle.

Staying in the U.S. or going abroad

When compiling your list of potential destinations, also consider how getting married in the United States versus abroad affects you and your guests. On one hand, traveling to an exotic place where you can marry and continue the festivities for days is thrilling and fascinating.

What's the downside? Traveling to destinations outside of the United States requires a passport for you and every guest who RSVPs. And if you don't speak the language or understand the currency, you may encounter frustration, not just during travel but when dealing with wedding vendors as you plan your wedding away. Furthermore, when you get married abroad, you have to contend with differing and sometimes confusing rules and regulations to make your ceremony legal (see the last section in this chapter).

Identifying destinations to avoid

Not every country is a wedding paradise. Destinations to strike from your list include regions that have war, civil unrest, a high crime rate, unpotable water, poor sanitation, dependably bad weather, lingering effects from a natural disaster, or a significant lack of facilities to hold a wedding. And because of the potential for bureaucratic delays, think twice about holding a legal ceremony in a place where weddings of foreign nationals (in this case, that would be you) aren't fairly routine.

Check the U.S. Department of State Web site (www.travel.state. gov) to read Travel Warnings and Consular Information Sheets for any countries that you're considering traveling to. These info sheets provide a steely-eyed assessment of characteristics of places that travel brochures ignore, such as the incidence of crime and disease.

Looking at Locales

The vast majority of couples who have a destination wedding choose a traditional property such as a hotel or resort. Such vacation lodgings usually have both the facilities and staff to host a destination wedding, which makes it easier and less stressful on a couple organizing a wedding in an unfamiliar setting from a distance. And by holding the ceremony and reception in the same location, you save on party rentals and transportation.

Nonetheless, for a variety of reasons, couples sometimes rely on a hotel strictly for lodging and look elsewhere for ceremony and reception venues. (I did the opposite: My wedding took place in a hotel's chapel, and we held the reception in an off-premise restaurant.) Properties other than hotels may provide something unusual and picturesque that guests can't find in their hometowns, and a once-in-a-lifetime opportunity to enjoy them. They may also provide lower-cost settings than commercial venues.

Checking in on hotel and all-inclusive resorts

Couples with active, love-to-party guests may find an all-inclusive resort the most cost-efficient option for their tribe. Not only can guests eat, drink, and play to their heart's content, their revelry remains safely within the perimeter of a protected property. The appeal of an all-inclusive is that you pay one price that covers food, drinks, lodging, sports, and entertainment during your stay. Spa treatments and excursions are normally extra.

To make their facilities even more enticing, some all-inclusive resorts offer a free basic wedding package to couples who commit to spending a minimum number of honeymoon days there after the ceremony.

Mexico and the Caribbean are home to the majority of all-inclusive resorts that promote wedding packages ranging from modest to spectacular. Nearly every one offers the choice of setting the wedding on the beach or in a gazebo, chapel, or tropical garden. (See Figure 6-1 for an example of a better all-inclusive resort.)

Figure 6-1: The beach at sunset provides a glorious setting for a wedding.

Find out more about the major all-inclusive resort groups that have free and upgraded wedding packages by visiting the following sites or speaking to a travel agent (more on travel agents in Chapter 11):

- Sandals (www.sandals.com)
- Beaches (www.beaches.com)
- SuperClubs (www.superclubs.com)
- Couples (www.couples.com)
- Iberostar (www.iberostar.com)
- Palace (www.palaceresorts.com)
- Secrets (www.secretsresorts.com)
- Dreams (www.dreamsresorts.com)
- Riu (www.weddingsbyriu.com)
- Occidental (www.occidentalhotels.com)
- Barceló (www.barcelo.com)
- Karisma (www.karismahotels.com)

If you decide to hold the wedding at an all-inclusive but some of your guests stay elsewhere, find out whether your hotel offers day (and night) passes. That way, nonguests can use the facilities and participate in on-property activities you arrange. *Note:* "Free" weddings only refer to the ceremony itself. It costs extra to have a catered reception, the price of which is figured on a per-person cost.

All-inclusives aren't the only hotels that aim to attract wedding parties. Although major hotel groups' city properties draw hometown weddings, their resort facilities are set up to host and accommodate destination wedding groups. Many of the best-known hotel brands dangle extras to induce couples to choose their facilities. Table 6-2 lists some major hotel groups and their perks.

Table 6-2: Wedding Offers from Major Hotel Groups

Hotel Group	Wedding Amenities	For More Information
Fairmont	Personal wedding specialist; free wedding Web site; sumptuous menus	Phone 800-257-7544; Web sites `www.fairmont.com`, `www.fairmontweddings.com`
Four Seasons	Ultimate luxury at hotels and resorts that customize every wedding element	Phone 800-819-5053; Website `www.fourseasons.com/weddings`
Hilton	Online form to submit a request for price estimate and find locations for wedding partiesof all sizes	Phone 800-HILTONS; Web site `www.weddingsbyhiltonfamily.com`
Marriott	Marriott Rewards points good for overnight stays are provided based on cost of wedding. Honeymoon registry available	Phone 888-236-2427; Web sites `www.weddingsbymarriott.com`, `www.marriottregistry.com`
Ritz-Carlton	High-end, comprehensive wedding services that yield classy events	Phone 800-241-3333; Web site `www.ritzcarlton.com/corporate/weddings/default.asp`
Starwood (includes Westin, Sheraton, Meridien, St. Regis, and W hotels)	Free wedding Web site and honeymoon concierge and gift registry program	Phone 888-625-5144; Web sites `www.starwoodhotels.com`, `www.spghoneymoons.com`

Although major hotel and resort groups are well-equipped to provide the venue and services you need to pull off a destination wedding, many smaller and more intimate properties are up to the task as well. Wherever you choose to base your event, understand that the vast majority of hotels and resorts can make a wedding really easy for you to plan when you choose a standard package.

Understanding the basic wedding package

Most hotels feature a standard wedding package that consists of a list of services and amenities the property provides at a set price. By bundling together those essentials, such as an officiant's services and flowers for the bride and groom, a property offers the convenience of a turnkey wedding where a couple need not fret over customizing every aspect, instead opting to use the tried-and-true elements provided. Couples who want to customize their wedding package, adding or changing options from a standard list the hotel provides, can still have a turnkey wedding, but should expect to pay a bit more.

A standard package can be ideal for a small, low-budget wedding. That's the kind of wedding we had, and it also included a well-lit makeup room for the bride and attendants, fresh floral arrangements in the chapel, and a wedding video. The following features are among those you're likely to find in a standard low-cost wedding package. This basic deal doesn't include the price of the reception, travel, or accommodations:

- ✔ Consultation with on-site wedding coordinator
- ✔ Assistance with document preparation
- ✔ Services of officiant
- ✔ Use of chapel or other scenic venue for the ceremony
- ✔ Small bouquet for bride and boutonnière for groom
- ✔ Sparkling wine and small, one-tier wedding cake
- ✔ Services of photographer (photographs may be extra)
- ✔ Prerecorded musical selections played
- ✔ Wedding certificate
- ✔ Inexpensive gift (such as T-shirts or keepsake glasses)

If you want to add something to the standard package, notify the property in advance of the wedding. Doing so allows you time to scrutinize and approve revised charges. Romantic add-ons to packages can include a post-wedding candlelight dinner, in-room spa massages for two, breakfast in bed, and other trip sweeteners.

Upgrading a basic package

Couples who are having a larger wedding or want something more elaborate can add to a basic package or request pricing on one they create. Typically hotels and resorts can provide a couple with a menu of services to choose from. If you have an idea for something unusual — whether it's setting up a fully furnished outdoor living room for cocktails before the ceremony or building a life-size sand castle for you to marry beside — put in a request with the wedding coordinator to find out whether the property can provide it and the cost.

Keeping to your budget and planning a modest wedding with a small guest list can leave you with money to splurge in some areas. Options to enrich the experience are vast and include the following:

- ✔ Add extra names to your guest list.
- ✔ Help out attendants and guests who have limited funds by subsidizing a portion of their travel costs.
- ✔ Treat yourselves to first- or business-class airfare.
- ✔ Upgrade from a standard guest room to a deluxe one or a suite.
- ✔ Arrange for limousine service to the marriage license bureau or to the reception site (if it differs from the ceremony location).
- ✔ Order a bigger bouquet or more elaborate wedding cake.
- ✔ Dress up your ceremony and reception spaces with more flowers and decorations.
- ✔ Book more time with the photographer or buy more shots.
- ✔ Fly in hair and makeup stylists from home.
- ✔ Add a cocktail hour.
- ✔ Include more gourmet items on the reception menu.
- ✔ Trade up from sparkling wine to genuine French Champagne.
- ✔ Plan a longer honeymoon or one at a more distant location.

Splurging on a designer destination wedding

Expanding on the popularity of their free and low-cost weddings, the two leading all-inclusive brands, Sandals and SuperClubs, have introduced more lavish wedding packages. Certain added frills cost a few thousand dollars, while elaborate packages can top $50,000, making some events twice as expensive as a typical hometown wedding.

Although over-the-top affairs obliterate the advantage of having an affordable destination wedding, I'd be remiss without telling you about some options if you do have cash to burn. Obviously the resorts are offering these types of glamorous destination weddings because some couples are willing to spend the money. If you crave a designer wedding, your first point of contact is still the wedding coordinator at either a Sandals or SuperClubs resort.

✔ **Preston Bailey Signature WeddingMoons at Sandals Resorts:** A floral and event designer who creates opulent party environments for celebrities, Bailey has conceived four preset wedding themes for couples marrying at Sandals and Beaches resorts. Each consists of an elaborately decorated setting.

Gazebos swirled with silk, flower-panel screens, satin-and-tulle chair covers, topiary centerpieces, and conch shells brimming with orchids are among the elements Bailey styled to prettify his namesake parties. These decorative enhancements (see Figure 6-2) range from under $2,000 up to $5,000.

Appealing to brides with a penchant for brand names, other Sandals temptations include wedding accessories (unity candles, photo albums, cake toppers, and barefoot jewelry) by Beverly Clark; cakes designed by Sylvia Weinstock; a line of destination wedding gowns; and Waterford crystal and china gifts. Sandals and Bailey can also conjure caviar-budget wedding packages featuring transportation via private jet, a musical concert by a well-known performer, and other extraordinary perks.

© Sandals Resorts

Figure 6-2: Preston Bailey's Signature "Water Lily" Collection for Sandals incorporates hot-pink lilies and cymbidium orchids.

✔ **"Wedding Bliss" and Sasha Souza "Oceans of Love" packages at SuperClubs:** Similar to Sandals, SuperClubs offers themed nuptial add-ons. These "Wedding Bliss" à la carte packages, which are upgrades to the free wedding offer, range from a sexy saxophone serenade for aisle walkers to a butterfly release to a newlyweds' sunset massage.

A West Coast wedding consultant and destination wedding planner, Sasha Souza designed her sky's-the-limit "Oceans of Love" package for SuperClubs' Grand Lido resorts that starts at $50,000 and includes everything from a honeymoon suite with Jacuzzi for five nights and six days, a spa package, private limo transfers for everyone, a live reggae band, a pool party, and a fireworks display.

Pondering the pleasures and perils of public places

Public places, such as a beach or park, allow you to save money on a ceremony spot that can be quite beautiful. *Public* doesn't necessarily mean *free*. And even in a public place, you may still need permission to use it for your wedding. Know that a facilities fee or permit may be required, or you may run into strict regulations about the number of people who can assemble there, putting up temporary structures, curfews, limits on amplified music, and other rules.

To find out whether you can stage your ceremony on public property, locate the person responsible for the space. The local municipality should be able to provide a name and contact number.

Beach weddings

Casual and romantic, beach weddings seem as if they couldn't be simpler: the two of you, an officiant, the crashing waves, an after-wedding run along the beach, or dive into the surf. The moment can be heavenly . . . or it can rain.

Still, lots of couples refuse to settle for anything other than a casual, toes-in-the-sand affair and are undeterred by passing showers. And to avoid hopping around on super-heated midday sand, they schedule early-morning or sunset weddings, which as an added benefit yield prettier pictures.

 If you're thinking of a public beach wedding, plan ahead and prepare for uncooperative weather (both heat and rain). According to bridal planner Sue Winner, fewer than 15 percent of beach weddings she's been involved with actually ended up taking place on the (hot) sand.

Buying out a property for your wedding

Movie stars and millionaires aren't the only people who buy out a place for a long weekend and convert it into a uniquely luxurious setting for an unforgettable party. Depending on the facility you select, the number of guests you invite, and the level of amenities, cuisine, and entertainment you provide, having a place all to yourselves may be within your reach. Taking over a multi-bedroom villa or an entire small inn or resort with your family and friends as its sole occupants can be the ultimate private pleasure.

Your planner or event director, working in concert with competent, agreeable staff, can customize every aspect of a wedding weekend at a place that provides 24-7 service, daily gourmet meals, and flowing cocktails for the duration of your stay.

Imagine this scenario: The two of you arrive on a Thursday. After unpacking, you savor a candlelight dinner on the beach. You sleep in on Friday. In the afternoon, you greet arriving guests, sunbathe by your private swimming pool, and then linger over your catered rehearsal dinner that night. The next day, while guests are off golfing or sightseeing, you prepare for the Saturday-night wedding.

Perhaps you're married poolside, its perimeter illuminated with candles. Then the entire party moves to your private terrace (overlooking the water, of course!) for a multicourse dinner prepared by the house chef. Much, much later that evening, when you return to your room, transformed now into a bridal suite with a path of rose petals that leads from the door to the bed, you sleep peacefully, knowing that your wedding was everything you hoped for.

Wimco (www.wimco.com) is a well-known company that arranges villa rentals in the Caribbean, Italy, the French Riviera, Greece, and Morocco. Also, hotels such as Half Moon in Jamaica (www.halfmoonroyalvillas.com) feature separate, fully staffed villa accommodations with access to the resort's facilities, including the spa, beachfront, and restaurants.

Weddings in a park or garden

The scent of flowers in bloom and their vivid colors in a public park or garden can provide a picture-perfect setting for a wedding — as long as you can establish some privacy.

Getting married in a public park or garden does have its drawbacks. Think twice before holding the wedding in a highly trafficked public place that is subject to the arrival of onlookers. Without private security guards, distinctive stanchions, and eagle-eyed staffers to steer away uninvited guests, you may end up having a bigger wedding than planned.

In addition, pipes and electrical cables may have to be run over the grass, and bathrooms cleaned and upgraded with candles, flowers, and amenities. Plus a crew may be necessary to comb the grass and bushes beforehand, clearing out trash and even animal waste.

Picking a private property

Couples who want a wedding in a more exclusive place where they can celebrate without prying eyes should look to a private property, of which you can find many different kinds. For example, golf and country clubs, thanks to their bucolic settings, are popular options to consider; even if you aren't a member, some clubs make their event spaces available for a fee.

Although a private facility's location or distinctive architecture may be very tempting, keep in mind that not all are equipped for a ceremony or reception and that many things that bring a party to life have to be rented.

If you're interested in a space that normally is used for parties and events, ask whether they keep a list of preferred vendors, which can make tracking down suppliers easier for you or your wedding planner. This section points out a few options for private property settings you may want to consider for your wedding.

College campuses

Many campuses have a chapel that can be used for a ceremony as well as banquet facilities and meeting spaces you can use for the reception. A majority of colleges also have parks or gardens or meadows on the grounds — great for photo ops.

Having your ceremony on campus may take several rounds of negotiations to persuade a school that had previously never allowed a private social event to take place there to host a wedding. But as long as one of you is an alum, you may have an advantage.

Offbeat opportunities

If you're looking for something even more nontraditional, consider the following types of properties for your destination wedding:

- ✔ **Historic sites:** A donation is usually expected, either in lieu of or addition to a facilities fee.

- ✔ **Art galleries:** For the right price, a gallery can close early or permit an after-hours event.

- ✔ **Aquariums and zoos:** These locations are fun, as long as they can provide a separate area for your party.

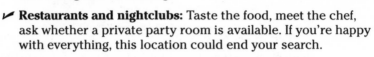

- ✔ **Private estates, country barns, and castles:** Event designers' dream venues, these sites allow for imaginative decorations.

- ✔ **Photography studios:** Open, well-lit spaces are perfect for picture taking and circulating.

- ✔ **Restaurants and nightclubs:** Taste the food, meet the chef, ask whether a private party room is available. If you're happy with everything, this location could end your search.

Nuzzling in natural settings

Perhaps you and your other half love spending time outdoors. If so, a wedding in a natural setting may be the obvious choice. Backdrops blessed with natural beauty require fewer flowers and less decoration to create a genuinely festive ambiance. This section looks at a couple of options. If you find one that interests you, contact the property directly or have your planner make the call.

Wedding in a winery

Wineries that are open to the public and have on-site restaurants are best equipped to host sit-down dinners, buffets, champagne receptions, and cake-cutting ceremonies where vintages from the facility flow. Because wineries cover many acres, you can stage different parts of your event in different spots, such as preceremony drinks and hors d'oeuvres on a terrace, the ceremony in the orchard, and then dinner under a tent. Many wineries have guest houses that the bridal party can use for the day, and others are full-service inns.

Given the choice between a hilltop setting and a flat one, go for the higher ground because it will be cooler in the summer and the photographs will be more dramatic.

Marrying atop a mountain

Normally couples feel on top of the world on their wedding day. And when they marry on a mountainside — where the air is fresher and the unobstructed views are thrilling — the experience can be literally breath-taking. (Check out Figure 6-3 for an example.)

Getting married atop a mountain may not be for everyone. Couples and guests who aren't acclimated may become light-headed, dizzy, and experience difficulty breathing in extremely high elevations.

Winter is prime time at ski resorts, so couples who schedule their wedding for after the season can expect to pay lower rates.

Figure 6-3: Summer wedding outside The Little Nell, Aspen, Colorado.

Pursuing active passions

Did an activity bring you together? If so, you may be able to stage your ceremony in a place that reflects the love you have for the pastime as well as each other. This section looks at a few options.

Sports venue weddings

Are the two of you absolutely crazy about a professional or semi-professional sports team? If so, why not get married at home plate, center court, or center ice? Couples are tying the knot everywhere from baseball diamonds to hockey rinks to scenic race tracks. (Figure 6-4 shows an example.)

Although you can't use a facility while play is underway, you may be able to rent it before the season or after the game. Some couples carry out the theme by sending invitations in the form of admission tickets and having their vows simulcast on the arena's electronic billboard.

Figure 6-4: He shoots, she scores! You can wed at your favorite sports venue, like these two fanatical hockey fans.

Theme parks

Perhaps the two of you are head over heels (literally) for roller coasters, thrill rides, and other theme park attractions. If so, why not consider getting married at an amusement park?

Wedding fantasies come to life at Disney parks (yes, Cinderella, you can arrive at the chapel in a horse-drawn pumpkin). Disney FairyTale Weddings (www.disneyweddings.go.com), at both the Anaheim and Orlando properties as well as at Hong Kong Disneyland, feature intimate (18 guests or fewer) and custom wedding (minimum of ten guests) packages, as well as cruise weddings aboard Disney ships. If you want a Disney wedding, check out Chapter 7 for in-depth info.

Popular theme parks where couples with kids and the young at heart can hold a wedding also include Busch Gardens (www.buschgardens.com), Knott's Berry Farm (www.knotts.com), and Sea World (www.seaworld.com). And at the indoor Great Wolf waterparks (www.greatwolf.com), neither seasons nor weather put a damper on events. As with other destination weddings, guests at theme-park weddings are expected to pick up their own travel costs, but you should plan on covering admissions charges.

Going the cruise ship route

It's usually smooth sailing for couples who marry aboard a cruise ship or in port. Not only are cruise weddings fun and affordable, with all the services and amenities you need already provisioned; they also send you off on your honeymoon without skipping a beat. Read about getting married on a ship in Chapter 10.

Making Your Destination Choice: The Actual How-To

You may be thinking, "So many locations and so little time!" And you really don't know where to start. Worrying is normal: You're planning one of the biggest days in your life.

To make your final destination decision, follow these helpful steps:

1. **List all the prospective locations you're considering.**

   Don't judge the locations now. Just brainstorm. Refer to the "Exploring Where to Go" section earlier in this chapter to inspire the list.

2. **After you have a list, start narrowing it down.**

   Assign a number, low to high, of how strongly you want a wedding in each location and how practical it is for you to go there.

3. **Focus on your top three choices.**

   With these three choices, do the following:

   1. **Visit the destination's official Web site to get the facts on marrying there and potential accommodations.**

   2. **Contact hotels you're interested in by phone or e-mail.**

      Ask whether wedding packages are available, what they include, the extras available, and complete costs.

   If you want an on-site reception, request menu options. And if you intend to honeymoon at the resort afterward, let it know that you're also interested in what the romance packages entail.

4. **Complete your research; now you're ready to decide where to hold the wedding.**

Review your list of potential places and see how many of the items that follow you can check off. The one that receives the highest number of marks is likely to be the best place to seal your vows.

- ❑ We have no major objections to the destination, property, and ceremony and reception sites.
- ❑ Our wedding date is available.
- ❑ The site can handle a wedding our size.
- ❑ We're satisfied with the local services.
- ❑ We will have an officiant who can conduct the ceremony the way we want it.
- ❑ The cost is within our budget.
- ❑ The amount of time it takes to travel to the place and the connections required are reasonable.
- ❑ We like the accommodations for ourselves and our guests.
- ❑ There's plenty to do and see nearby.
- ❑ We have dealt with people who are helpful and who we trust to help create the wedding we envision.

Test-Driving Your Destination Wedding Site

Have you narrowed your options down to a couple of places and are not quite sure yet which one is right for you? Or are you concerned that a place that looks great on paper or online won't impress in person? You could take a trip to inspect potential destination wedding locations to help you make your final decision. Some couples schedule a series of long weekends to a variety of places before making their final decision. Others rely on their wedding planner to do the legwork. Still others take advantage of test-drive packages, which provide a quick overview but are primarily sales pitches.

If every detail — food, flowers, ceremony and reception spaces, accommodations, and so on — must be just so in order for you to feel comfortable with the wedding plans, then personally checking out a destination and making the major decisions well in advance of the wedding is imperative. When you have a big and elaborate wedding in mind, you simply can't find a substitute for showing up ahead of time (and as far in advance as possible) in order to suss out whether a spot is right for you.

However, if you're more easy-going and trust serendipity and the experienced wedding providers you've hired at a distance to deliver what they promise, save your money. Many twosomes who organize a small, turnkey wedding don't show up until the event or a few days before. (I was one of such brides. The entire wedding had been planned remotely, and everything went smoothly.)

What to look for during an inspection

As soon as you arrive at a destination, a series of impressions will bombard you. Everything from the distance of the airport to the property to the way the hotel staff greets you is important, so keep a notebook handy to write down your observations.

Be on the lookout for four key atmospherics at any site you inspect. When any of the following are missing, seriously consider moving on to the next place or vendor on your list:

- ✔ **Cleanliness:** Is every area you visit spotless, from the floors to the restrooms? Presumably you've given the property advance warning that you were coming. If they didn't clean up in anticipation of your visit, the place will unlikely sparkle on your wedding day.

- ✔ **Attentiveness:** Were you greeted politely within moments of your arrival? Was it clear a staff member was expecting you? Did he begin to discuss your tour, and ask whether you wanted to be shown anything in particular? Answering "yes" to these questions are all good signs that a facility wants your business, is professionally managed, and will work to make your experience positive.

- ✔ **Flexibility:** Unless you're 100 percent delighted with the layout of the place and the particulars of the wedding package, ask what it would involve to make a specific change such as an alternate site, time, or menu. You can gauge how amenable they are as hosts by their reactions. If every change you propose is cause for an additional fee, do some tough negotiating before signing anything.

- ✔ **Helpfulness:** Did the property's tour guide take an active or passive role? Was she basically a note-taker, or did she present you with a reasonable number of options? She knows the place better than you, so you should be able to count on her to make suggestions where appropriate.

Seeing the sites

The most efficient way to check out specific sites and interview as many vendors as possible is by having a car and driver at your disposal. You can set this up in advance through your hotel or the local tourism office. Although airport taxi drivers sometimes offer their services for an entire day at a fixed rate, you have no way of knowing how trustworthy or reliable one is.

After you arrive at a destination, check out the following to ensure the locale is right for your wedding:

- ✔ **Potential ceremony and reception locations:** These site visits are the most important because they're where the main events take place. If you plan an outdoor wedding, ask what options are available in case of rain, heat, insects, or other environmental issues. Ideally, a facility will reserve both an indoor and outdoor space for you, and you should be able to decide to use either one with same-day notice.

  Ask how many people each space you're shown can accommodate. You don't want to crowd people in, nor do you want them in a room that overwhelms. You can fit more people in an area set up for a cocktail event than a sit-down dinner.

  If the party space is undecorated, request to be shown pictures of what it looks like when dressed for a wedding. Be sure you understand what is provided at no additional cost and what requires a fee.

- ✔ **Accommodations:** Knowing that friends and family will be bunking at the resort, ask to see a range of rooms, from the cheapest accommodations to the more expensive suites. Are some guests traveling with young children? They may need quarters that include kitchen facilities to store snacks or warm a bottle. If handicap accessibility is an issue, make sure that the ceremony and reception sites are compliant as well as the rooms.

- ✔ **Private party spaces:** Find out what choices you have for holding a rehearsal dinner on-site and whether you can have a private space to yourselves.

- ✔ **Recreational areas:** Is there a pool, a beach, a spa, hiking trails, or a sports or fitness center on the premises? The more facilities on-site and the better their condition, the fewer reasons you'll have to leave.

Asking the right questions

Come prepared to ask as many questions of your host or wedding planner as you need to during your inspection. Receiving straight and clear answers is both desirable and reasonable. The following questions are relevant to ask:

- ✔ Is the date we want for our wedding available? Does the price change based on the time of day or other variables?

- ✔ How many weddings take place here in an average month? On a typical day?

- ✔ Do you have on-site wedding coordinators? What does she do? Is there a fee for her services?

- ✔ Can we count on assistance acquiring a marriage license?

- ✔ How many different types of guest rooms do you have, and can we see one of each category?

- ✔ What amenities does a bridal couple receive?

- ✔ Can you accommodate all our guests on that date and the day(s) before and after? Is a group discount available?

- ✔ If you don't have enough rooms for our guests, where are the closest places they can stay?

- ✔ What kind of wedding ceremony and reception packages are offered, what do they include, and how're they priced?

- ✔ Do you charge a facility-usage fee?

- ✔ What are our options for ceremony and reception locations?

- ✔ How far apart are the ceremony and reception spaces we prefer? If our ceremony and reception sites are beyond walking distance, what are the transportation options?

- ✔ Can we use a caterer, florist, musicians, and officiant of our choice, or are we obligated to work with your vendors?

- ✔ How are the spaces normally decorated? Are there particular themes available? What is the price range?

- ✔ Do you have a curfew or volume restriction on music?

- ✔ What types of activities can our guests participate in before and after the wedding?

- ✔ Are children permitted at the resort? If so, what facilities exist for them?

✔ Has the property been hit by bad weather recently and suffered any damages?

✔ Are any renovations planned, and if so, will noise disturb the festivities?

✔ Does the property carry liability insurance? Is it necessary for us to buy additional event insurance?

✔ Who would be our primary contact person if we decide to book our wedding here? Can we meet with him before we go?

✔ How much of a deposit is required, under what circumstances is it refundable, and when is the final payment due?

✔ How soon should we plan on arriving before the wedding?

Getting direct answers that you're comfortable with can confirm that you've come to the right place to hold your destination wedding.

Visiting with vendors

Schedule time during your trip to meet with potential vendors, such as the florist, caterer, and so on. If they're located on-site at a hotel or resort, it will certainly save you travel time getting to them. Regardless of where they do business, when making an appointment, let potential vendors know that you intend to do more than chat when you encounter them face to face: You want to sample their wares and get their input. For more information on choosing vendors, check out Chapter 5.

For many couples, the quality of food served at their wedding is paramount. So you need to taste everything that may be served. Even though you may have your heart set on one menu, ask to try the chef's specialty. It may be so delicious that you decide to substitute it for some standard fare.

Florists can be expected to prepare a sample bouquet for a nominal fee along with photos of their previous work. And if you plan to have your wedding hair and makeup done locally, put those stylists through their paces, bringing along a photo or tear sheet from a magazine to show the look you want them to emulate.

Toward the end of any vendor meeting, pose an open-ended question, such as "Is there anything I haven't asked you about that could make my wedding even more special?" You never know what someone may propose.

Selecting a Destination Where You Can Legally Marry

When you're deciding on a destination, one of the most important points to consider is whether you can get legally married there. Follow these steps to ensure your destination wedding will be valid:

1. **Meet the area requirements to obtain a marriage license.**

2. **Show up together in person and acquire the license.**

3. **Participate in a ceremony led by an officiant whose credentials are accepted where the wedding is held.**

   Afterwards, the officiant signs, stamps, or notarizes your license.

The reason to concern yourself with this is that destinations outside the United States have their own rules and regulations in order for a wedding to be legal. That's why you need to contact the local office that issues marriage licenses to determine whether you can meet a destination's specific requirements before making wedding or travel plans. Don't depend on unofficial Web sites for this information, because license requirements can change.

If you find that overseas wedding laws are too restrictive or burdensome to comply with, consider quietly taking care of the legalities with a private civil ceremony before you travel. You can then go ahead with any kind of destination wedding you like, seal your vows with a kiss, and your guests need not be any wiser that your "first" wedding took place in your hometown courthouse.

This section takes a general look at the requirements for getting married both inside and outside the United States to emphasize how requirements differ. Specific legal requirements may cause you to rethink a destination. Chapters 7–10 provide more detailed info about locations and their specific marriage license laws.

Tying the knot in the United States

Every municipality in the United States is entitled to have its own set of requirements that must be met before it issues a marriage license. Most places don't require U.S. citizens to be residents of the wedding destination. Furthermore, states recognize weddings between members of the opposite sex performed in other states.

To find out what the specific regulations are and where to apply for a license, contact the clerk of the city or county you want to marry in. Typically you'll need to bring proof of age, identity, citizenship, and your social security card. A U.S. marriage license is normally valid for a few months after it is issued.

If you want to have a religious ceremony away from home but still in the United States, contact the church or synagogue office at your wedding destination to inquire about the possibilities. Religious leaders may be reticent about conducting ceremonies for couples who don't belong to their congregation. They may require regular attendance for a period of time, premarital counseling, or other programs before agreeing to solemnize your marriage.

Getting married in another country

As a general rule, marriages that are performed legally abroad are also valid in the United States as long as they adhere to the laws of the country where the marriage is performed. However, acquiring a marriage license overseas can be more difficult than getting one at home. Each country has its own rules and requirements, and in the strictest nations, only a couple who are citizens of the country may marry there.

The place to start, if you haven't yet left home, is with the country's tourism bureau or consulate. If you're already in the country where you want to wed, the U.S. embassy can also provide guidance. Neither a consulate nor an embassy official is authorized to perform marriages in foreign countries. However, their offices are the best place to find the appropriate source to contact.

Offices that process marriage licenses in other countries typically require a variety of documents from a couple. You may be expected to produce the following items in order to obtain a license to wed:

- ✔ Proof of identity (such as an original birth certificate or one with a raised seal, a passport, or a driver's license)
- ✔ Divorce decree or death certificate, if this isn't a first marriage
- ✔ Filing and paperwork fee, which may be required in cash

In addition, some localities also require some of the following:

- ✔ Blood test
- ✔ Residency requirement
- ✔ Proof of citizenship (your passport suffices)

✔ Tourist card, visa, or other proof of arrival in the country

✔ Parental authorization for couples under 18

✔ Premarital counseling

✔ Waiting period

✔ Witnesses and copies of their passports

✔ Posting of banns (wedding notice)

✔ Paperwork processing time

✔ Document translation

✔ Notarization

✔ *Apostille* (a document that certifies the legality of another document, such as a birth certificate or a divorce decree)

The U.S. Department of State authenticates documents mailed to it for a fee of $7 per document. The address is available at www. state.gov/m/a/auth. If you're out of the country and require an apostille, contact the nearest U.S. embassy or consulate for assistance. You can find a list of these at http://usembassy. state.gov. Click on *U.S. Citizen Services,* if you can't find a home-page link to the information. Obviously, the more documents and translations required, the more time-consuming obtaining a marriage license in another country is.

Chapter 7

Staying Close to Home: The United States and Canada

....

In This Chapter

▶ Selecting a Las Vegas wedding that fits your style

▶ Heading to Hawaii for a wedding on the beach

▶ Finding fun and frugal spots in Florida

▶ Toasting friends and family at a Wine Country wedding

▶ Uncovering uncommon wedding destinations across the United States

▶ Exploring romantic Canadian cities to say your vows in

....

*W*hen a couple first begins to think about having a destination wedding, they often picture themselves in a faraway place such as a sophisticated city, a pristine mountaintop, or a secluded island. In reality, they may not have to go that far to reach the type of setting they dream of. With venues of almost every kind in the United States and Canada, staying relatively close to home may make sense for you. That way, you can spend more of your funds on the wedding and reception and less on airfare to distant points.

Keep in mind when shopping around for destinations that the less expensive the cost of travel is, the more likely guests will accept your invitation.

Friends and neighbors, Canada and the United States are both excellent choices for a destination wedding. In addition to sharing a common border and language, they both have a high standard of living and low crime rates in the locations I recommend. This chapter looks at some of the more popular destinations in the United States and Canada. Transportation between the two is efficient and easy, and you don't need a passport until mid-2009 at least.

Considering the Hot Picks in the United States

Did you know that almost two-thirds of U.S. couples who have a destination wedding stay inside the country to marry? The United States is so vast that every state, not to mention every major city, attraction, and hotel, has its own Web site filled with information to convince you that it's the perfect place for your wedding. One of them may well be.

Because I don't have enough room in this chapter to include all the great U.S. destinations, I encourage you to continue researching on your own if you don't see the perfect place on these pages. To find additional wedding locations in the United States, pick up one of the big U.S.A. guidebooks. If you prefer to use the Web, check out www.seeamerica.org, which links to state tourism offices or use Google (www.google.com) or a destination-focused site such as About.com Travel (www.about.com/travel), simply pairing the name of the destination you want with the word *weddings*.

Living it up in Las Vegas

Saying "I do" in Las Vegas is so easy, affordable, and fun that more than 100,000 couples do it annually, making it America's number-one spot for destination weddings. Any time of year, you can witness couples of all ages and sizes, garbed in all styles of wedding apparel, on the Las Vegas Strip. You also find them inside casinos, restaurants, hotels, and streaming in and out of the Clark County marriage license bureau downtown.

Your options are vast in Vegas. Whether you and your other half dream of a traditional or a quickie wedding, a *Honeymoon in Vegas* scenario, or a helicopter ceremony, contact the facility you're interested in by phone or e-mail. Just about every Vegas chapel on the Strip and in its casino hotels explains its wedding packages on its Web site and also provides a toll-free phone number and e-mail address that put you in touch with a representative from the wedding department. Although many couples choose freestanding chapels for cost, convenience, and kitsch, hotel and theme weddings are eclipsing quickie Strip weddings in popularity.

Las Vegas wedding basics

If you're wondering what's involved in getting married here, it's pretty simple. Just follow these steps:

1. **Pick up a license.**

   The Las Vegas Marriage Bureau is open daily from 8 a.m. until midnight at 201 Clark Avenue, which is in downtown Las Vegas, three blocks off the Strip. Applications can be downloaded online (`www.co.clark.nv.us/clerk/ Marriage_Information.htm`) but must be submitted in person. You can contact the bureau at 702-671-0600.

   To get to the Marriage Bureau, catch a taxi in front of any hotel or take a bus down the Strip. If you prefer to travel in style, look for a wedding facility that offers limo service to and from the Marriage Bureau as part of a wedding package.

2. **Choose a chapel.**

   When selecting a Vegas chapel, you have two types of options:

   - **Freestanding chapels on the Strip:** Most people associate getting married in Las Vegas with these chapels where you can show up at 4 a.m., get married by an Elvis impersonator (check out Figure 7-1), and even drive through. A wedding here won't cost a lot of money (as long as you have a small, brief ceremony and resist buying the upsells).

Figure 7-1: Viva Las Vegas! You can have an elegant wedding in a fine hotel chapel or a kitschy one on the Strip with an Elvis impersonator.

Fun, old-fashioned Strip facilities include the Little White Wedding Chapel (www.littlewhitechapel.com; 800-545-8111), Little Chapel of the Flowers (www.littlechapel.com; 800-843-2410), Viva Las Vegas Wedding Chapels (www.vivalasvegasweddings.com; 800-574-4450), and Graceland Wedding Chapel (www.gracelandchapel.com; 800-824-5732). Most of them have built-in Webcams, and you can e-mail nonattending guests the time to log on to the chapel's Web address to watch your ceremony. (For more info on Webcams and your wedding, check out Chapter 15.)

Although you may be able to walk into one of these wedding chapels on the Strip without a reservation, I recommend reserving the time, the specific chapel, and the package in advance to get what you want.

- **Chapels inside hotel-casinos:** Couples who believe that a wedding ought to be a refined and dignified occasion, regardless of where it's held, will prefer the decorum as well as the decor of a hotel chapel. Not only are these chapels newer than their Strip competitors, but they also make a real effort to provide couples with a tasteful ceremony.

Chapels both on the Strip and in casino hotels have wedding coordinators, and they're responsible for helping you pick the package that you want, scheduling the wedding, notifying the officiant, wrangling the witnesses (if necessary), and making sure that all the elements you signed up for are provided.

Theme weddings in Las Vegas

Because every Las Vegas casino hotel has a theme, ranging from ancient Rome (Caesars Palace) to urban mash-up (New York New York), couples can easily slip into one of these virtual worlds for a pre-wedding, wedding, or post-wedding celebration that extends the theme. Although conventional weddings are the rule at casino-hotel chapels, tempting fun themes include

- ✔ **Gondola wedding:** Held at The Venetian hotel (for info, contact via www.venetianweddings.com or call 866-548-1807). No need to travel to Venice, when you can be serenaded on this hotel's Grand Canal.

- ✔ **Disco wedding:** Marry inside the Forever Grand Chapel in the MGM Grand and celebrate afterwards in its Studio 54 nightclub. You can find details at www.mgmgrand.com or by calling 800-646-5530.

✔ **Star Trek wedding:** The Trekkie Wedding at Las Vegas' Star Trek: The Experience inside the Las Vegas Hilton takes place on a replica of the Star Ship Enterprise bridge. A Klingon can act as your witness, and "intergalactic" music serenades the ceremony officiated by a minister dressed in a Starfleet uniform. Beam yourselves over to www.startrekexp.com or call 702-697-8750.

✔ **Roller-coaster wedding:** Experience the thrill of the Sahara Hotel's Speed — The Ride NASCAR attraction. Go to www.saharavegas.com or call 800-398-6928 for a topsy-turvy wedding to remember.

✔ **Paris romance wedding:** Say your vows atop the Eiffel Tower in the Paris Las Vegas hotel. Go to www.parislasvegas.com or call 877-650-5021 if you're interested in Las Vegas l'amour.

Elegant weddings in Las Vegas

Traditional-minded couples and those who want a formal, dignified affair can find many pretty, romantic spots that can suit their needs in Las Vegas. The best casino hotels in town (see the following list) have beautiful wedding chapels and offer packages that start at affordable and go to sky's-the-limit:

✔ **Mandalay Bay:** Its chapel design is sleek and sophisticated, with garden views. See for yourself at www.mandalaybay.com, or call 877-632-7701.

✔ **Bellagio:** This casino hotel has two chapels that can accommodate 30 and 130 guests, and locations throughout the hotel provide Tuscan-like backdrops for photos. Go to www.bellagio.com or call 888-987-3344 for more info.

✔ **Caesars Palace:** Offering a choice of five indoor and outdoor settings that can fit from 35 to 196 guests, Caesars offers a menu of "unforgettables" that include invitations and gown and tuxedo rentals. To check it out, visit the Web site (www.caesars.com) or call 877-279-3334.

✔ **Wynn Las Vegas:** The top of the line, Wynn Las Vegas is the world's only five-star, five-diamond casino hotel. Its three wedding salons have upholstered pews and flattering lighting and can accommodate from 65 to 120 guests. Browse its Web site (www.wynnlasvegas.com) or call 877-770-7077.

Just because you want an elegant wedding in Vegas doesn't mean you have to go into debt, take out a loan, or get a second job. If you want to get an idea of what things cost and compare a low-budget and a luxurious destination wedding, refer to Chapter 4.

Vegas yes, Strip no

The fastest-growing city in America, Las Vegas features more wedding places beyond its famed Strip. Two fairly new hotels that have upped the ante in luxury also boast facilities that can accommodate larger weddings. Both properties are a short cab ride from The Strip, so you can marry in their chapels and luxuriate in their beautiful surroundings, then head to the action for great gambling and restaurants:

 ✔ **JW Marriott Las Vegas:** Large rooms, lush grounds, indoor and outdoor ceremony venues, and all-inclusive wedding packages await couples. Go online to www.jwlasvegas resort.com or call 702-869-7034 for info.

 ✔ **Ritz-Carlton Lake Las Vegas:** Whether you choose an intimate or extravagant wedding here, the settings are Vegas's most romantic. See www.ritzcarlton.com/resorts/lake_las_ vegas or call 702-567-4700.

Restaurant receptions

Las Vegas has recently turned into a foodie city, with many of the world's best chefs opening high-end restaurants inside hotels. You and your party can dine at desert outposts of Los Angeles's Spago and Nobu, New York's Rao's and Aureole, New Orleans's Commander's Palace, and even Paris's L'Atelier de Joël Robuchon.

Fortunately, the city also has a wide selection of affordable off-Strip restaurants for receptions. Two favorites are Carluccio's Tivoli Gardens (702-795-3236), an old-fashioned Italian restaurant, and Pamplemousse (www.pamplemousserestaurant.com; 702-733-2066), a Rat Pack–era French eatery with exceptional food and service.

Check out a listing of Las Vegas eateries at www.vegas.com/ restaurant, where you can make reservations.

Getting hitched in Hawaii

America's 50th state and number-one honeymoon destination, Hawaii (www.gohawaii.com; 800-464-2924) is also a prime wedding spot for couples — especially those coming from the West Coast who can fly direct in about five hours. Exquisite sunsets, gorgeous Pacific ocean views, and residents born of the gentle Polynesian culture all add to the loveliness of Hawaii (see Figure 7-2). Visitors also eat well here, tempted by everything from fresh fish to succulent pineapples, piquant Maui onions to rich Kona coffee.

Figure 7-2: Orchid leis, a tropical bouquet, and a kahu officiant add authenticity to a Hawaiian wedding.

Thanks to dependably warm and sunny days cooled year-round by trade winds and astoundingly beautiful Hawaiian sunsets, outdoor weddings are very popular. All it takes to arrange a ceremony on one of the state's clean and wide public beaches or parks is securing an available date and a paid special-use permit. Receptions aren't normally allowed.

If you want to marry on a secluded beach, hiring an island wedding planner who can direct you to places that only locals know about is your best option (see Chapter 4 for more on wedding planners). And if you're bringing a group of 20 or more to Hawaii, look into Hawaiian Airlines' (www.hawaiianair.com) Wedding Wings program 60 days ahead of the wedding to request an upgrade for the two of you.

For information on getting a marriage license valid throughout the state, go to http://www.hawaii.gov/health/vital-records/vital-records/marriage/index.html.

Maui

The highest percentage of destination weddings takes place on Maui, consistently voted "best island in the world" by readers of a leading travel magazine. Maui (www.gohawaii.com/maui; 800-464-2924) has four areas where its best hotels are located: Kaanapali Beach, Kapalua, Wailea, and Hana.

Borrowing local Hawaiian traditions

Whether you crave a formal ceremony or barefoot beach affair, you can get married your way in Hawaii. Couples who want to give their event a stronger sense of place may adapt local traditions. The following are a few examples of what you can do:

✔ Some ceremonies begin with a wedding chant initiated by a *kahu* (nondenominational officiant) who subsequently blows a conch shell to signify the bride's entrance. He may lead the wedding party down to the water's edge to be honored with a hula and blessed with a gentle sprinkling of sea water before beginning the vows.

✔ A husband and wife can do an orchid lei exchange at the beginning or the end of the ceremony to represent their unity and commitment to one another.

✔ Some couples integrate a *sand ceremony,* where two different shades of sand, symbolizing bride and groom, are blended together to fill a keepsake vessel.

✔ Flower circles on the vast beach mark a distinct space for a marrying couple to stand inside. Bamboo tiki torches often surround them.

✔ Instead of a traditional recessional, everyone walks to the edge of the beach and throws flower petals into the ocean following a blessing by the minister.

✔ Hawaiian love songs or instrumentals played on a super-resonant Hawaiian lap steel guitar provide an authentic serenade before and after the ceremony.

To incorporate any of these traditions into your Hawaiian wedding, discuss it with your wedding planner. If you don't have one, talk it over with the officiant.

Thanks to the island's dramatic geography, you can find ample sites beyond hotel ballrooms, terraces, and their adjacent beachfronts to get "Maui'd." Check out the following options:

✔ Pause at the lush Maui Tropical Plantation (www.mauitropical plantation.com; 800-451-6805), where exotic flowers and the spectacular West Maui mountain range serve as a backdrop.

✔ Stop beside a remote waterfall on the drive to heavenly Hana. The 52-mile-long road to Hana traverses some 600 curves and dozens of bridges. Around each bend, the scenery delights and surprises. Search Google Images (images.google.com) for *hana waterfalls* to see what this looks like.

✔ Feast at the Old Lahaina Luau (www.oldlahainaluau.com; 800-248-5828); wedding chants and fare evoke old Hawaii here.

✔ Ascend to a sunrise ceremony atop dormant, 10,000-foot Mount Haleakala volcano. Trips via tour bus and helicopter are available through www.viator.com, along with bicycle-down adventures.

Oahu

The most crowded and commercial of the Hawaiian Islands, Oahu (www.gohawaii.com/oahu; 800-464-2924) is also home to Waikiki Beach, ringed by hotels overlooking the crescent shore. Each hotel can serve as a ceremony venue and provide reception space.

The largest hotel in the state, Hilton Hawaiian Village (www.hilton hawaiianvillage.com) recently added the Ocean Crystal Chapel. Set in a tropical garden, the chapel can seat up to 70. Smaller venues are also available on the 22-acre, waterfront property.

Thanks to its popularity, Oahu also offers unique spots to tie the knot in. Among them are

- ✔ **The Polynesian Culture Center:** A tropical setting that offers entertainment for family members of all ages. Visit www.polynesia.com or call 800-367-7060.

- ✔ **Byodo-In Buddhist Temple:** A tranquil, photogenic setting with lovely Japanese gardens. See it at www.hawaiiweb.com/oahu/sites_to_see/byodo-in_temple.htm.

- ✔ **Haiku Gardens:** Features an over-water gazebo that serves as an open-air chapel. Check out www.haikugardens.com or call 808-247-0605 for more info.

Other options include working with a wedding planner to stage a wedding in one of Oahu's five botanical gardens, taking guests on a sunset cruise, or gaining access to a private estate or golf course.

The Big Island

The largest and least-crowded Hawaiian island, the Big Island (www.bigisland.org/romance; 800-464-2924) is a nature-lover's paradise that has remained relatively unspoiled. Black-lava beaches; tumbling, blue waterfalls; verdant tropical gardens; and the flame-orange Kileaua Volcano exhibit the color and energy of the island.

The size of the Big Island is comparable to the state of Connecticut, so deciding on which side to hold your wedding is important. Although you can drive to all parts of the island, select-ing the nearest airport (Kona or Hilo) as your starting point is the most time-efficient method. Kona has some luxurious hotels:

- ✔ **Kona Village Resort** (www.konavillage.com; 808-325-4372), whose unique black sands remind visitors of the island's origin. Accommodations are luxurious thatched-roof huts.

✔ Immensely beautiful and renowned for superlative service, the 3,200-acre, oceanfront **Mauna Lani Resort** (www.maunalani. com; 800-367-2323) has a dedicated weddings and romance director.

Other options on the Big Island for your wedding include

✔ **Outdoor venues:** Weddings also can be held outdoors at Hulihee Palace (808-329-1877) and Puuhonua O Honaunau National Historical Park. Check out www.nps.gov/puho or call 808-328-2288.

✔ **Parker Ranch:** The 225,000-acre Parker Ranch (www.parker ranch.com) is one of the oldest and biggest ranches in the country and offers numerous wedding locations, including gardenia and rose gardens, a lavender arch, a koi pond, and a formal dining room. You can visit the Web site or call 808-885-5898 for more info.

✔ **Hawaii Tropical Botanical Garden:** Considered one of the most beautiful spots in the islands, the Hawaii Tropical Botanical Garden (http://htbg.com) on the Hamakua Coast (fly into Hilo) has a wedding site overlooking Onomea Bay. Its wedding package includes a minister, tropical bouquet for the bride and lei for the groom, a golf cart to ferry the couple and parents to the site, CD of digital pictures, and more. For more details, check out the Web site or call 808-964-5233.

Kauai

The oldest and most verdant of the Hawaiian islands, Kauai (www.gohawaii.com/kauai; 800-464-2924) is a wonderful place for an outdoor wedding. Many claim it has the best beaches in the state. Couples can dig their toes into the sand from the broad, sandy, uncrowded swaths of Shipwreck Beach on the south shore's Keoniloa Bay (conveniently located near a Hyatt hotel) to those beside sheltered Hanalei Bay on the north side. Afterward, a private luau or a sail along the breathtakingly beautiful Napali Coast can cap an utterly romantic wedding.

In addition to Kauai's beaches, coves, hotels, and restaurants, other appealing wedding sites that a local planner can hook you up with include

✔ **Fern Grotto:** A very popular natural amphitheater beside the Wailua River, Fern Grotto is a unique setting for a scenic destination wedding. It takes 40 minutes to reach it via riverboat, and after a short walk on pavement to the grotto, couples marry at this Eden-like spot where tropical vegetation covers volcanic rocks.

- ✔ **Ninini Point Lighthouse:** This site is open sporadically, but the building and grounds provide a picturesque setting and excellent views of Nawiliwili Harbor.

- ✔ **Na ʻĀina Kai Botanical Gardens:** If you're looking for a beach, waterfall, Japanese teahouse, or lake settings, this location has them all. Check out www.naainakai.org or call 808-828-0525.

- ✔ **Waioli Huiia Church:** In Hanalei, Waioli Huiia Church, built by Christian missionaries, has stained-glass windows, and waterfalls surround it.

 Couples need not stand still to pledge their vows on Kauai. For an action-packed ceremony, consider marrying beside a waterfall you reach via horseback, hopping aboard an ATV, and roaring up a mountainside. Or you can mouth the words "I do" over the noise of a helicopter that sweeps over Waimea, known as the Grand Canyon of the Pacific. A local tour company, resort concierge, or wedding planner can help you turn these fantasies into reality.

Finding the magic in Florida

Florida's tropical weather and azure waters, its variety of natural and manmade wonders, and the availability of cheap, direct flights from many domestic airports all make this state a prime place for destination weddings. No wonder that nearly 30 percent of couples who marry within the state of Florida aren't residents.

Prices for everything from bridal bouquets to wedding cakes vary widely and are likely to be highest along the Gold Coast, stretching from Palm Beach down to Miami, and in Disney World. However, you don't have to bring a pot of gold to get married there. The following looks at some options for a Florida wedding.

Florida for the frugal

If you've dreamed of getting married in sunny Florida and you want to stay on a budget, you're not out luck. Fortunately, many of Florida's state parks (www.floridastateparks.org) include beach frontage, perfect for informal and inexpensive weddings. To arrange one, first contact the park manager to request permission.

Another option: Way down the coast, in the Florida Keys, edged by the Atlantic on one side and the Caribbean on the other, water plays a large part in inspiring couples as to where to tie the knot. You can take your vows on the beach at sunset, and then invite up to 30 guests to board a paddlewheeler that plies the waters off Key Largo for a reception. And for something different, marry at a dolphin facility with the friendly mammals as your witnesses. Visit Florida Keys tourism site at www.fla-keys.com or call 800-358-5937.

Weddings in Walt Disney World

Young-at-heart couples and ones with children in tow can't help but get excited by the prospect of marrying inside Disney World (www.disneyweddings.com; 321-939-4610). The Orlando park goes all out to make events the stuff of magic. However, if your guest list favors sophisticated and child-free couples, Disney isn't the place for you.

What makes a Disney wedding desirable? Check out some of the following perks:

- ✔ **Classic Disney magic:** The bride can be delivered to the wedding pavilion in Cinderella's glass coach driven by two footmen and pulled by six Welsh ponies. Or you can have your ceremony end with a white dove release or invite Disney characters to dance at the reception. And Disney recently debuted its own Fairy Tale Wedding Dress collection, so a bride can walk down the aisle looking like a princess.

  Neither Mickey nor Minnie Mouse is permitted to officiate, but couples can arrange for the characters to mingle with guests at the reception, pose for pictures, and "cut in" on the first dance.

- ✔ **On-site wedding coordinator:** In addition to booking your ceremony time and space and helping to customize the event, a Disney coordinator can present options for post-wedding celebrations.

- ✔ **Couture weddings.** Couples who want elaborate decorations (crystal chandeliers, gilt mirrors) at their Disney wedding and reception can opt for one of four dramatic looks conceived by designer David Tutura.

- ✔ **Personalized wedding Web site:** Couples who book a Disney wedding receive a wedding Web site where they can fill in all the details they want guests to know. After your big day, your wedding pictures are posted to the site.

- ✔ **Lodging:** One advantage of inviting friends and family to celebrate with you is the wide choice of accommodations. Budget-conscious guests can stay in the park's value or moderate resorts. Those who can afford to splurge can choose a deluxe hotel such as the retro Grand Floridian (407-824-3000), which has honeymoon suites, or the new Animal Kingdom Lodge (407-938-3000). You can find complete information and rates on accommodations by clicking on "Resorts" at www.disneyworld.com.

> ✔ **Theme park access:** What's the point of a Disney World wedding without a visit to the Magic Kingdom, EPCOT, Disney-MGM Studios, the Animal Kingdom Park, and then Downtown Disney at night? You can hit them all on a wedding-and-honeymoon combo, visiting the hot spots with your guests or on your own.

Four nights is the minimum length of time required for a couple to stay in order to purchase a Disney World wedding package. But with two water parks (Typhoon Lagoon and Blizzard Beach), four theme parks (Magic Kingdom, Epcot, Disney-MGM Studios, and Animal Kingdom), golf courses, and spas, few couples consider that requirement a deterrent.

You can book Disney weddings up to a year in advance, although last-minute couples who want a small wedding may be accommodated (if the date is available) as soon as 21 days in advance.

Wedding in Wine Country

Surrounded by natural beauty, wineries make ideal venues for outdoor destination weddings. Perhaps the best-known Wine Country destinations, Sonoma County (www.sonomawine.com) and Napa Valley (www.napavintners.com) north of San Francisco are home to hundreds of wineries. Ones open to the public have tasting rooms, and those where weddings are routinely held feature more-extensive facilities such as banquet halls.

In addition to California, a number of other states, as you can see in the following list, have wine-growing regions with wineries available for celebrations:

> ✔ **New York (www.newyorkwines.org):** Several regions of the state, including the East End of Long Island, the Finger Lakes, and the Western tier produce award-winning wines.
>
> ✔ **Oregon (www.oregonwine.org):** Small-production wineries offer intimate spaces for weddings.
>
> ✔ **Pennsylvania (bvwinetrail.com):** Lodgings in Brandywine Valley are mostly limited to B&Bs.
>
> ✔ **Texas (www.texaswinetrail.com):** Hill Country also has plenty of spas, art galleries, and even cooking classes to entertain wine-loving wedding parties.
>
> ✔ **Virginia (www.virginiawines.org):** Boutique wineries in this state stretch from near Washington, DC, to Richmond.
>
> ✔ **Washington (www.washingtonwine.org):** Only California surpasses this state in the number of wineries.

If tying the knot in a winery sounds idyllic to you, look for wineries with on-premise restaurants that prepare food conceived to complement the house vintages. Even more convenient are wineries with an inn on the premises or nearby that can house your guests.

Exploring more U.S. locations

Spanning the 3,200 miles from northern Maine to southern California are countless other places well-suited for a destination wedding. Whether your taste runs to the charming, the luxurious, or the unusual, you can find a wonderful place to wed.

Churches, synagogues, catering halls, restaurants, and hotels win the lion's share of wedding business (you can find them in almost any city; check the Yellow Pages), but many more options are available for couples who want something different or want guaranteed-gorgeous wedding photos. Imagine a backdrop of a national or state park, outside a lighthouse, on a ferry or riverboat, on horseback at a dude ranch, or in a private estate or mansion. The choices are endless, depending on your own tastes and budget.

Southern charms

Weddings in a southern location can take you back in time. Often the focus is on tradition and heritage, and "good old Southern cooking" invariably delights wedding guests. Outside the big cities, weddings in the South tend to be less expensive than in other parts of the country. A few of my top southern picks include

- ✔ **Sevier County, Tennessee:** Dotted with wedding chapels and home to Dollywood, Gatlinburg, and Pigeon Forge, this affordable mountainous destination (www.smokymountain-guide.com) is the only county in the United States where a couple can pre-apply for their marriage license online (https://sevier-tn.mygovonline.com/clerk/modules/marriagelicense) and pick it up at the courthouse after they arrive.

- ✔ **Asheville, North Carolina:** Comfortable even in summer, this city (www.exploreasheville.com; 828-258-6101) is surrounded by the Blue Ridge Mountains (in other words, you have to make an effort to get a bad wedding picture outdoors), and Asheville activities range from hiking to gallery-hopping.

Mountaintop marriage

Winter is prime time for ski resorts, and nothing is as beautiful or exhilarating as boarding a gondola with your guests (or even leading the way from a chairlift), arriving at a specially prepared perch, and reciting your vows surrounded by snow-capped mountains.

If you want to marry atop a major mountain and don't have a favorite one, visit www.skiusa.com or call 800-754-7669 to research the possibilities, which are organized by state. After you have a ski resort in mind, find and visit its Web site. Then call or e-mail to ask to speak for someone who can provide wedding information.

The downside to a winter mountaintop wedding (aside from the big chill) is this: During the short snowy season, couples may find getting the full attention of vendors frustrating. Not only are ski resorts more crowded then, but many outdoor venues aren't even open in winter. So you have fewer choices, bigger crowds, and higher prices.

The largest ski resort in the United States, Vail, Colorado, has a Web site for summer visitors with a section devoted to weddings (vail.snow.com/summerhome.asp). Vail presents summer lovers with a choice of venues on the mountain, in the village, and in nearby places such as ranches, parks, and other outdoor locations.

Ski resorts are eager for business during the warmer months, which is when the majority of weddings take place. Some ski resorts are open only for a short summer season that extends from just before Independence Day until right after Labor Day. To attract vacationers, they add all kinds of activities, from mountain biking and bungee jumping to horseback riding and hot-air ballooning.

Be sure to find out when a particular resort has the best wedding weather (and is open for business) before deciding on that destination. Depending on the region, ski season starts as early as Thanksgiving and stretches (out West at least) into early spring. The biggest crowds come for the holidays — Thanksgiving, Christmas, New Year's — when hotel prices soar and availability drops. So if you have your heart set on a winter wedding, January and anytime up until winter break will be most affordable and least crowded.

Coastal capers

Having your wedding in a quaint coastal town may be your fantasy. If so, the best place I can think of is Newport, Rhode Island (www.gonewport.com).

This small city on the New England seacoast seems custom-made for romance, and has a dedicated Web site to help you plan a wedding (www.yournewportwedding.com). In America's sailing capital, you can choose a beach wedding, a picnic reception in Fort Adams

State Park in full view of the harbor, or even a ceremony and reception inside a turn-of-the-century mansion (`www.newport mansions.org`).

You take Manhattan

New York City is drawing an increasing number of couples to tie the knot, primarily because this booming metropolis is such a fascinating place for a honeymoon. Broadway theater, the best shopping, museums that hold the world's treasures, superior restaurants in every price range, great hotels, authentic ethnic enclaves, and landmarks that include the Statue of Liberty, the Empire State Building, and the United Nations make New York a must-see at some point in every couple's life. Both `http://gonyc.about.com` and `www.nycvisit.com` can guide you around the city.

Some New York options include

- ✔ **Museums and more museums:** New York is home to museums grand and small, and many of them make spaces available for wedding celebrations. Find a list with approximate rental fees at `http://nymag.com/weddings/listings/locations`.

- ✔ **Puck Building:** At the edge of New York's SoHo neighborhood, the landmark Puck Building (`www.thepuckbuilding.com`) is on the National Historic Register and a favorite with couples who want to create a unique environment starting from the bare walls.

- ✔ **The Waldorf Astoria Hotel:** The gold standard for a New York wedding is the Waldorf Astoria (`www.weddingatthewaldorf.com`). It contains more than three-dozen gilded banquet rooms that can accommodate parties ranging in size from 20 to 2,000 under glittering chandeliers.

Contrary to the ultra-high costs of most weddings in Manhattan, you do have a modest option: the private, nondenominational chapel of the City Clerk's office (`nycmarriagebureau.com`). On a typical day, about 40 couples tie the knot there at a cost of $40 for the license plus $25 for the civil ceremony.

Following a downtown ceremony, frugal folks can head for the nearby Brooklyn Bridge walkway. On the bridge you can pose for dramatic pictures against the East River and city skyline. To keep the event low-cost, either head back into Manhattan's Chinatown or cross over to the Brooklyn side and walk to Atlantic Avenue for a Middle Eastern wedding feast.

Coupling in Canada

Ranked as the world's best country in which to live by the United Nations, Canada is a clean, safe, progressive nation whose natural beauty stretches from coast to coast. Add to that a favorable exchange rate, cosmopolitan cities as charming and cultured as many in Europe, and a polyglot society that reflects the country's English, French, and Native American roots, and you've got a country to marry in that's both foreign and familiar.

Each province has its own set of regulations that must be met to obtain a marriage license. Weddings are conducted as civil ceremonies. Following that service, couples can also be blessed by a religious officiant. Although seven out of ten Canadians identify themselves as either Roman Catholic or Protestant, Canada is a multicultural nation where many different spiritual beliefs are followed and respected.

On July 20, 2005, Canada's Equal Marriage Bill was proclaimed into law in Canada, making it legal for same-sex couples to exchange vows there. Since then, Canada has emerged as a favored destination for gay and lesbian weddings. However, the U.S. doesn't legally recognize marriages of gay U.S. citizens in Canada.

On the following pages, you can read about what entices couples to marry in Canada's leading cities and get links to official tourism sites. For general information, you may find these resources helpful:

- ✔ **Canada tourism online:** The main Web site for gathering information on Canada online is `www.explore.canada.travel`. Every province, territory, and mid-to-big city also has its own dedicated Web site.

- ✔ **Air Canada discounts:** Group Express is the name of Air Canada's reduced-fare program for ten people or more traveling together. To find out how to arrange a trip for your group, go to `www.aircanada.com` or call 800-268-0024.

If you or any members of your wedding party are traveling between the United States and Canada, be sure to carry and present a valid passport. For more info on passports, see Chapter 11.

Weddings with a French accent

Canada's Québec province offers many of the same charms as France — fine food, historic treasures, Paris chic, *joie de vivre* —

without the obstacles of marrying in that country. In its two major cities, Montreal and Québec City, you're as liable to hear French spoken as English. Both are ports along the Saint Lawrence Seaway, accessible via car, bus, train, air, and even cruise ship. To find out what it takes to get legally married in Québec, go to www.justice.gouv.qc.ca/english/publications/generale/maria-a.htm.

When you call a phone number in Quebec, you'll first hear French spoken. Start speaking in English, and the person on the other end will respond in English.

Marrying in Montreal

The French-speaking capital of Canada, Montreal (www.tourisme-montreal.org; 877-266-5687) is a sophisticated metropolis with a vibrant historic district that overlooks the waterfront.

In addition to private rooms in Montreal's excellent hotels and restaurants serving the finest cuisine this side of the Left Bank, couples can get married in

- ✔ A casino shaped like an ocean liner (www.casino-de-montreal.com/montreal/nav/en/home)

- ✔ Montreal Botanical Garden (www2.ville.montreal.qc.ca/jardin/en/menu.htm)

- ✔ A riverboat (www.bateau-mouche.com)

- ✔ Chapel of the Sacred Heart in the 1672 Notre Dame Church (Catholics only) (www.montreal.com/tourism/churches.html)

And the ceremony and reception sites aren't the only places that are uncommonly charming. Montreal has abundant spots for a wedding party to explore before and after the main event. From the top of Mount Royal to La Ronde amusement park, from the horse-drawn *caleches* that clip-clop along cobblestone streets to the fun of a *bateau-mouche* river cruise, this is a city to love.

If you're interested in getting married in Montreal, contact the tourism office to request a recommendation for a local wedding planner or work with a coordinator at a local hotel.

Ambling down l'aisle in Québec City

Québec City (www.quebecregion.com/e/mar-index.asp; 877-783-1608), capital of the province of Québec, presents the perfect backdrop for utterly romantic weddings. This city is the heart of French civilization in North America, and couples have long been drawn to its ancient walled center, where narrow, winding streets date back four centuries to the city's 1608 founding.

Civil ceremonies and receptions in Québec City are typically held indoors at restaurants and aboard riverboats. The city is also home to many beautiful churches, and its wedding office (418-649-3501) can recommend specific venues.

The hotel that towers above the St. Lawrence River and overlooks the old city is the castle-like Le Château Frontenac (www.fairmont. com/frontenac; 418-692-3861), which has hosted many wedding over the years, ranging from small parties in suites to major fetes in its Grand Ballroom. (See Figure 7-3.)

Figure 7-3: A romantic setting in front of the Frontenac in Québec City.

Québec winters can get very cold, but hearty couples may still want to consider scheduling their destination wedding to coincide with the city's annual winter carnival, the biggest in the world. For carnival dates and info, check out www.carnaval.qc.ca.

Another amazing place to chill is Québec's Ice Hotel (www.ice hotel-canada.com; 877-505-0423), which has a dedicated chapel and several wedding packages to choose from. Its season extends usually from early January to April 1. The ceremony takes place within the hotel, and a bar is available for a cocktail reception. Afterward a couple can repair to a wedding-night suite, snuggling into a sleeping bag or under a heavy fur blanket and keeping each other warm until morning.

Saying vows in Vancouver

Year after year named "best city in the Americas" by a leading travel magazine, vibrant, multicultural Vancouver (www.tourism vancouver.com; 604-683-2000) lies between the Coast Mountains and the Pacific Ocean and offers couples an impressive array of facilities and activities. Here you can find sites just right for a destination wedding — both out in nature and in the comfortable indoors. The place to look for information on marrying in British Columbia is www.vs.gov.bc.ca/marriage/index.html.

Couples who don't feel like choosing between indoors and outdoors ought to consider marrying aboard one of the boats that cruise Vancouver harbor (www.boatcruises.com; 604-688-7246). Catered wedding packages provide food and drink for four-hour receptions.

The great outdoors

Thanks to Vancouver's mild weather (snow is rare and fresh ocean breezes keep the sunniest summer days comfortable), well-kept parks, and public access to most waterfronts and beaches, opportunities to marry outdoors abound.

Thousand-acre Stanley Park, the second largest in North America, extends from the city's downtown to the water's edge. The park has a number of breathtaking settings where couples hold wedding ceremonies. Groups up to 50 can use many of the city's fresh-air locations without prior permission. However, no chairs, tents, awnings, tables, decorations, alcohol, rice, or confetti are allowed. If an outdoor ceremony followed by a picnic is your style and your group is larger than 50, you can reserve a site at www.city. vancouver.bc.ca/parks/info/picnic/index.htm.

Unique adventures for you and your guests await before and after the wedding. Guests can go on a guided kayaking trip, take a treetops hike 100 feet above the forest floor (www.capbridge.com), golf, snowboard on Grouse Mountain, join a whale-watching expedition, or simply detox inside a seaweed wrap. (For more info, check out Vancouver's tourism Web site, mentioned at the beginning of this section.)

Inside story

Vancouver has several top hotels alongside its waterfront that boast extraordinary views from their reception spaces and guest rooms.

✔ **Herons at the Fairmont Waterfront:** This hotel (www.fairmont.com/waterfront; 800-257-7544) has two-story, floor-to-ceiling windows with panoramic harbor views of the mountains, Stanley Park, and cruise ships gliding into port. The hotel's catering team is super-experienced in orchestrating weddings large and small.

✔ **The Pan Pacific Vancouver:** This hotel (www.panpacific.com/Vancouver; 800-937-1515) boasts equally stunning views and 20 different event rooms to cater to weddings of all sizes.

Other indoor venues include the Stanley Park Pavilion (www.stanleyparkpavilion.com; 604-602-3088), adjacent to the park's gorgeous Rose Gardens. Because the facility offers all services — catering in your choice of cuisine, floral arrangements, horse and carriage tours in the park, photo and video, music, wedding cake — it's convenient for out-of-town couples to have a turnkey reception here. With its sparkling chandeliers, raised altar, and private bride's room, the Chapel at Stanley Park (www.thechapelatstanleypark.com; 604-688-0770) is a compatible setting for the ceremony.

This multicultural city also boasts more than 5,000 restaurants, including ones that specialize in French, Asian, Greek, and Italian, as well as Afghan, Lebanese, and Malaysian fare. So whatever your culinary tastes, you can find a restaurant to hold a reception in. Go to www.vancouver.com/restaurants for a list. When you find ones that appeal to you, call to ask whether they have a private dining room to host a wedding, what menu options they offer, the prices, and date availability.

Athletes and spectators from all over the world will converge in Vancouver for the 2010 Winter Olympics, so think twice before scheduling a wedding there for the second half of February 2010.

Investigating other Canadian locations

Although you can find a variety of wedding destinations in Montreal, Québec City, and Vancouver (see previous sections), Canada has so much more to offer (I could probably write a book on Canada wedding destinations alone). And this discussion wouldn't be complete without taking a look at what Toronto and Niagara Falls have to offer.

Info on marrying in Ontario, the province that contains both Toronto and the Niagara region, is available at www.cbs.gov.on.ca/MCBS/ENGLISH/marriages.htm.

Tying the knot in Toronto

Even if you haven't visited Toronto (www.torontotourism.com; 800-499-2514), you've probably seen it on film. Toronto has appeared in countless movies that needed a clean, affordable urban location. And thanks to the favorable exchange rate, prices for wedding parties are as reasonable as they are for film crews.

Toronto has all the amenities one would expect in a major city (excellent hotels as well as a wide range of fine and ethnic restaurants). The city has a vital waterfront and Paramount Canada's Wonderland (www3.paramountparks.com/canadaswonderland; 905-832-8131), the largest and most popular theme park in the country. You can also give diverse, progressive Toronto its props for being the first North American city to legalize weddings for gay couples, including nonresidents.

Niagara nuptials

There are two cities named Niagara Falls: one in Canada and one in New York State, across the river from each other. Facilities on the Canadian side are more extensive and better tended than those of their U.S. neighbor, so it's worth crossing the border.

Less than a two-hour drive from Toronto, the iconic honeymoon spot and natural wonder that is Niagara Falls (www.niagarafalls tourism.com; 800-563-2557) makes a memorable wedding destination or an entertaining day trip from Toronto or Buffalo, New York, for you and your guests. Couples can be married in wedding chapels and gardens near the Falls, overlooking the Falls, and hovering atop the Falls in a helicopter. You can even get hitched in the wedding chapel inside Niagara Fallsview Casino (www.niagara fallsviewcasinoresort.com; 866-789-8697).

If you bring your own officiant, you can get married on a Maid of the Mist riverboat (www.maidofthemist.com), which comes thrillingly close to the Horseshoe Falls (no reservations accepted). Afterward, you can grab a bite at one of the Fallsview hotel restaurants, avoiding the tourist traps clogging the waterway.

Just a 20-minute drive north of the Falls, but a world apart, Niagara-on-the-Lake (www.niagaraonthelake.com; 905-468-1950) is a scenic village resplendent with gazebos and gardens perfect for romantic summer weddings. The town center is one of Canada's National Historic Sites. Niagara-on-the-Lake is also home to a large number of wineries and small inns, many of which provide sylvan settings for weddings and fine fare for receptions.

Chapter 8

Heading to the Tropics and Islands

*T*ropical fantasies captivate many an engaged couple as they picture themselves running away from it all to avoid an over-priced, overproduced at-home wedding. Yet it need not be a fantasy; having a destination wedding in the tropics is a real possibility. Brides and grooms in search of great beaches, crystal-clear waters, and weddings that are both easy-going and easy to organize are choosing island getaways in record numbers.

Deciding on a tropical location requires an understanding of the different features these destinations offer. Caribbean islands such as Jamaica offer a wide choice of all-inclusives where weddings are an everyday occurrence. Resorts along the coasts of Mexico add spice to a tropical wedding. So if you're tempted by tropical locales, this chapter introduces you to the major ones where couples wed.

The Truth about Tropical Destination Weddings

More than anywhere else, the tropics attract couples who want to situate their wedding in a warm place where they can take advantage of a full-service hotel and its amenities, soft-sand beaches, outdoor sports, and romantic nights under starry skies.

Pondering the pros of a tropical wedding away

If the idea of transporting yourselves alone or with guests to marry in a sun-drenched setting with an endless supply of frosty tropical drinks appeals to you, look at both the advantages and disadvantages before investing in an industrial-size tube of SPF30. Here are the pros.

In addition to the it's-a-wedding-and-a-beach-vacation-rolled-into-one aspect and all the fun you can have, you can also count on:

- ✔ **The ease of a turnkey wedding.** The majority of destination weddings are turnkey affairs, which means you can get married with a minimum of fuss, especially if your guest list is small and you're basically okay with the standard options included in a wedding package. Just about every good resort in the tropics has played host to a wedding, if not hundreds or even thousands of them. If it doesn't have a coordinator on-site, the resort can put you in touch with vendors it recommends. And if your guest list expands — or if you'd rather be on the beach than bargaining with a caterer — bring down your own wedding planner or hire a local one. Wedding planners can also advise you as to the best ceremony spots and wedding packages.

- ✔ **The exhilaration of outdoor activities.** Water lovers can snorkel around reefs and wrecks, take boat tours, wind surf, scuba dive, fish, and sail. On land, couples and guests can spend time golfing, horseback riding, and unwinding in a spa.

- ✔ **The flavor of foreign fare.** Even in the most remote spots, you can find familiar Continental fare, such as steak and seafood dishes. Couples who want to spice things up can choose authentic local dishes at restaurants and receptions.

- ✔ **The charm of new people and cultures.** Similar to tropical temperatures, people of the tropics tend to be warm, too. They're proud of their surroundings and respond to you with warmth and friendliness when you put out that vibe to them.

Considering the cons of getting married where it's hot, hot, hot

Is there trouble in paradise? Could be. So it's wise to approach a wedding in the tropics with eyes open. Here are some cons:

- ✔ **Passports required:** With the exception of Puerto Rico and the United States Virgin Islands (which I discuss later in this chapter), you'll be required to carry a passport by mid-2009. Find out how to get a passport in Chapter 11.

- ✔ **Heat:** You have to love heat and not mind humidity if you choose to marry in most torrid climes, although breezes and ascents to higher elevations can mitigate those concerns. Mold can also be a problem in hotel rooms in humid locales, which makes a preliminary visit to sniff around a good idea.

- ✔ **Bugs:** Tropical winds keep insects away from beach areas, but if you're going to be spending time in a jungle or rainforest, don't say I didn't warn you. You can find bugs the size of cocker spaniels in those places. Okay, I exaggerate. But bring bug spray. And a leash.

- ✔ **"Island time":** Vendors who operate with an unhurried don't-worry-be-happy attitude aren't for control-freak couples. Everything gets done in time — but on their schedule.

- ✔ **Evidence of poverty:** Many tropical nations don't enjoy the same standard of living as the United States. You may encounter people whose lives are hard as you travel around. In some Caribbean and Mexican areas, crime rates are high. Check out the situation in your destination by reading its Consular Information Sheet at `travel.state.gov`.

Contemplating Your Choices for a Caribbean Wedding

Centuries ago, explorers brought back news of the treasures of the Caribbean: A sultry climate fanned by trade winds, trees bearing luscious fruit, miles of pristine beaches, and warm crystalline waters the color of blue jewels. Today couples are still drawn to the region for those same natural wonders, enhanced by a variety of vivid cultures, myriad land and water activities, extraordinary cuisines, and carefree weddings.

Hurricane season in the Caribbean stretches from (June 1– November 30). Risk-aversive couples ought not book weddings during that period. However, experienced travelers know that most island days will be hot and sunny during that period. And if it rains, the weather is more likely to bring just a passing shower.

If you're hesitant about having a tropical wedding because you don't think you can afford one in the Caribbean, you have options. The Web site www.nofrillswedding.com, for instance, links to planners on Jamaica, Antigua, St. Lucia, Nevis, and St. Kitts who arrange beach weddings for couples on a tight budget. Information on the most popular islands for destination weddings follows, along with suggestions for other alluring spots.

Loving it up in Jamaica

One of couples' favorite places for a destination wedding — thanks to its numerous beaches, countless waterfalls, and multitude of all-inclusive resorts (read about the advantages of all-inclusive weddings in Chapter 6) — Jamaica has a soul and spirit all its own.

The rhythms of reggae infuse Jamaica, one of the biggest islands in the Caribbean. With 200 miles of sandy shores, nearly every coastal Jamaican resort has a private beach. Visitors willing to tear themselves away can fit in a trip to Dunn's River Falls and the Bob Marley Museum. Uncommon adventures beyond those range from ATV safaris to river tubing to horseback rides that start up at the cliffs and end with hooves splashing in warm, shallow waters.

To get married in Jamaica, apply for a license before leaving home and wait 24 to 48 hours after arrival (hotels require the extra day) to hold the ceremony. Full details are at www.visitjamaica. com/vacation_themes/weddings_and_honeymoons/getting_ married_in_jamaica.aspx.

Weddings at all-inclusives and other resorts

In Jamaica, all-inclusive hotels and resorts are popular places to get married in. Leading all-inclusive resorts you may want to check out include the following:

- ✔ **Sandals:** Jamaica is where Sandals (www.sandals.com), originator of the *weddingmoon* (wedding-honeymoon combo) concept, got its start. Couples can choose from seven different locations on this island, including the newest, Sandals Whitehouse, designed to resemble a European village.

  Basic weddings at all Sandals properties (refer to Figure 8-1) are free for couples who stay for at least seven nights. If that's more sun 'n' fun than you can handle, weddings (complete with free consultant services) start at $750. With add-ons such as a $1,200 photo package, a bride's personal dressing assistant ($75), and even a destination wedding dress ($500) that you can buy on the premises, the total cost can spike. To work out the details for your wedding, check out Sandals' Web site or call 888-SANDALS.

Figure 8-1: Sandals Resorts' free weddings (with a weeklong stay) are simple affairs.

If you're bringing children along to the wedding, you can stage a weddingmoon at Sandals' family-friendly sibling, Beaches resorts (www.beaches.com). Together, the two host more than 15,000 weddings a year in Caribbean locations.

✔ **SuperClubs:** Another adults-only all-inclusive, SuperClubs (www.superclubs.com or 877-467-8737) also has a kid-friendly brand, Breezes (www.superclubs.com/brand_breezes/ specials.asp). Similar to Sandals and other all-inclusives, these resorts are considered by some couples to be "mills" that conduct weddings all day long — but you can't beat the price when it's free.

✔ **Couples Resorts:** Exclusively for grown-ups (topless bathing permitted), Couples Resorts offers free basic wedding deals like the other all-inclusives mentioned. Visitors to the Couples Resorts Web site (www.couples.com) can reserve a wedding date and time online, or you can call 800-268-7537.

Regular Jamaican resorts, where you pay separately for food and drinks and that are known for hosting great weddings, include

✔ **Royal Plantation:** Run by the daughter of Sandals' owner, this next-generation property (www.royalplantation.com) is more intimate and upscale than dad's digs. Its small beachside gazebo provides a lovely setting for an intimate wedding.

✔ **Jake's:** Casual beachfront weddings at this hip Negril hide-away (www.islandoutpost.com) start at around $1,000. Reception menus offer grilled lobster and bananas flambé.

✔ **Half Moon:** For more than half a century, couples have had weddings alongside Half Moon's (www.halfmoon.com) crescent beach. Following a wedding here, some couples plant a tree on the grounds, and then return to visit on their anniversary.

Uniquely Jamaica

Ceremonies in Jamaica aren't limited to resorts and all-inclusives. Alternate venues, which you can learn more about at www.visit jamaica.com include these scenic spots:

✔ The Blue Lagoon in Port Antonio

✔ Lover's Leap at the South Coast

✔ Cliffs of Negril

✔ Gardens in Ocho Rios

✔ Former Plantation Great House in Montego Bay

Although Jamaica has many charms, couples should be aware that this country has problems with crime and poverty outside resort areas. And insistent vendors, offering to sell you everything from hair braiding to ganja (marijuana), congregate in public areas at the edges of vacation spots. You can brush off most of them with a simple, "No thanks."

Island-hopping in the Bahamas

A short 35-minute flight from Miami, the Bahamas (www.bahamas.com) are the closest tropical islands to the U.S. mainland. Quintessential beach getaways, the Bahamas consist of 700 islands with soft, coral-sand beaches.

Just 20 of the islands are inhabited, and most of the action takes place on New Providence, which includes Nassau and Paradise Island. Because many of the islands are fairly close to one another, couples sometimes marry on one that provides a wide array of wedding services and then island-hop via ferry or small plane to another that is more remote for their honeymoon.

Wherever you stay in the Bahamas, getting married is relatively hassle-free. The Ministry of Tourism maintains a Weddings and Honeymoon Unit to answer questions and make recommendations. To contact an officer, call 888-687-8425 toll-free or e-mail romance@

`bahamas.com`. Marriage license requirements are online at `www.bahamas.com/bahamas/experience/templrgstandard.aspx?sectionid=49290`.

Major island resorts

So what are your options? More than nine out of ten couples who wed in the Bahamas do so at a resort hotel because everything you need is at your command: ceremony sites, connections to officiants, coordinators to do your bidding. Some of my top picks include

- ✔ **Atlantis:** The biggest resort in the Caribbean, action-packed Atlantis (`www.atlantis.com`) keeps adding more reasons to get you there. The latest are Aquaventure, a 63-acre water park, and The Cove, an adults-only retreat (those with kids are welcome in three other towers). On-site wedding specialists handle arrangements, and outdoor events have a designated alternative area in case of rain.

- ✔ **Sandals Royal Bahamian:** A honeymoon haven with four-poster beds, lavish bathrooms, and upgrades to suites with private plunge pools and butler service, the resort offers Sandals' stay-seven-nights-get-a-free-wedding deal (`www.sandals.com/general/wedding.cfm`).

- ✔ **Pelican Bay at Lucaya:** This resort can accommodate parties of up to 80 people and has a just-for-two wedding package priced under $3,000. Pelican Bay's Web site (`www.pelican bayhotel.com/weddings/realweddings.asp`) displays stories and photos from actual on-site weddings.

Although the majority of people do marry at a resort hotel, do-it-yourselfers can tie the knot at two public beaches on New Providence, Goodman's Bay and Cabbage Beach. For local flavor at the reception, include delicacies like frosty Bahama Mamas and the fruits of the sea, including lobster, crab, conch chowder, and fritters.

Although public sands are regularly groomed, seaweed washes up overnight. At a hotel, you can be confident that the beach will be swept before your wedding — and if it isn't, there's always someone on-site to address your concerns.

Off the beaten path

If you want a more intimate Bahamian experience, you have plenty of choices. Pure, scenic, and uncrowded, Bahamas Out Islands (`www.myoutislands.com`) offer miles of empty beaches and a scattering of small towns. Places where weddings are most memorable include the following:

✔ **Abaco Beach Resort:** Set beside crystal-clear turquoise waters on Abaco Island, basic weddings start at $645. You can find a form to check wedding-date availability and room rates on the Web site (www.abacobeachresort.com).

✔ **Fernandez Bay Village:** This family-friendly, Cat Island resort (www.fernandezbayvillage.com) hosts informal sunset tiki-torch ceremonies on the beach or atop Mount Alvernia with bridal bouquets composed of flowers picked in its garden.

✔ **Four Seasons Resort:** The magnificent Emerald Bay Beach, a tropical garden, and a stone church atop a bluff on Great Exuma are among the settings this luxury resort's wedding specialists can arrange. Access the Web site at (www.fourseasons.com/greatexuma).

Beachcombing in Barbados

Among the southernmost islands in the Caribbean and the one that lies farthest to the east, Barbados is at the outer edge of the hurricane belt. Although it remains susceptible during the rainy season, Barbados has been more fortunate weather-wise than many neighbors to the north.

Barbados is the most popular spot in the Caribbean for British couples in search of warmth and sun and also is welcoming to sophisticated Americans. A member of the Commonwealth, Barbados maintains a distinct British accent and visitors note that this island is a bit more formal and reserved than other islands. For example, jackets are required for men at the island's smartest restaurants at dinner.

You can find marriage requirements along with links to local wedding planners and other vendors at www.barbados.org/weddings.htm.

Couples can wed in Barbados the day they arrive, although you may want to spend time first exploring the island. Barbados has a lot to offer, keeping you and your guests occupied with activities that can include seaside horseback rides, ocean sails, tours of historic plantation houses, visits to flower forests and wildlife preserves, and the excitement of attending a cricket, polo, or rugby match. Taking a driving tour that encircles the island, from its western Caribbean shore to its rugged northern coast to the eastern beaches pounded by the Atlantic is also great fun — especially if you stop off for a sampling at a rum distillery.

Flying fish — you can actually see them leap out of the water — are a Bajan delicacy. Other local seafood to enhance a reception meal include freshly caught lobster, swordfish, and snapper.

Scenic ceremony settings

In Barbados, you have a choice of picturesque places to hold your wedding. Ceremony venues that local planners can book include churches, sunset cruises, plantation estates, under the shade of a flamboyant tree, beside a cliff, on the beach, as well as the following locations. Each has its own staff, so you don't necessarily have to work with a planner to wed there:

- ✔ **Flower Forest:** A 50-acre preserve with a gazebo used for weddings that is surrounded by colorful blossoms.

- ✔ **Orchid World:** Six acres abloom with 20,000 vivid specimens.

- ✔ **Harrison's Cave:** Underwater waterfalls and rock formations create an otherworldly ambiance.

Checking out the resorts

Couples who come to Barbados to marry tend to stay in one of its resorts. Many of these resorts offer first-class accommodations, beautiful settings, and standard wedding packages that can be embellished to suit your needs. Places well-equipped include

- ✔ **Almond Beach Club:** This all-inclusive (www.almondresorts.com/Resorts/AlmondClub) has standard rooms and luxury suites. The basic $400 wedding package includes breakfast in bed the morning after your wedding.

- ✔ **Cobblers Cove:** A beachfront hotel (www.cobblerscove.com) reminiscent of an English estate, Cobblers' $900 wedding package includes the basics plus transportation to acquire your marriage license.

- ✔ **Crane Beach Hotel:** The extraordinary cliff-top setting of Barbados' first hotel (www.thecrane.com) overlooks the beach way down below. A basic wedding package starts at $600.

- ✔ **Fairmont Royal Pavilion:** Weddings are completely customized at this stunningly romantic beach resort (www.fairmont.com/royalpavilion), which is child-free from November through April.

- ✔ **Little Arches:** This charming, ten-room, adults-only hotel (www.littlearches.com) has a private wedding garden that can accommodate 40 guests.

Making waves in Bermuda

Way out in the Atlantic Ocean, 600 miles off the coast of North Carolina, Bermuda has been a favorite destination of wedding and honeymoon couples for generations. Unlike the Caribbean islands, its climate isn't tropical year-round; winters can get nippy. But that doesn't stop couples who like to golf, sail, and tool around pretty Bermuda on rental mopeds from visiting during the cooler months.

Bermuda's British tradition and high standard of living also differentiate it from most neighbors to the south. You don't see grinding poverty here. In fact, prices are on par with the United States, and even modest accommodations can be pricey. In the following sections, I suggest some lovely Bermuda locations.

Marrying in Bermuda isn't complicated but does require advanced planning because the law insists that a Notice of Intended Marriage be published in local papers 15 days prior to the wedding. For more info, go to www.bermudatourism.com/weddings/pdf/ Marriage.pdf. Check out the dedicated Bermuda weddings Web site (www.bermudatourism.com/weddings) to find local planners and download a free wedding brochure.

Discovering where love's in bloom

Come summer, Bermuda is at its peak with flowers everywhere and waters warm enough to swim in. Although most couples choose to marry at their hotel (usually beside its beach or on a terrace overlooking the water), other popular spots that a local wedding planner can help arrange include churches, gardens, cliff tops above the sea, aboard sailboats, and the following locations (for info on hiring a wedding planner to help, see Chapter 5):

- **Astwood Cove:** A beachfront park with a stone stairway that leads down to the water's edge

- **Horseshoe Bay Beach:** A wide crescent beach with pink sands

- **Gibb's Hill Lighthouse:** A timeless backdrop for photos

You may also want to get married or at least have your picture taken under Bermuda's romantic *moongates* (see Figure 8-2). You can find these round archways across the island. Legend has it that a couple who kisses under one (no time limit posted) will have a long, happy life together.

Figure 8-2: Pose under a moongate for luck if you wed in Bermuda.

Accommodating your desires

Lodgings on Bermuda that are well-equipped to handle wedding parties range from small inns to cottage colonies that hug the shore to large resort hotels. My faves include

- ✔ **Ariel Sands:** This collection of cottages (www.arielsands. com) is anchored by a hip main building with a restaurant overlooking the ocean and decorated with personal photos of its owner, actor Michael Douglas. Many couples opt to marry on the beach here, arriving via horse-drawn carriage. The resort can put you in touch with the outside planner they use.

- ✔ **Pink Beach Club:** Bermuda's legendary pink sand adds to the allure of this charming cottage colony (www.pinkbeach.com) that even has its own moongate.

Sporting times

A haven for golfers, Bermuda boasts the highest concentration of golf courses per square mile in the world. Other activities a destination wedding party may enjoy include visiting the Royal Naval Dockyard (crafty types can paint commemorative wedding plates at Bermuda Clayworks), a snorkel safari, and kayak tours. Bermuda's gorgeous beaches, with their countless romantic coves and inlets, are a delight for swimmers and smoochers.

Want to go "semiformal" to your wedding? For the groom that can mean wearing a tuxedo jacket . . . and Bermuda shorts! It looks perfectly appropriate here, even when the bride dons a long gown.

Exploring other Caribbean locales

With a total of 28 territories and more than 7,000 islands in the Caribbean, the area's appeal is vast. For an overview, pick up a copy of *Caribbean For Dummies* by Darwin Porter and Danforth Prince (Wiley). To start researching on your own, look into these other contenders for a wedding away:

- ✔ **Antigua:** Proud of its 365 beaches, breezy Antigua (www.antigua-barbuda.org) has secluded spots for weddings as well as full-service resorts that offer complete packages.

- ✔ **Aruba:** Lying outside the hurricane zone, beachy, Dutch-accented Aruba (www.aruba.com) hosts weddings year-round.

- ✔ **Dominican Republic**: Affordable all-inclusive resorts that cater to families dot the country's rapidly expanding Punta Cana region. Explore it at www.dominicanrepublic.com.

- ✔ **St. Lucia:** Pretty St. Lucia (www.stlucia.org) makes it easy to get married on the day of arrival. Local planners (check out www.aweddinginstlucia.com) can even work with cruise ship passengers to arrange in-port weddings.

- ✔ **Turks & Caicos:** The next great place and under major development now, T&C (www.turksandcaicostourism.com) is growing in popularity, thanks to the vast, untouched beaches on its 40 tranquil islands.

Going to the Caribbean without a Passport

Because both Puerto Rico and the United States Virgin Islands (USVI) enjoy the status of U.S. territories, no passports are required to travel in or out of these islands. However, if you do have a passport, bring it. Otherwise you need to present a certified birth certificate and photo ID to apply for a marriage license. I go into more detail about these territories in the following sections.

Preferring Puerto Rico

The prospect of land and water adventures, getting lucky at a casino or golf course, and staying in a big full-service resort or a small inn that offers personal attention entices couples to wed in Puerto Rico (find out more and explore attractions at www.gotopuertorico.com).

Judges or clergy perform legal marriages in Puerto Rico. For complete details on requirements, which include a blood test, call the Demographic Registry (787-767-9120) before plunging into the island's turquoise waters and icy piña coladas.

Tying the knot at resorts and hotels

Capital city and site of the international airport, San Juan has the island's biggest, splashiest casino hotels and outposts of Hilton, Marriott, InterContinental, Sheraton, and Radisson hotel brands.

Have you been saving up frequent-guest points or frequent-mileage rewards? Consider exchanging them for free hotel nights in San Juan to curtail wedding costs.

Some of the most romantic spots to marry in San Juan include

- ✔ **El Convento Hotel:** A former nunnery in the center of charming Old San Juan, El Convento (www.elconvento.com; 800-468-2779) works with designated local planners plus its in-house events team to produce weddings anywhere from the original chapel of the Carmelite convent to its outdoor restaurant patio and romantic hotel ballroom.

- ✔ **The Horned Dorset Primavera:** Two hours east of San Juan Airport, the Horned Dorset (www.horneddorset.com; 800-633-1857) is a Relais et Châteaux property, which means every aspect of a wedding there is custom-tailored.

- ✔ **Ritz-Carlton, San Juan:** Reception spots at the elegant Ritz-Carlton (www.ritzcarlton.com/en/Properties/SanJuan; 787-253-1700) range from an intimate private dining room to the ballroom, which has a capacity of 500 guests.

For those on a budget who like to get close to nature and want to experience less-urban Puerto Rico, family-run *paradores* (www.gotoparadores.com) are small country inns in picturesque locations. Spanish is the first language, so having a local planner is an asset. Ask the tourism bureau for recommendations.

Hanging loose and having fun

Because Puerto Rico is a relatively small island, just 100 miles wide and 35 miles from north to south, you can experience the following highlights during a stay regardless of where you hold the wedding and spend nights:

- ✔ **Old San Juan:** Windswept El Morro fort overlooks San Juan Bay. Across the water from it, the Bacardi Rum Distillery offers tours and samplings of its world-famous rums.

✔ **El Yunque Rainforest:** Waterfalls rush beside hiking trails, and you can swim in natural pools while *el coquí,* Puerto Rico's tree frogs, serenade.

✔ **Río Camuy Cave Park:** The world's only tropical cavern with an underground river, Río Camuy has trams and trolleys that lead deep into a dramatically illuminated 170-foot-deep cave.

Uncovering the pleasures of the USVI

Couples who appreciate the familiarity of the United States, the fun of water sports, and the relaxation of beach resorts flock to the U.S. Virgin Islands (www.usvitourism.vi), which consists of three main islands: St. Thomas, St. Croix, and St. John.

St. Thomas, the most developed of the islands, is a magnet for shoppers as well as a beautiful beach location. St. Croix is home to Buck Island National Monument, which has a unique underwater nature trail with live coral grottoes and resplendently hued fish. Most of St. John is a U.S. National Park, so its pristine protected areas are plentiful.

To download a USVI wedding and honeymoon brochure that recommends wedding planners and other vendors, go to www. usvitourism.vi/en/pdfs/wedding_guide_MECH.pdf. You can retrieve a marriage information fact sheet as well as the marriage license requirements and application at www.usvitourism.vi/en/pdfs/marriage_app.pdf.

Top resorts for romance include the following:

✔ **The Buccaneer** (www.thebuccaneer.com; 800-255-3881) on St. Croix gets top marks from couples for ceremony locations, catering, and vendors. Services of a wedding coordinator are included in packages. (See Figure 8-3.)

✔ **Caneel Bay** (www.caneelbay.com; 888-767-3966) on St. John is upscale and unplugged. Weddings, organized by the on-site team, are held overlooking Turtle Bay Beach.

✔ **The Ritz-Carlton, St. Thomas** (www.ritzcarlton.com/en/Properties/StThomas; 340-775-3333) has a wedding advisor on the property who sets up events ranging from a beachfront wedding for two to a ceremony for up to 49 aboard the hotel's own catamaran.

Figure 8-3: A simple floral arch marks this wedding spot at The Buccaneer Resort in the U.S. Virgin Islands.

> ✔ **Frenchman's Reef & Morning Star Marriott Beach Resort**
> (`http://marriott.com/hotels/travel/sttfr-frenchmans-reef-and-morning-star-marriott-beach-resort`; 340-776-8500) is a big St. Thomas family-oriented resort that includes a Webcast in its four wedding packages (priced $850 to $2,650).

In addition to those traditional resorts, the USVI also has very affordable, environmentally sustainable places to wed. Mount Victory Camp (`www.mtvictorycamp.com`) on St. Croix consists of platform dwellings and bungalows. The entire camp sleeps 22 and can be booked for under $500 nightly, depending on the season. On St. John, Maho Bay Camps (`www.maho.org`) has tent cottages overlooking the Caribbean. Barbecue areas and fresh water are available at nearby hiking trails and plantation ruins.

Marrying in Mexico

Exotic yet close, Mexico has long been a favorite destination of travelers from the United States. Sunny, hot, and affordable, this country offers couples a choice of venues that range from all-inclusive resorts with free weddings, to places of rare charm and natural beauty, to historic sites and ancient ruins. With so much to savor (not to mention that zesty cuisine and those thirst-quenching margaritas), Mexico (`www.visitmexico.com`) makes a great case for combining both a wedding and honeymoon.

Mexico is almost as vast as the United States. To save flying time, couples who live near the U.S. East Coast tend to set their south-of-the-border weddings in places along Mexico's Caribbean coast. Those who reside closer to California and the West choose destinations along Mexico's Pacific coastline. Midwesterners take their pick of both.

Marriage laws in Mexico vary from state to state, just as in the United States. The office of the *Registro Civil* (civil registry) in the jurisdiction where you plan to marry can supply complete details about the requirements. Be advised that in some locales a blood test and a chest X-ray (that you get after arrival) are necessary. Results must be in Spanish, and foreign documents must be translated into that language. Learn more at www.mexperience.com/guide/weddings/getting_married.htm.

Getting married at an all-inclusive

Similar to the Caribbean, Mexico is home to many all-inclusive resorts. If you plan on vacationing in this country for a specified number of days, you can take advantage of free basic wedding packages or pay for upgraded affairs at them. Each of the following hotel groups has properties on both Mexican coasts. As you look into them, you can find family-friendly all-inclusives and adults-only ones. Many are quite lavish, yet cost considerably less than similar resorts in the United States and the Caribbean.

✔ Barcelo Hotels (www.barcelo.com)

✔ Palace Resorts (www.palaceresorts.com)

✔ Dreams Resorts & Spas (www.dreamsresorts.com)

✔ Occidental Hotels & Resorts (www.occidentalhotels.com)

✔ Sol Meliá Hotels & Resorts (www.solmelia.com)

Checking out the Caribbean coast

Beaches and bath-warm waters have made Mexico's Yucatan Peninsula the country's biggest tourist draw. Most of the action takes place along the Riviera Maya, a 75-mile-long coastal stretch that includes Cancun, the island of Cozumel, and Playa del Carmen across from Cozumel.

The Riviera Maya (www.rivieramaya.com) has more all-inclusive resorts than anywhere else in Mexico. Check out the preceding section for a list of resorts in both eastern and western Mexico.

Resorts belonging to the following groups are exclusive to the Caribbean coast, provide free on-site coordinators, and offer free basic weddings as well as more-elaborate affairs.

- ✔ Iberostar Hotels & Resorts (www.iberostar.com)
- ✔ Karisma Hotels & Resorts (www.karismahotels.com)
- ✔ Secrets Resorts (www.secretsresorts.com)

Not all Riviera Maya weddings take place in hotels, of course. Those who want a unique historic experience can marry at a bare-foot Mayan Indian ceremony (www.weddingsinplaya.com/weddings_mayan.html) performed by a shaman.

Couples who are their most amorous in aquatic settings can marry at the Occidental Grand Cozumel Hotel (www.grandcozumel.com). This property's underwater wedding package includes boat rental, diving equipment, ceremony, flowers, cake, and champagne. The latter three are to be savored above sea level.

Picking Mexico's Pacific coast

The warm Sea of Cortez meets the Pacific Ocean in Los Cabos at the southernmost tip of the Baja California peninsula. One of Mexico's most popular resort areas, Los Cabos gets 350 days of sunshine a year and is home to the resort towns of Cabo San Lucas and San José del Cabo, separated by 20 miles.

Spicing up your Mexican wedding

For a wedding that reflects Mexico's color and cultures, consider adding these elements to your fiesta:

- ✔ **Dress:** Guayabera shirt for him and cotton Mexican wedding dress for her
- ✔ **Decorations:** Colorful *loteria* playing cards, Talavera ceramics, and *papel picado* banners
- ✔ **Special events:** Tequila tastings and tours of ruins
- ✔ **Hors d'oeuvres:** Tiny, filled tortillas
- ✔ **Tableware:** Hand-blown Mexican glassware and painted pottery at the reception
- ✔ **Music:** Mariachi band or acoustic guitarist
- ✔ **Wedding cake:** A traditional sweet *tres leches*

All-inclusive fans can find upscale resorts in Los Cabos. But by searching for the term *Los Cabos hotels* on www.tripadvisor.com, you can identify alternate accommodations with low prices and high ratings. For example, the admired ten-room Bungalows Hotel (www.cabobungalows.com) can host up to 50 people for a wedding.

Because your upcoming wedding is (one hopes) a once-in-a-lifetime affair, don't overlook Los Cabos' luxury lodgings. Even if you can't afford to overnight in them for long, you may want to arrange a pre-wedding meal or spa event on their premises. If this idea sounds good to you, be sure to check out the following, and should you want advice, get in touch with their on-site wedding coordinators.

- ✔ **Marquis Los Cabos:** Here (www.marquisloscabos.com) you can experience the only Torah in Baja California, which is meaningful to Jewish couples.

- ✔ **One & Only Palmilla:** This resort (www.oneandonly resorts.com) has a traditional, white-washed Mexican chapel on the premises where you can hold your wedding ceremony. (Check out Figure 8-4.)

- ✔ **Las Ventanas al Paraiso:** You can work with a dedicated Director of Romance here (www.lasventanas.com), who can customize every aspect of the wedding.

Figure 8-4: A traditional Mexican chapel at One & Only Palmilla.

Other Pacific coast cities worth considering for their settings and breadth of hotels and wedding facilities are Puerto Vallarta (www.visitpuertovallarta.com) where cobblestone streets and the broad malecon invite post-wedding processions, and Ixtapa-Zihuatanejo (www.ixtapa-zihuatanejo.com), which lures visitors. You can research this topic more in depth in *Mexico's Beach Resorts For Dummies* by Lynne Bairstow and David Baird (Wiley).

Hitting the Rain Forest

Do you and your other half have a true affinity for the environment and want to visit places where few tourists have visited? Do you enjoy being outdoors trekking off the beaten path, encountering wildlife in their natural environment, and getting to know residents in a capacity other than as people hired to serve you? Then lush Central America may fulfill your desires.

Tourism has become increasingly important to the following peaceful Central American countries, yet they haven't become overdeveloped. You can still find bargain accommodations and pristine natural beauty.

Diving into Belize

On the Caribbean Sea between Mexico to the north and Guatemala below, English-speaking Belize (www.travelbelize.org) boasts the largest barrier reef in the Western Hemisphere. It also has abundant wildlife, Mayan temples, miles of unspoiled coastline, and a jungle filled with chattering toucans.

Belize weddings can take place on an island, in the rainforest, and at resorts, where packages include rooms, license, minister, cake, and flowers. At Belizean receptions, tacos made with roasted pig add a local delicacy. Fish lovers can feast on freshly caught shrimp, lobster, and snapper. Belize, which requires a three-day residency, makes it relatively easy to get married in the country. You can find wedding requirements online at belize.usembassy.gov/getting_married_in_belize.html.

If you envision a large, grand-scale destination wedding complete with a gushing fountains of chocolate and a 30-piece orchestra, Belize isn't right for you. Because this country doesn't have any major hotel chains and accommodations max out at about 50 rooms, Belize appeals to couples who want an intimate, modest, and casual getaway. Most lodgings are very affordable, with rates that seem from an earlier time. One thing you don't want to forego is air conditioning, though; it's a jungle out there.

Accommodations options include the following. Contact the hotels directly for help planning a wedding.

- ✔ **Five Sisters Lodge:** As part of its wedding package, Five Sisters Lodge (www.fivesisterslodge.com) accompanies a couple's first kiss with a release of iridescent blue morpho butterflies.

- ✔ **Kanantik Reef and Jungle Resort:** This resort (www.kanantik.com) has a 7-night/8-day wedding-and-honeymoon package featuring roundtrip flights from Belize City to Kanantik's private airstrip, meals, three tours, room service, a candlelight dinner on the beach, plus marriage license, officiant, bridal bouquet, photographer, videographer, wedding cake, and a chilled bottle of champagne for $2,465.

- ✔ **Placencia Hotel:** At the (relatively) high end of the spectrum, Placencia Hotel (www.theplacencia.com) features beachfront villas and an on-site wedding chapel.

Choosing Costa Rica

The opportunity to get really close to nature on kayaks, whitewater rafts, surfboards, canopy tours, and horseback attracts active couples to Costa Rica (www.visitcostarica.com). Biologically diverse, this country's varied terrain includes ocean and jungle, hot springs, waterfalls, and lagoons. Although much of Costa Rica is hot year-round, highland locations can be cool and comfortable.

To tie the knot anywhere in Costa Rica, you need to involve a local lawyer. Some attorneys insist on a document that attests both of you're single, which must be translated into Spanish. Papers have to be in order at least a month before the wedding. Find complete details and a lawyer to assist you at usembassy.or.cr/consfaq.html#marriage.

Hotels provide the settings for most weddings, and they're your best resources for wedding planning services. I recommend these:

- ✔ **Four Seasons Costa Rica at Peninsula Papagayo:** At the country's top hotel (www.fourseasons.com/costarica), couples can marry aboard a catamaran, just one wedding option.

- ✔ **Los Altos de Eros:** Staff at this intimate boutique hotel (www.losaltosdeeros.com) with only five guestrooms, personally arrange all aspects of a destination wedding.

- **Paradisus Playa Conchal:** This family-friendly luxury resort (www.paradisusplayaconchal.travel) has banquet rooms that can hold wedding parties that range in size from 50 to 400.

You can also find plenty of unique places to say "I do," including the following:

- **Arenal Volcano:** Couples with fiery temperaments may want to consider a wedding at the edge of this volcano. Costa Rica Weddings in Paradise (www.costarica-weddings.com/volcano-weddings.htm) can assist with planning, secure the site, and provide legal assistance.

- **La Paz Waterfall Gardens:** A magical site (www.waterfall gardens.com) equipped with viewing platforms and established trails. Both stateside and on-site coordinators are available.

Opting for an Oceania Paradise

Secluded and remote, the island nations of the Pacific Ocean appeal to couples with a strong desire to marry in an exotic place as close to paradise and as far away from civilization as anywhere on earth. Romantic over-water bungalows built just for two, pristine beaches without another soul or structure in sight, and ancient cultures that invite you to share their traditions are all part of the appeal of having a destination wedding in this part of the world.

Getting to these islands involves considerable flying time. Direct flights from Los Angeles to Papeete's Faa'a Airport in French Polynesia, serviced by Air New Zealand, Air France, and Air Tahiti Nui, take about 7 1/2 hours. From New York's JFK Airport, Air Tahiti Nui flies to Papeete in 13 hours. Flights to Fiji, the Cook Islands, and the Maldives are even lengthier and may involve additional short flights to reach even more distant spots.

Marriage, Fijian style

At a Fijian wedding, the bride can make her entrance on a *bilibili,* a bamboo raft that glides under palm trees, escorted to the altar beside the sea by a fully costumed warrior. After the vows, a choir serenades the couple and is followed by a group of ceremonial *meke* dancers decked in garlands of flowers. Then you take part in the *lovo* feast, featuring meat roasted underground, and finally a sacred *kava* ceremony, where the community honors the couple.

Journeying to Fiji

Consisting of more than 330 small islands in the South Pacific, Fiji is a remote destination where the food, customs, and even the architecture are unfamiliar. Colorful wedding customs, good-natured residents who treat visitors with kindness, and places of spectacular beauty and privacy inspire couples to marry at either a traditional white wedding or one that integrates local rituals.

A range of accommodations, from moderately priced hotels with wedding packages to private-island resorts, is listed at www. bulafiji.com/index.cfm?go=main.wedding. Lodgings in Fiji often consists of traditional *bures,* thatched-roof huts that have been updated with modern conveniences.

Marrying in Fiji is easy. (See the requirements at travel.state. gov/law/citizenship/citizenship_771.html.) You don't have a waiting period or minimum stay. Do note, though, that Fiji doesn't have any nondenominational ministers.

Keeping the law on your side: Tropical marriage requirements

Every region has its own set of regulations to issue a marriage license, and they do change from time to time. Regardless of the specifics of a destination, each location typically requires you to produce the following:

- ✔ Your passports
- ✔ Official birth certificates
- ✔ Proof of divorce or death certificate if this isn't a first marriage
- ✔ Parents' written consent for underage couples (the definition of underage varies by country)
- ✔ Registration fee

In most locales, you're expected to show up in person together to apply for the license, and you may have a waiting period before it is issued. In some cases, you may need to pay to have documents translated into an island's official language or take a blood test that checks for HIV or venereal disease.

To find current official island requirements, use the link or phone number provided for each location in this chapter.

Picking Polynesia

The two best-known destinations in Polynesia are the Cook Islands, which belong to New Zealand, and Tahiti, a French territory. Surrounded by pristine waters, both spots are ideal for couples who want a wedding event that includes extraordinary water sports — from underwater spear fishing to paddling outrigger canoes to deep-sea diving among some of earth's most exotic species in living, breathing, still-growing reefs. Read the following to find out more about what these islands have to offer:

✔ **The Cook Islands:** This location consists of 15 peaceful islands. Rarotonga, the capital, is encircled by white beaches fringed by palm trees. A short flight north, the even less populous Aitutaki Island is sheltered by a vast coral reef teeming with marine life.

Lovers are welcomed on these islands, and you'll have few impediments to marriage as long as you apply to the Registrar of Marriages for your license three days before the wedding. Visit www.cook-islands.com for further details and lodging info.

✔ **Tahiti:** Gorgeous Tahiti invites you to honeymoon there but makes it difficult to legally marry. This location has a one-month residency requirement, impractical for all but residents and bazillionaire beachcombers. But don't let that stop you. You can marry before leaving home and have a symbolic wedding here (see an example in Figure 8-5). To find out more info about marrying in Tahiti and to check out accommodations, go to www.tahiti-tourisme.com.

A traditional Polynesian wedding celebration, which can be arranged by your hotel with advance notice, can take place at the Tiki Village Theater (www.tikivillage.fr/mariage/en) on Tahiti's neighboring island of Moorea. A village chief with his high priest in attendance conducts the service. Both bride and groom don leis and crowns of flowers. After the ceremony, the couple can board a royal canoe and sail toward the sunset, serenaded into the night by local musicians.

How far from civilization do you want to go? *Motu* (small islands) off the larger islands have no roads or restaurants. For complete seclusion, arrange a *motu* wedding or a daylong escape with your hotel.

Figure 8-5: Tent and chairs set up for the arrival of the wedding party and guests at the InterContinental Resort in Tahiti.

Chapter 9

Wowing and Vowing in Europe

*T*he Grand Tour of Europe was long considered to be the proper initiation into adult society for newlyweds. Those who experienced it returned home with a mark of culture, an appreciation for the Continent's fine food and wine, a deeper understanding of art and architecture, and a broader definition of the good life.

Today's couples now look to Europe not only as a honeymoon destination but also as the ultimate place to hold a wedding. I devote the majority of this chapter to Western Europe's most popular countries for weddings abroad — the United Kingdom, France, Spain, Greece, and Italy — and also recommend two of Eastern Europe's hottest spots to marry in.

Considering a European Wedding: The Pros and Cons

Europe, where wedding traditions have evolved over centuries, is the number-one destination choice of sophisticated couples. For generations, couples in love have pledged their vows everywhere from the Continent's ancient town halls to its enchanting castles to holy places such as the Vatican.

If you don't mind traveling far from home, appreciate foreign cultures, and can afford Europe, no place else on earth is as enchanting. But before you pull out your passports (information on obtaining them is in Chapter 11), consider the pros and cons of marrying in Europe.

Pondering the pluses

Couples can find unique advantages to marrying in Europe. Regardless of the country you choose, the following distinguish a destination wedding in Europe:

- ✔ **Culture:** From the Louvre in Paris to the West End theaters of London, from La Scala Opera House in Milan to the bold Gaudí structures of Barcelona, Europe is considered the apogee of culture. Its magnificent art, architecture, music, and theater represent the highest accomplishments of civilization.

- ✔ **Cuisine:** French and Italian chefs are the undisputed leaders in world cuisine, and you can sample their mastery on native soil. You also have the gustatory delight of complementing fine European cuisine at your reception and other wedding events with equally refined European wines.

- ✔ **History:** Ancient castles, cityscapes dominated by age-old stone churches, lush vineyards, mature gardens, vast fields of lavender and heather, and cliffs overlooking the timeless sea provide inspiring settings to begin celebrating a future together.

- ✔ **Romance:** The most romantic figures in history — Romeo and Juliet, King Henry VIII and Anne Boleyn, Abelard and Heloise — didn't hail from Ohio. They came from Europe, where the land is infused with a drama and beauty that inspire eternal love.

- ✔ **Tradition:** Thousands of years of European history have forged customs that today's couples can borrow to add meaning to their own ceremony. In some small villages in France, children stretch white ribbons across the bride's path, which she must clip to reach her intended. In Italy, newlyweds lead a procession to the town plaza accompanied by friends, family, and local well-wishers. And following a Greek ceremony, the best man places gold crowns or orange-blossom wreaths linked by a silk ribbon on the bride's and groom's heads, identifying them as the king and queen of the day.

Considering the cons

The best approach to a wedding away is with eyes wide open. By understanding the obstacles that may present themselves, you may either decide to marry elsewhere or make adjustments in your plans to accommodate differences.

✔ **Strict marriage requirements:** At the end of each country in this chapter is a link to its specific marriage requirements. Several require a lengthy residency period before issuing a license, making it simpler to have your legal wedding at home and a symbolic one in Europe.

✔ **Language differences:** In countries outside the United Kingdom, English isn't the first language. Although many people in big cities speak English, not all do. A local planner who speaks English can help you search for appropriate venues and vendors and communicate your wishes; an interpreter can help couples who are planning on their own.

To obtain a local planner in Europe, contact the country or city tourism office to ask for a recommendation, or ask a local planner where you live for a referral, search online, or ask a facility or vendor in the destination.

✔ **Difficulties with documents:** Even in countries where non-citizens can marry, the process of securing (and, in non-English-speaking countries, translating) required documents can be lengthy.

✔ **August vacation:** Europeans have more vacation time than Americans do. Every August, people take the month off. This lengthy break comes at the same time when tourism soars. So don't count on top service and attention this month.

✔ **Weather:** Recent summers have seen alarming heat waves, and winters can be cold and miserable. But balladeers sing of "April in Paris" for a reason (check out the section on Paris later in this chapter for more info).

✔ **Cost:** Western European countries have a high standard of living, and prices for everything from food to flowers in some locales are steeper than at home. Prices also vary daily, depending on the current exchange rate. Add to that the cost of travel, and a European wedding can be pricey. You can find out more about dealing with overseas currency in Chapter 4.

Not every European wedding costs a fortune. Couples marry inexpensively in historic town halls across the Continent, many with magnificent architecture. If this is what you want, advance reservations usually are needed.

✔ **Distance:** Considering the flying time involved from North America to Europe, a weekend wedding is impractical (the jet lag alone could have guests nodding out just when you're ready to say your vows). But if your party consists of the two of you alone, Europe is a spectacular place to combine a wedding and honeymoon.

Jumping the Pond to the U.K.

In England, Scotland, and Ireland, the locals' accents are charming, and they're speaking your language. That's the good news. The bad news: The average wedding in urban areas costs as much or more than an average one this side of the Atlantic. However, Ireland and Scotland remain more affordable than England.

Online resources for couples who hope to marry in Great Britain are plentiful. The www.weddingplanner.co.uk site lets you search for planners and vendors by major city or the county in England and Scotland in which they operate. Another site, www.confetti.co.uk, helps couples find wedding venues and other necessities in those countries. You can use www.irishweddingsonline.com to access locations and helpers in Ireland. This section breaks down the United Kingdom to provide info on having a destination wedding in England, Ireland, or Scotland.

England

England (www.visitbritain.com) offers couples a vast choice of wedding locations that include cosmopolitan London, the scenic Cotswolds, ancient Canterbury, prehistoric Stonehenge, the Roman town of Bath, the Victorian Keswick in the Lake District, Shakespeare's Stratford-upon-Avon, the Beatles' Liverpool, and the world-renowned university towns of Cambridge and Oxford.

Within these places are a myriad of potential sites to hold a wedding: parks, gardens, museums, hotels, restaurants, pubs, country inns, private homes, and even castles. In England, only licensed venues can hold weddings, and they run the gamut from traditional to unusual. As with any destination you aren't familiar with, I advise you to hire a local planner who can present a suitable choice of venues and also secure necessary permissions.

The following highlight a few English locations you may want to consider:

✔ **London** (www.visitlondon.com), England's sophisticated capital, is also one of the world's most expensive cities. So planning an affordable wedding here and also choosing among the city's many hotels is a wallet-stretching challenge. Find help at www.visitlondon.com/city_guide/weddings/ planning.html. Nontraditional venues registered to hold weddings include the following:

- London Eye's capsule (www.londoneye.com), 440 feet over the city, is specially decorated and offers a champagne toast.

- The Chelsea Town Hall (www.rbkc.gov.uk/venues chelsea/general), located on King's Road, is a charming setting for civil weddings.

- Madame Tussauds (www.madame-tussauds.co.uk), the original wax museum, can provide the setting for melting moments.

- London Zoo (www.zsl.org/zsl-london-zoo) opens its doors for private events, although it doesn't cost peanuts.

- Ironmongers' Hall (www.ironhall.co.uk) is a historic guild with a hall for hire.

- Shakespeare's Globe Theatre (www.shakespeares-globe.org) rents space and can also provide catering and entertainment.

✔ **Bath** (http://visitbath.co.uk/lovebath) is a World Heritage site and one of Britain's most romantic cities, thanks to its Georgian architecture, hot springs, rolling hills, and intimate scale. More than half the weddings that take place here are for nonresidents. Country houses, hotels, the Pump Room (cited in Jane Austen novels), and the famous Roman Baths are among the town's 30 venues that hold wedding licenses.

✔ **Cotswolds** (www.the-cotswolds.org) is England's prettiest countryside, featuring classic gardens resplendent with roses, welcoming pubs, and historic houses and cottages. Stonehouse Court Hotel (http://stonehousecourt.co.uk) is a 17th-century manor with an outdoor license to host weddings of 10 to 150 people. It also has 36 bedrooms for overnight guests.

If you're considering getting married in England, make sure you're aware of the banns. Required by the Church of England, *the banns* refers to the public announcement of an intended marriage three weeks before the wedding. Similar notice must be displayed in a register office 15 days prior to civil marriages in England and Wales. Legal marriages in England also require a week of residency. You can find full requirements at www.gro.gov.uk/gro/content/marriages.

Irish traditions for lovers

The Irish definitely have an affinity for traditional symbols of love. If you're planning on an Irish wedding, you may want to add some authentic romance to your visit. The following are a few examples of Irish culture:

✔ Ireland's iconic claddagh ring — consisting of two hands holding a single heart — can be a lifelong reminder of an Emerald Isle wedding. Used as a marriage ring or given in friendship, it makes a unique wedding-party gift.

✔ Engraved Celtic rings feature an endless spiral, the symbol of an enduring marriage.

✔ Stop kissing one another long enough to plant one on the Blarney Stone in County Cork, said to confer the gift of eloquence.

Ireland

Green and welcoming Ireland (www.discoverireland.com) appeals to couples with a love of the outdoors and a taste for fine spirits. Its many castles and gardens, the mystical fog that envelops the land, and the magical incantations of home-grown crooner Van Morrison all contribute to the beauty and romance of the Emerald Isle. Outdoor enthusiasts choose Ireland for its abundance of destination wedding activities, including golf, fishing, hiking, and horseback riding. History lovers want to spend time exploring Ireland's castles and ancient monuments, perhaps searching for their own Irish roots.

Ireland's major cities — Dublin, Galway, and Belfast — continually refresh themselves, adding to or upgrading their many hotels that provide shelter and sustenance to wedding parties. Tops in each:

✔ **Shelbourne in Dublin:** Landmark 182-year-old city-center hotel (marriott.co.uk/Channels/hotels-uk/hotels/travel/dubbr-the-shelbourne) with a grand ballroom (holds 360) and smaller suites for intimate weddings.

✔ **g hotel in Galway:** Chic and au courant, the g (www.theghotel.ie) has six event suites and can accommodate parties of up to 100.

✔ **Ten Square in Belfast:** Boutique hotel (www.tensquare.co.uk) with opulent event space.

Working with a local planner, couples can save on a site by arranging to have a wedding outdoors or away from a major city. Check out the following options:

- ✔ **Belle Isle:** This site (www.belleisle-estate.com) is a working farm in Northern Ireland that also happens to include a castle that hosts civil weddings. Its lodgings range from a coach house to private cottages.

- ✔ **Castle Oaks House Hotel:** On Limerick's River Shannon banks, this hotel (www.castleoaks.ie) has 25 years' experience hosting weddings.

- ✔ **St. Stephens Green:** Dublin's 27-acre St. Stephens Green is popular with wedding parties and provides beautiful backdrops of flowers and water fountains.

Irish weddings require three months' notice of the intended event. Complete details are at www.groireland.ie/getting_married.htm.

Scotland

Today one out of four couples who marry in Scotland (www.visitscotland.com) are visitors, and many choose the village of Gretna Green (http://weddings.gretnagreen.co.uk). Couples can still wed in its Old Blacksmith's Shop, now a tourist attraction (the original proprietor doubled as a minister). Some combine it with a reception at the adjacent Smiths Hotel (www.smithsgretnagreen.com). Elsewhere in Scotland, couples tie the knot in castles and churches, on golf courses and country estates, and in hotels in the Highlands and the two major cities, Edinburgh and Glasgow.

By using the form on the Destination Scotland Web site (at www.destinationscotland.com/romance/venue.asp), you can describe your needs and receive recommendations on where to marry. Scotland's unique and charming venues include

- ✔ **Eala Bhan:** If you're not worried about the Loch Ness monster showing up as an uninvited guest, consider marrying aboard this wooden sailboat that plies the waters of the Scottish Highlands and sleeps 12 (www.highlandvoyages.co.uk).

- ✔ **Glencorse Old Kirk:** Couples can marry outside of Edinburgh in the woodland setting author Robert Louis Stevenson described as "the finest spot on earth" or in the ancient stone church where he worshiped (www.glencorsehouse.com).

Romancing at a castle wedding

To feel like royalty on your wedding day, consider marrying in a castle. These fairy-tale settings promise a "happily-ever-after" event in authentically historic surroundings. Beyond a castle's turreted structure often lie formal gardens with mature plantings; large, open lawns; and waterways where swans glide by — all of which present magnificent backgrounds for wedding photos. Inside you can anticipate a wealth of antiques, walls covered with tapestries, and beamed ceilings wrought by hand centuries ago.

Many castles that host weddings today have been restored with modern facilities added. Although they aren't cheap to rent, you can still spend less on a small wedding in a castle than a large one at home. Following is a sampling of European castles that proffer the keys to the kingdom . . . if only for a day or a weekend.

English castles

- **Amberley** (www.amberleycastle.co.uk) has stood in the English countryside for nine centuries.

- **Leeds** (www.leeds-castle.com) is located on an island accessible by car. It has 20 bedrooms for guests, its own florist, a wine cellar, and hot-air balloon flights.

- **Swinton Park** (www.swintonpark.com), which dates from the 1600s, is operated as a 30-bedroom hotel and has won numerous hospitality awards. Swinton Park is the ancestral home of the Earl of Swinton and is a licensed wedding venue surrounded by a 200-acre estate (see the following photo).

© Felicity Lister

Irish castles

- **Ashford** (www.ashford.ie/weddings.html) is a 13th-century lakeside estate outside of Galway.

- **Crom Castle** (www.cromcastle.com) in Northern Ireland is a good option for smaller weddings. It can sleep 12 people and fit up to 35 for a ceremony in its conservatory.

✔ **Dromoland** (www.dromoland.ie) is a castle hotel outside of Shannon.

✔ **Knappogue** (www.shannonheritage.com/Knappogue_Wed.htm) is a 15th-century tower with a medieval-style banquet hall near Shannon.

Scottish castles

✔ **Blair Castle** (www.blaircastleweddings.co.uk), dating in part from 1269, is conveniently located close to a railway station. Its indoor sites include an intimate library, Georgian dining room, and ballroom for 40 to 445 guests.

✔ **Guthrie Castle** (www.guthriecastle.com) is located between Edinburgh and Aberdeen. This circa-1468 castle hosts weddings ranging in size from 2 to 360. Up to 22 guests can overnight here.

✔ **Wedderburn Castle** (www.wedderburn-castle.co.uk) outside of Edinburgh has 14 bedrooms and can accommodate up to 50 for a reception.

Find an expanded list of Scottish castles, along with information on their lodgings and features, at www.castles.org/Chatelaine/weddings.htm.

French châteaux

✔ **Château d'Esclimont** (www.jpmoser.com/chateau_d_esclimont.html), built in 1543 and on 150 acres, is close to Versailles and Paris.

✔ **Château Rayssee** (www.chateaudordogne.com) in the Dordogne region features a medieval castle, two swimming pools, seven bedrooms, and 20 acres.

✔ **Château de la Chèvre d'Or** (www.chevredor.com) is set high on a promontory in the ancient village of Eze overlooking the Mediterranean. It has 33 bedrooms, a heated pool, and a private room for weddings.

Italian castles

✔ **Castello 7** (www.rentvillas.com/PropertyDetail.aspx?Catalog=3247) outside Florence proves that not all castles are hulking or expensive. This one sleeps only four and doesn't have catering facilities, but what you save on lodging you can apply to an outside reception.

✔ **Odescalchi Castle** (www.odescalchi.it/first.htm) was the site of the Tom Cruise–Katie Holmes wedding seen 'round the world.

✔ **Sicilian Castle** (www.5stardestinations.com/sitepages/property1758.php) from the 15th century stands on the waterfront, has a private beach, contains nine bedrooms, and is equipped with a chef and a housekeeper.

Include Scottish customs in your wedding: Grooms who want to look authentic can rent a kilt rather than a tuxedo. For luck, a bride can tuck a sixpence in her shoe and add a sprig of heather to her bouquet. And up in Shetland, having a "second night" after the wedding, dedicated to drinking and dancing, is traditional.

 Although a residency period isn't required for couples who want to marry in Scotland, prior notice of at least three weeks is needed. Get information and downloadable forms at www.gro-scotland. gov.uk/regscot/getting-married-in-scotland/index.html.

Affirming L'amour in France

You would think that the country that touts itself as the world's most romantic would make it easier for couples to marry there. But no. France (www.francetourism.com) insists outsiders fulfill a 40-day residency requirement to acquire a marriage license. So I advise having a civil ceremony at home first and bringing your marriage certificate to France.

Whether you decide simply to have a symbolic wedding or put down roots in France for more than a month, you can find incredibly romantic places to say "I do." In fact, more than 20,000 hotels, inns, and other lodgings in the country, government-rated according to five comfort levels, are available. The most romantic ones offer perks such as champagne breakfast in bed, bouquets of flowers, petits fours, limousine rides, and more.

 If you're determined to wed in France, you can find marriage rules at www.info-france-usa.org/visitingfrance/marriage.asp.

Paris

Chic Paris (www.parisinfo.com) is a magnet for romantics. Views of the Eiffel Tower and the Louvre; the Arc de Triomphe and Notre-Dame Cathedral; Paris' seductive cuisine and street-corner cafés; splendid architecture; world-renowned theaters, cabarets, and opera; and the indelible style of Parisians are enough to seduce any visiting couple to want to marry on the spot. You can't right away, but you can set plans in motion.

Paris For Dummies by Cheryl A. Pientka and Joseph Alexiou (Wiley) can help you sort out the city's neighborhoods and evaluate its hotels. Alternative venues include the following:

✔ **Bateau-mouche:** These slender boats (`www.bateauxdeparis.com/paris-wedding.php`) ply the River Seine, and several feature lunch and dinner cruises and dramatic nighttime sails.

✔ **Dali Museum:** If the entire notion of getting married seems surreal, no place in Paris is more apropos than the Dali Museum (`www.daliparis.com`), which rents out reception rooms.

✔ **La Mairie:** Civil ceremonies (the only ones recognized by law) are conducted in town halls, including the stately one in Paris's 7th Arrondissement.

Elsewhere in France

France also has plenty of charming and scenic locales for a destination wedding outside its capital. The country is divided into 22 tourism regions, each with its charms. Highlights include

✔ **Western France:** Beaches and gardens, parks and cathedrals, Loire Valley vineyards and châteaux, and Disneyland Paris all lure lovers to France's Atlantic coast.

✔ **Eastern France:** At the medieval crossroads of Europe, Alsace, Burgundy, and Champagne-Ardenne contain storybook villages.

✔ **Southern France:** Stretching from the Atlantic down to Spain, the region includes Biarritz and Bordeaux, center of winemaking.

✔ **Provence and the French Riviera:** Ancient villages overlooking the Mediterranean and renowned resort towns such as Nice, Cannes, and St. Tropez draw lovers to the sea. And Provence's lavender-scented fields, cuisine, and Roman ruins bring out the romantic in everyone.

A local planner is necessary to effect wedding arrangements, and you can locate one through `www.weddingsinfrance.com`. Venues throughout France include hotels and historic monuments, chapels and nightclubs, private homes, and rented yachts.

Saying "I Do" in Spain

Similar to France (see preceding section), weddings in Spain (`www.spain.info`) require at least a month in residence, making it a logical destination for a symbolic ceremony. Both religious and nonreligious ones can be held in a multitude of venues, unlike legal ceremonies that have specific rules about locations. You can find information on requirements to marry in Spain at `travel.state.gov/law/citizenship/citizenship_763.html`.

Growing ever more fashionable as a vacation destination, Spain's sophisticated cities and scenic regions provide distinctive locations for weddings. The country's wealth of castles and historic buildings, beaches and gardens, as well as haciendas and luxury hotels can all serve as settings for destination wedding parties. Because I don't have room to cover every city, here are a few of my favorites:

- ✔ **Barcelona:** Artistic and sophisticated Barcelona (`www.barcelonaturisme.com`), home of Gaudí's architectural masterpieces, is also a major Mediterranean port. As Spain's most cosmopolitan urban center, its local wedding planners have access to churches with English-speaking priests, plus photographers and other vendors who understand the language.

- ✔ **Marbella:** On Spain's Costa del Sol, Marbella (`www.andalucia.com/marbella`) wedding venues range from castles in the foothills of the Sierra Nevada to seaside hotels and private homes, golf courses, and the beach itself.

- ✔ **Seville:** Charming and historic Seville (`www.exploreseville.com`), scented with orange blossoms, was the home of the immortal lover Don Juan. In nearby Granada, couples can marry in the Alhambra Palace's tiny chapel.

Paradores are one-of-a-kind, government-sanctioned inns where couples can hold a ceremony and reception and also lodge guests overnight. They include converted monasteries, former palaces, and other upgraded historic places. Some feature pools and spas, and serving regional food and wine to company is a matter of pride. For more info on paradores or to locate one in a specific region, go to `www.parador.es/english`.

Becoming a Couple in Greece

The movie *My Big Fat Greek Wedding* was set in Chicago, but the joyous spirit of celebration it portrayed originated in sun-bleached Greece (`www.gnto.gr`). This island nation's warm climate, rain-free days, sea breezes, relaxed atmosphere, tasty cuisine, and long history — plus the ease in which marriages can legally take place (there's no residency requirement) — make it one of Europe's premier places for destination weddings.

To find a wedding planner in Greece, contact the tourism bureau or ask for a recommendation at a hotel that you might consider getting married in. To find out what the marriage license requirements are in Greece, go to www.usembassy.gr/us_citizen/ac_marriage.htm.

Athens

Ancient and modern life exist side by side in Athens, regarded as the birthplace of civilization. Its skyline is dominated by the rocky Acropolis plateau crowned by the Parthenon, sacred temple of the goddess Athena. Historic districts, vibrant street life, cafés, and tavernas that stay open till the wee hours all add to wedding fun. Hotel options include:

✔ **Athens Atrium Hotel:** This traditional hotel (www.athens atrium.gr) has a ballroom that holds 200 guests.

✔ **Economy Hotel:** Aptly named, this modest hotel (www.economy hotel.gr) is well-regarded for its staff and affordability.

✔ **Fresh Hotel:** This hip hostelry (www.freshhotel.gr) has an outdoor rooftop lounge with a view of the Acropolis and reception rooms that can hold 40 to 140 people.

The Cyclades

This group of 56 islands — the most notable of which are Andros, Mykonos, Naxos, and Santorini — lies in the Aegean Sea south of Athens. Groves of olive trees, a blazing sun that sparkles off aqua waters, and exquisite sunsets behind whitewashed limestone buildings are the quintessential picture of Greece.

Santorini (www.santonet.gr), which stands on the rim of a volcano with the sea 1,000 feet below, is one of the world's most beautiful islands on which to wed (see Figure 9-1). Venues range from the Byzantine Chapel of Saint Irene to private hotel terraces and decks of vintage sailing ships, spectacular settings for sunset ceremonies. All are in high demand, so reserve a spot well in advance.

Figure 9-1: Wedding on a Santorini terrace overlooking the Aegean Sea.

Sporades

This archipelago consists of 700 islands north of Athens. Skiathos
(www.skiathos.gr/html/tourismos/en/index.html), with
more than 60 beaches, lures sun-and-sea lovers. Thanks to its popularity, it has many hotels and their prices are competitive.

Magic Hotel (www.magic-hotel.com) offers couples the option of
using its wedding consultant or simply providing vendor recommendations. Another perk of having a destination wedding in
Skiathos: Every major beach has a watersports center, a launching
point for water-skiing, jetskiing, windsurfing, and parasailing
adventures. Wedding parties who rent a boat for a day can sail to
an uninhabited island, drop anchor, and swim to a secluded beach.

Singing "That's Amore" in Italy

Revel together in the romance of Italy (www.italiantourism.com) —
the food, the wine, the art — in world-renowned cities such as
Rome, Florence, and Venice as well as dazzling coastal communities
along the Mediterranean and villages that stretch up to the Alps.
Couples who hope to wed here need to know that Italy can get very
crowded during the peak summer season and is fairly expensive.

Nonetheless, you'd be hard pressed to find lovelier settings to
marry in from the tip of "the boot" to the northern Lake District.

Applying for a Vatican wedding

For Roman Catholic couples, getting married in St. Peter's Basilica is a high honor and blessing reserved for the truly religious. The process must begin with the couple meeting with their own parish priest, who informs them of requirements they must satisfy. Home of the American Catholic Church in Rome, the Church of Santa Susanna (www.santasusanna.org/weddingsRome/stPeters.html) conducts weddings in English and is also the source for information on Vatican weddings.

Many town halls in Italy date back centuries, are ornately decorated, and provide exquisite settings for civil weddings. Other options include hotels, private villas (see Figure 9-2), farmhouses, castles, or even the Holy See. There is no residency requirement to marry in Italy, but you do have to deal with bureaucratic paperwork. You can find guidelines for marrying at italy.usembassy.gov/acs/marriage/general-marriage.asp.

© Joanne Dunn, www.joannedunn.it

Figure 9-2: Ancient sites, long-held traditions, and incomparable food and wine all contribute to the appeal of a wedding in Italy.

Italy has many spectacular places to marry in, including the following (Web sites, when available, are noted):

✔ **Gardens of Augustus:** Only reachable by boat, the Gardens of Augustus, built atop ancient Roman ruins in Capri, overlook Mt. Vesuvius and the sea.

- ✔ **Hotel Luna Convento:** The private chapel of Hotel Luna Convento (www.lunahotel.it), a former 12th-century monastery on the Amalfi coast, echoes with timeless love.

- ✔ **Grand Hotel Gardone Riviera:** Beside Lake Garda in northern Italy, Grand Hotel Gardone Riviera (www.grangardone.it) has a lakeside promenade above its private beach.

- ✔ **Palazzo Cavalli:** Serenaded by an operatic gondolier, couples can sail to Palazzo Cavalli on the Grand Canal, the most famous wedding hall in Italy and property of the city of Venice.

- ✔ **Red Hall:** Opulent is the only way to describe Red Hall in the 13th-century Palazzo Vecchio of Florence; this location was once a Medici residence but is now used for civil weddings.

- ✔ **Verona:** From around the world, couples flock to Verona to marry in Guarienti Hall near the tomb of Juliet, Shakespeare's most tragic heroine.

Work with a local wedding planner to marry in any of these sites; www.weddingitaly.com is one you may find helpful.

Eyeing the Eastern Options

More affordable than their neighbors to the west, some Eastern European countries have become smart destinations for couples on the cutting edge. Several better hotel groups have opened properties in major cities throughout this part of Europe. However, in smaller towns, the lack of English-speaking wedding vendors can be an obstacle to those who don't know the local language. Two of the most popular locations include

- ✔ **Czech Republic:** Lively and charming Prague, spa towns that date from the 15th century, and 2,000-plus castles across the country are attracting couples to situate their destination wedding in the Czech Republic (www.czechtourism.com). Fifty of those castles have been converted to hotels, so brides and grooms can house guests as well as have a ceremony conducted in those magical spots. You can find the requirements for marrying in the Czech Republic at prague.usembassy.gov/getting_married_in_the_czech_republic.html.

- ✔ **Croatia:** The long coastline of Croatia (www.croatia.hr) faces the Adriatic Sea, making it appealing to those who want to wed in a sunny Mediterranean climate. Visitors liken it to Greece, Tuscany, even the French Riviera — but without big crowds and steep costs. (To find information on marrying in Croatia, go to www.usembassy.hr/acs/marriage.htm.)

Chapter 10

Cruising on a Love Boat

. . . .

In This Chapter

▶ Deciding whether a wedding at sea is right for you

▶ Working out the details of your cruise wedding

▶ Hosting shipboard and portside weddings

▶ Obeying marriage laws where you sail

▶ Celebrating your honeymoon on the water

. . . .

*P*icture yourself and your honey exchanging rings on a cruise ship deck as your closest friends and family stand nearby. The breeze blows in your hair, and you smell the saltwater. What could be more romantic?

Getting married at sea is one of the simplest ways to have an affordable destination wedding. This fact alone may convince you to get on board: The average cost of a shipboard wedding with a two-hour reception for 100 guests on a premium cruise line is $7,000. The average cost of a land-based hometown wedding for the same number of guests is close to $27,000.

In addition to being cost-effective, a shipboard wedding allows couples to combine their ceremony and reception with a cruise honeymoon. (In fact, a bridal couple must sail if they want a cruise-hosted wedding.) Are you tempted to board a cruise ship for your wedding? If so, this chapter reveals what you need to know.

Sailing into Matrimony: The Benefits of a Cruise Wedding

Cruise weddings range in size from intimate ceremonies with bride, groom, officiant, and witnesses to parties of, well, titanic proportions.

In addition to the affordability of cruise ship weddings, this type of destination wedding also offers marrying couples the following:

- **Extensive amenities.** On the newest ships, amenities are equal to those of fine resorts: spas that pamper, swimming pools, and even concierge and butler service. In ports of call, you can participate in land and water sports, tackle an extreme adventure, tour historical and cultural points of interest, and shop for duty-free goods.

   On sea days, ships offer activities to engage people of all ages — unless you prefer to simply gaze at the ocean from deck chairs, holding hands as you watch the world go by. At night, you can sip cocktails on the deck under moonlit skies, dance to live music, see a Broadway-style show, and try your luck in a casino. And with satellite telephone service and 24-hour Internet access, a couple can stay connected with friends and family at home — or cut loose completely.

- **Extraordinary value.** All-inclusive pricing covers meals (but not liquor or soft drinks), accommodations, and entertainment so a couple knows in advance what a trip will cost (although shore excursions, specialty restaurants, spa treatments — and the wedding itself — add to the bottom line).

- **Professional help from an experienced cruise wedding coordinator at no charge.** And because cruises are already staffed with expert florists, chefs, bakers, photographers, and musicians, you have access to the help you need to produce an event that meets your specifications at a party that lasts for four days (or longer!), rather than four hours.

Booking and Coordinating a Cruise Wedding

Does a cruise wedding sound right for you? If so, you need to first find out whether the cruise ship has the number of cabins available that your party requires (work with a travel agent on this), then book your event, calling upon the ship's wedding coordinator. Even if you desire the most basic ceremony and supply your own officiant and a bouquet of silk flowers, you still need to go through the coordinator, who is responsible for scheduling all onboard passenger weddings. This section helps you determine some of the details, such as who to invite, how much you can expect to spend, how to coordinate and customize your cruise ship destination wedding, and how to book your cruise.

Setting sail with friends and family

One of the biggest considerations a couple must make when deciding whether to have a cruise wedding is how much to include guests in the celebration. Many brides and grooms fear that they will have little alone time when Aunt Patty is knocking on their door every 30 minutes to make sure they save a seat for her at bingo. However, other couples find the idea of spending the entire cruise with the people they love the most ideal honeymoon vacation. Before booking your cruise wedding, you must decide what's preferable to you.

Couples have three options when deciding how to include family and friends in their destination wedding at sea:

✔ **Let them board as nonsailing guests for the ceremony.** To accomplish this, you hold the wedding aboard the ship either when it's in the embarkation port or in another port where the majority of guests can join you. A wedding like this is similar to a traditional wedding in that it lasts only a few hours — but it takes place on a ship. (No stowaways allowed!)

✔ **Welcome your guests to join the festivities in port.** Here again, you need to choose a port convenient to most guests and then book a nearby site such as a hotel or restaurant for them to come celebrate with you. There's more coordination required for an affair like this because it may call for transportation from the ship to the venue. Outside catering and decoration decisions can add to the bottom line as well.

✔ **Invite them to cruise along with you.** When you ask guests to sail with you, you can stage the ceremony at any point during the journey, and in any port as well. You also can plan it as a trip that turns into a family reunion and multigenerational vacation, providing quality time with guests. You can share meals, go sightseeing as a group, and sit by the pool or in a hot tub together. Some ships provide a private meeting room during the cruise for you to gather in, or you can schedule a private cocktail party and perhaps even get the captain to pop in.

The choice is up to you. Just remember that at sea as on land, you're not responsible for picking up the tab for the cruise portion of the trip for wedding guests who want to sail along with you. And you may engender some hurt feelings if you invite some people to come along, but not others.

Cruise ship wedding packages

Cruise wedding prices start at around $1,000 for the most basic package. The cost typically includes the ceremony on the ship with an officiant, bride's bouquet and groom's boutonnière, champagne, a small wedding cake, and the services of a photographer. Carnival's package, which starts at $750, is the cheapest among major cruise lines that sail from the United States. For most couples, though, the basic package is just the starting point.

Royal Caribbean Cruise Lines recently introduced its Explorer Weddings program, which enables couples to marry in uncommon settings beyond the chapel. New onboard venues include the ship's surf simulator, its miniature golf course, and even the ice-skating rink. Explorer Weddings coordinators also can organize weddings in port, with experiences that range from saying vows undersea to tying the knot atop an Alaskan glacier.

The top cruise lines in Table 10-1 all host weddings. Prices reflect the minimum for a basic ceremony only; license and registration fees and reception costs are extra.

Table 10-1: Weddings on Major Cruise Lines

Cruise Line	Info	What's Special
Carnival	www.carnival.com Wedding info: 800-933-4968 Cruise booking: 888-CARNIVAL (227-6482)	The most affordable choice, Carnival's "Just for the Bride & Groom" packages on its party-hearty ships start at $750. Weddings must be booked no fewer than 35 days prior to sailing.
Celebrity	www.celebrity.com Wedding info: 866-535-2352 Cruise booking: 800-647-2251	Celebrity passengers tend to be slightly older and more sophisticated than the norm. Kids are few, and food is gourmet. Customized deck weddings under a white canopy start at $1,400.
Costa	www.costacruises.com Wedding info: 877-580-3556 Cruise booking: 800-247-7320	Choose from a Caribbean- or Italian-style wedding starting at $1,300. The latter includes Roman pillars at the ceremony location, a passage in Italian read at the ceremony, traditional Italian wedding music, a Venetian-style bridal bouquet, and a bottle of sparkling Italian wine.

Cruise Line	Info	What's Special
Disney	www.disneycruise.com Wedding info: 321-939-4610 Cruise booking: 800-951-3532	Bring the kids! Great for multigenerational wedding parties, Disney Fairytale Weddings at Sea start at $1,900 for a shipboard wedding, $2,900 for a Castaway Cay private Caribbean island package.
Holland America	www.hollandamerica.com Wedding info: For cruises to North America and Canada: 888-475-5511; 604-940-1181 For cruises to Europe: 877-580-3556; 305-577-3358 Cruise booking: 877-724-5425	Holland America cruises attract mature passengers. Dining room assignments are for the duration of the cruise, and a formal night is usually included. Weddings start at $1,295 for North American and Caribbean sailings and $1,900 for European sailings.
Norwegian	www.ncl.com Wedding info: 800-392-3472; 305-421-1280 Cruise booking: 800-327-7030	"Wedding Aisles"packages start at $1,100. And this cruise line offers *freestyle cruising,* which means you eat when, where, and with whom you want — and you have more dining choices on NCL than on other cruise lines.
Princess	www.princess.com Wedding info: 866-444-8820 Cruise booking: 800-PRINCESS (774-6237)	Princess is the only major North American cruise line where the captain can perform a ceremony at sea. "Tie the Knot" package prices begin at $1,800 for the ceremony. Princess ships sail everywhere from Alaska to Tahiti.
Royal Caribbean International	www.royalcaribbean.com Wedding info: 888-933-7225 Cruise booking: 866-562-7625	A favorite with active vacationers, RCI ships — the world's largest — offer the most to do onboard plus separate pools for kids and adults. "Royal Romance" packages start at $1,100.

(continued)

Table 10-1 *(continued)*

Cruise Line	Info	What's Special
Windstar	www.windstarcruises.com Wedding info: 877-580-3556 ext. 1034 Cruise booking: 800-258-SAIL (7245)	Small Windstar motorized yachts can ease into secluded coves, and entire ships can be chartered for a wedding cruise. No-fee dawn and sunset ceremonies are splendid. The attitude is informal. No wedding coordinator is on board.

Note: All prices were accurate as of November 2006 and are subject to change without notice.

Finalizing the details

Cruise ship vacations are becoming more and more popular, so booking in advance is very important. If you have a particular ship and sailing date in mind, don't delay. At minimum, start planning three months ahead of time; many experienced cruising couples actually book their next cruise a year or more in advance.

Travel arrangements for a cruise wedding can be complex, involving flights and overnight hotel stays on either end of the voyage itself if you don't leave from and return to a port within driving distance of where you and your guests live. So I suggest you turn to a travel agent to make your reservations. See Chapter 11 for how travel agents can help plan your wedding.

Before you contact an agent and book a cruise wedding, ask yourselves these questions. Doing so can make it easier for the agent to tailor recommendations based on your needs.

Will it float? Try before you buy

Two cruise lines, Celebrity and Royal Caribbean, offer a Testing the Waters package that allows a couple to inspect a ship before committing to having a wedding on it. For under $200 (more if extra people tag along), you can get a tour of the pier, port, and ship led by a wedding coordinator, view potential reception and ceremony venues, discuss photography and decorations, and have a buffet lunch in the ship's café.

✔ **Who is sailing with us?** Do we expect family and friends to join us on the cruise? If so, the travel agent may be able to secure a group discount. You may even get a free cabin for yourselves if you meet the cruise line's definition of a group.

✔ **What is our budget?** Knowing what you can spend helps identify the most affordable cruise lines for you. Keep in mind that the cost of the cruise is separate from that of the wedding.

✔ **Where do we want to sail?** Caribbean itineraries are popular with Easterners and Midwesterners. Cruises to Alaska, Mexico's Pacific coast, and within Hawaii are most convenient for West Coast residents. But that needn't affect your decision. If you've always dreamed of sailing to Tahiti or through the Panama Canal, go for it!

✔ **When do we want to sail?** Although cruises leave from ports year-round, summer is prime sailing season, and you have the widest choice of ships and itineraries at that time of year.

✔ **How long a cruise should we take?** Budget is a factor in the length of any cruise. The more you can spend, the longer you can sail. Itineraries range from overnight cruises "to nowhere" to 100-plus days at sea on a round-the-world cruise. Most voyages are in the five- to eleven-day range.

Working with the pros

Cruise weddings are as close to a turnkey affair as a couple can get, yet a lot of planning still goes into the simplest affairs. Having a wedding coordinator onboard can make you grateful to have someone to help guide you through the process.

Look to your coordinator to handle all the wedding details from booking to bon voyage. The responsibilities that fall to the wedding coordinator include

✔ Answering your questions

✔ Informing you of the legal requirements, helping you to get required documents, and making sure that your ceremony will be valid in the port you choose

✔ Reserving a place and time for the ceremony and reception

✔ Arranging preboarding for you and your guests

✔ Securing the officiant

✔ Coordinating with the ship's florist, baker, photographer, and other providers who are crew members

✔ Communicating the catering order

✔ Making sure your spaces are clean and well lit

✔ Being available for last-minute changes and emergencies

✔ Handling transportation to a port location, if required

To get started planning your destination cruise wedding, contact the cruise line and ask to speak to a wedding coordinator (find phone numbers for the major cruise lines earlier in this chapter). As with any wedding vendor, your coordinator should strike you as someone you can count on and can call with questions and concerns.

Cruise wedding coordinators only manage the wedding portion of your trip. Your coordinator can help you figure out what type of cruise ship wedding package you want to purchase (check out the next section). You'll still need to work with a travel agent to book cabins and such.

Customizing your ship wedding

If you want to personalize aspects of the wedding, give your coordinator (she is your point person throughout) ample time before you board to produce those elements to your liking. You may be perfectly happy with what's included in your onboard wedding package or you may still want a few extras to enhance your cruise wedding. I cover some of the options in the following sections.

Ceremony enhancements

Not all ships offer the same elements, but the following are widely available:

✔ **Decorations:** Think a silk canopy or tulle-wrapped archway adds the perfect touch? Add it to your list.

✔ **Flowers:** Love a particular kind of flower or want a special type of bouquet? Most likely, your wedding coordinator can help you get what you want.

✔ **Photography:** On some ships, basic wedding packages include the services of the photographer only — and photos themselves cost extra. Other packages include a limited number of photos. Choose photo options in advance to avoid being surprised.

✔ **Religious elements:** Ships that contain wedding chapels usually have a podium for the officiant and a table next to it. If you want an altar to take communion or kneeling benches, or a chuppah for a Jewish wedding, request this in advance.

✔ **Tuxedo rental:** Ships that have formal nights usually have a place on board where you can rent a tuxedo, which is more convenient than having to pack one and return it after the trip.

✔ **Videography and Webcam transmission:** Not part of a basic package, video and Webcam pictures help to share the memories with those who aren't with you. (Check out Chapter 17 for how a Webcam can transmit your ceremony.)

Reception elements

Some couples think that a big, festive reception is the best part of an onboard wedding, even though it escalates the affair into another budget bracket. Most basic wedding packages include a small cake and domestic champagne toast afterwards. The following are a few reception upgrades you may want to consider:

✔ **Premium cake and Champagne:** To make the after-ceremony even sweeter, trade up to French Champagne and a two-tier cake.

✔ **Catering:** You can choose from a buffet table, hors d'oeuvres and cocktails, or a four-course sit-down dinner. Specialty restaurants on ships, which are smaller than main dining rooms, make good reception spots because they can be closed for your private party.

✔ **Dining-room decorations:** Beautify surroundings with flowers on the tables, a fountain that gushes champagne, garnished and carved fruit and marzipan, or an ice sculpture with your initials on it.

✔ **Music and entertainment:** CDs are fine, but true music fans with guests who like to dance appreciate the services of a DJ, piano or keyboard player, vocalist, or the ship's own live band.

✔ **Sound and lighting:** Music needs to be amplified, and you and the entertainment deserve to spend time in the spotlight.

If you're spending a substantial amount on the wedding, don't be shy about asking to have a few extra perks included gratis. And get the price of each component in writing beforehand. You don't want the honeymoon ruined by a tariff that takes you by surprise.

Finding Locations on Land and Sea

Although cruise weddings typically take place while the ship is in port, you need to choose in advance whether to have your wedding onboard the docked ship or at a nearby land location. Whether your wedding guests join you just for the day or sail along with you

may help you decide whether getting married on the ship or in
port is a better choice. This section looks at your options on where
you can tie the knot on a cruise wedding.

Saying "I do" onboard the ship

Couples who marry onboard have the choice of different areas in
which to hold the ceremony and reception. Depending on the ship,
you may have your ceremony in the wedding chapel, on deck, in a
lounge, library, restaurant, your private suite, or elsewhere.
Weddings are often scheduled between noon and 2 p.m. because
the majority of ships leave port around 5 p.m. The ceremony itself
lasts about half an hour, leaving two hours for a reception.

A ship's wedding chapel is the obvious choice because it's dedicated to that purpose and can be decorated according to a couple's
wishes. (See the section "Customizing your ship wedding," earlier
in this chapter, for more info).

The newest ships launched by Princess, Royal Caribbean, Norwegian,
and Carnival cruise lines all feature dedicated wedding chapels.
These intimate indoor spaces are usually located on a top deck to
allow sunlight to stream in during the day. (Check out Figure 10-1
for an example.)

Princess Cruises' *Golden Princess* and *Grand Princess* both have a
Webcam in their wedding chapel, making it possible for nonsailing
guests to witness the wedding in real time. ***Remember:*** Webcams
don't record images, so request videography if you want a moving
visual record of the wedding.

Figure 10-1: Royal Caribbean's *Freedom of Seas* wedding chapel.

To facilitate embarkation, your cruise wedding coordinator arranges priority check-in and boarding for you and your guests before the rest of the passengers. She also makes sure all nonsailing members of the wedding disembark half an hour prior to departure.

Marrying in port

Today nearly 40 percent of the United States population resides within a half day's driving distance of a port. If you and most of your guests live near Miami, New York, Boston, Baltimore, Charleston, Galveston, Tampa, San Francisco, Seattle, or New Orleans, where many ships sail from, a cruise wedding is especially convenient for friends and family who prefer not to fly.

If you decide to get married in port, you can ask your cruise wedding coordinator to help with the details or put you in touch with a professional at the location. Can you pull off a port-side ceremony and reception yourselves? If you're willing to handle a slew of details without help from an experienced hand, yes — just remember to get back on board before the ship sails.

For many cruise lines, the cost of a wedding varies by port and is based on demand and local economic conditions. Whether most of your wedding guests are traveling with you — or your wedding party includes just the two of you — you have a wealth of scenic and romantic harborside locations to choose from on all seven continents. Some popular shore destinations include the following:

- ✔ **Alaska:** May through September, outdoor cruise weddings can take place against magnificent backdrops. With assistance from the ship's excursions desk, your coordinator can help to organize a ceremony for you amidst scenic Tongass National Forest or another protected wildlife environment; invite guests to a salmon bake followed by panning for gold; be surrounded (and perhaps serenaded) by canine athletes at a sled dog and musher's camp; or fly to the top of a glacier and pledge your troth in an icy, pristine wilderness (see Figure 10-2).

- ✔ **Europe:** European ports open up another world of possibilities for an on-shore ceremony that your wedding coordinator can help to arrange. Parks and gardens, castles and private estates, chapels and former monasteries are all potential venues. (Check out Chapter 9 for more on European destinations.)

Figure 10-2: Royal Caribbean's Explorer Weddings can whisk couples off to exotic spots like the top of a glacier for a ceremony while in port.

Used with permission of The Wedding Experience.

✔ **The Caribbean:** Many cruise ships call at Caribbean ports, where wedding locations in those countries range from wide public beaches to hotel terraces that overlook the sea, to private suites and big ballrooms. One resort, Half Moon (www. halfmoon.com) in Jamaica, now offers cruising couples who sail into Montego Bay a quickie one-day wedding package complete with roundtrip transportation to the pier. (For more info, see Chapter 8.)

✔ **New Orleans:** The port was closed following Hurricane Katrina and recently reopened. Now it's the least-expensive port to marry in, remains popular with Southerners, and passengers can enjoy the city's famed cuisine before and after sailing.

Although weddings in port have their good points, you may want to consider how such weddings differ from onboard ones (other than the location):

✔ **Cost:** Shore weddings are more expensive than shipboard ones because transportation to the venue must be factored in and you also may have to pay to rent a venue. Some ports are barren, industrial places, so if you're planning a wedding on shore, you may need a space elsewhere.

✔ **Time:** Any minutes spent getting to and from a location shorten the amount of time for the ceremony and reception.

Getting hitched on a private island

Several cruise lines that regularly sail Caribbean itineraries — including Holland America, Royal Caribbean, NCL, and Disney — have their own private island that only their ships call at. These private-island locations provide good settings for casual, toes-in-the-sand weddings, the sun high above and a steel band drumming in the background.

Holland America's unspoiled Half Moon Cay has a beautiful, white-washed wedding chapel on the island as well as a trolley that can help to transport less-mobile guests to the location (see the following photo). This traditional Bahamanian chapel stands in a garden overlooking the sea. Guests often wear tropical attire, and champagne and cake are served following the ceremony.

Only ship passengers have access to ships' private islands, which makes this option best for couples who are traveling with their entire wedding party.

© Holland America Line

Vowing to Be Legal Onboard

After a ship enters the waters of a sovereign territory, any weddings conducted onboard or in port must conform to the laws of that territory in order for the marriage to be legally recognized. That includes obtaining a license from that location, having the ceremony conducted by a person authorized to sanction a marriage in that territory, and in some cases requiring specified language to be included in the vows.

As a result, some couples decide that getting a wedding license at home, before they sail, followed by a small courthouse ceremony is easier, cheaper, and more convenient. On the ship or in port, the couple can then proceed with a symbolic wedding ceremony complete with officiant and spoken vows.

The need to attend to legal details underscores the value of working with an experienced cruise wedding coordinator. She is able to tell you what the rules and regulations for that territory are; what paperwork, documentation, and fees are necessary; and what forms you can file in person versus through the mail. Be sure to work out these details with her well in advance.

The officiant a ship supplies may be a religious, nondenominational, or authorized civil representative. Civil authorities are generally justices of the peace or notaries. Holland America always has a priest onboard, and a minister and rabbi sail during holidays as well. Couples who prefer to be married by a specific person must arrange in advance to bring the individual onboard and pay for that person's services separately.

Many people have a misconception that a ship's captain can perform wedding ceremonies. You can find only one exception: Princess Cruises, which is registered in Bermuda, can issue a Bermudian license in international waters — and Princess captains can marry a couple onboard while the ship is at sea. Weddings on all other cruise ships can only take place when the ship is docked, and couples must abide by the laws of the location unless they have a purely symbolic wedding.

Hiring a private boat and captain

The ultimate in luxury, a private yacht allows you to truly set your own course. And renting a yacht isn't as expensive as you may think. More and more couples, groups of friends, and families are chipping in to spend their vacation flying to a warm destination such as the Caribbean, where they meet the boat. They sail in and out of secluded coves, swim in warm turquoise waters, head into port for some sightseeing and shopping, and yes, find time to get married either by bringing an officiant onboard or having the ceremony in port.

To do the coordinating yourself, start by contacting a company such as The Moorings (www.moorings.com), which arranges yacht charters all over the world.

Overcoming Your Fears

If you've never cruised, one or both of you may have some questions or feel anxious about the cruising experience and having a wedding at sea. Relax. Millions of people cruise annually without incident. Here I address some of the common concerns that newbie couples have about cruising to help put your mind at rest.

- ✔ **What if our entire wedding party gets seasick?** That's highly unlikely, because most weddings take place when the ship is docked. Also, modern ships have stabilizers that keep things rolling smoothly. If you hit rough waters, your cabin steward or the ship's doctor can supply something to calm your stomach.

- ✔ **What if a guest misses the boat?** Weddings that take place onboard are scheduled for hours before the ship sails. If you plan to be married after departure, your guests can fly and meet you at the next port.

- ✔ **Will we be bored after the wedding?** You won't have time to sample all the activities on sea days. In port, you can choose from a variety of excursions and adventures, ranging from swimming with dolphins to hiking on the edge of a volcano.

- ✔ **Will we gain weight?** Maybe — but hey, you'll be married by then. Cruise food is plentiful, always available, and scrumptious. To counter its effects, you can go swimming, use the jogging track and fitness center, take yoga and aerobics classes, and call upon a personal trainer. Vegetarian and healthy selections are served at every meal.

- ✔ **Can we catch the Norwalk virus?** After the epidemics a few years ago, ships became much more conscientious about sanitation. Now many cruise lines provide antibacterial hand soap for passengers to use before each boarding. To find out a particular vessel's sanitation rating, see www.cdc.gov/nceh/vsp.

- ✔ **Will we be surrounded by older people?** Yes — and young people. And parents with kids. And couples in love. Fact is, different cruise lines have different features that attract different types of passengers. A smart travel agent can steer you to a ship that's right for the two of you.

- ✔ **Do we have to eat meals with strangers?** Most ship dining rooms have a majority of tables that accommodate six to eight people, and passengers are assigned to their tables for the length of the cruise — which is perfect if you're traveling with a small group. If you prefer to eat by yourselves, ask your travel agent to request a table for two or choose a Princess or Norwegian ship, where diners choose a different table each night. Specialty restaurants on ships are also a good option for dining *à deux*.

After the Wedding: Creating a Honeymoon Haven at Sea

Whether you're sailing on alone or with your wedding party, you're entitled to some private honeymoon time on your journey. You'll find that cruising can be incredibly romantic, whether it's the two of you on deck at night under the stars, kissing on your private balcony, steeping in a Jacuzzi after everyone else has gone to bed, slow dancing to live music in one of the lounges, or indulging in a spa massage for two.

Any travel agent who's on the ball will notify the ship that it's your honeymoon, and you may get special treatment. Some ships host a special cocktail party for newlyweds, but don't leave all the honeymoon planning up to them. If you can afford it, book a stateroom with a queen- or king-size bed and private balcony. Want to really splurge? Trade up to a suite with a butler or concierge, and have them deliver room-service meals with champagne!

Part III
Getting the Destination Wedding You Want

The 5th Wave   By Rich Tennant

"Well, apparently not all the natives were told to replace rice for the darts in their blow guns."

In this part . . .

When the time comes to focus on the nitty-gritty of planning your destination wedding, this part drills down to the details. Chapter 11 helps you navigate the travel aspect, whether you work with a travel agent or on your own, and steers you toward getting the best rates for yourselves and your guests. You also find information on securing a passport if you're leaving the country.

Chapter 12 gives you the inside scoop on how to pull together the party elements — invitations, food and drink, music, flowers, photography, plus welcome-bag essentials for guests. In Chapter 13, I lead you to the altar and show you how to get it looking great for your ceremony. Chapter 14 does the same for the two of you, with advice from fashion insiders on what the well-dressed destination bride and groom should wear, plus how to transport your wedding gear so it looks as fresh as it did when you first tried it on.

Chapter 11

Making Travel Arrangements

In This Chapter

▶ Discovering how your wedding date can affect travel costs

▶ Acting as your own trip planner

▶ Knowing when to use a travel agent

▶ Keeping guests apprised of travel plans

▶ Arranging transportation at your destination

*P*art II discusses many locations you and your other half may want to consider for your destination wedding. After you decide on a place, the next step is to ensure that you and your wedding party arrive there safely and on time.

Before you begin making any travel arrangements, be reassured that your job is to be the bride or groom, not double as a travel agent. Your responsibility is neither to make all your guests' arrangements nor pay for their trip. However, you're expected to scout possibilities and inform friends and family of travel and lodging options. Whether you're experienced travelers or first-timers, this chapter can help to lay the groundwork so that saying "I will attend" is a no-brainer for attendants, family, and guests.

What You Need to Know Before Making Travel Plans

Before jumping in to plan your wedding travel, it's important to make some preliminary decisions so that you can communicate productively with travel sellers and get what you want from them.

Whether you assume trip planning yourselves or are assisted by a travel agent, you need to focus on the following:

- ✔ **Know your dates.** Decide on the optimal day and time you want to go. If you're flexible and willing to travel earlier or later, better rates may be available. (See the next section, "Choose Wisely: How a Date Can Influence How Much You Pay".)

- ✔ **Keep good notes.** Even if you know your destination well, you may not yet have decided on the hotel where you want to stay or the ideal flights. As you research or your travel agent suggests locations, keep track of the most appealing places and offers.

- ✔ **Choose refundable or nonrefundable rates.** Nonrefundable, nonexchangeable rates are cheapest but more restrictive. Choose refundable rates if cancellations are a possibility.

- ✔ **Consider buying travel insurance.** Normally I don't recommend travel insurance, but with so much at stake for a wedding, insurance can protect you and your investment should trouble occur. To compare policies, visit www.insuremytrip.com. Read the small print on any policy you consider because coverage varies.

Choose Wisely: How a Date Can Influence How Much You Pay

After deciding to get married and then choosing to have your wedding out of town, selecting a date is the next most important decision you need to make. It can influence how much you pay for travel services and even affect who from your group can attend.

The further in advance your group buys airline tickets and reserves hotel rooms, the less likely you are to be disappointed and shut out of what you really want — and the less you generally have to pay. On the flip side, if you wait until six weeks beforehand to make any travel arrangements, don't be surprised if you don't get the hotel or flight you really want or if you have to pay a hefty premium.

Looking at seasonal rates

Have you heard the term *high season* or *low season?* They refer to the rates at hotels when a destination is most popular with tourists (high season) and when rates are most affordable (low season). Knowing what these terms mean can help you understand price variations that can affect your budget.

Hotels in many vacation areas adjust their rates based on the season. For example, rates in the Caribbean, Florida, and southern cities traditionally go down when low season begins April 15. They dip even more when hurricane season begins on June 1. Rates start to rise again around Thanksgiving, peak at Christmas, and then decline again in the spring. The same generally holds true for ski resorts. In Europe, summer is high season; rates soar and many nationalities consider the entire month of August vacation time, leaving hotels and restaurants short-staffed.

Although weather may not be ideal during a low season, holding a wedding after the crowds are gone yields cost savings; plus, planes are usually less full, hotel rooms are easier to get, service people are less overwhelmed, and special requests are more easily met.

Considering holidays and guests' schedules

Should you hold your destination wedding over a long holiday weekend, such as the Fourth of July or Labor Day? Although doing so seems like a good idea — most people have time off from work, so they aren't likely to lose pay — it may not be. You need to take into account the extra traffic and higher hotel and airline prices surrounding major holidays.

Check the calendar of events for any destination you're considering. Anything from a national holiday to a major convention can affect your plans, hotel prices, the availability of venues, and the level of service you receive.

You know your friends and family best. Do they always spend the holiday the same way or with the same people? Then breaking with tradition may disturb them. If they're more free-spirited, they may look to a holiday wedding as the best way to spend a long weekend.

Be ultrasensitive to the schedules of people whose presence you consider essential to your wedding. That way, you can avoid scheduling your wedding at a time that conflicts with their own important personal days, such as a pregnancy due date, a child's birthday, or even the day that a long-labored-over project is due.

Planning the Trip Yourselves

Although a bride and groom can personally arrange travel itineraries for members of their party, doing so would add many more responsibilities to manage. Besides, you already have a wedding to plan! However, if you're a do-it-yourself type of couple, the best scenario is when you have a very small group to organize or it's just the two of you traveling together.

Before you start making reservations, be prepared. Do the primary travel research yourself using current travel guidebooks and the Web. I find Frommer's destination titles (published by Wiley) especially helpful and user-friendly, because they provide literally hundreds of ideas for wedding settings and long-weekend stays.

If your guest list is sizeable or you haven't done much traveling, consider using a professional to handle the actual booking. Some travel agents don't charge a fee, and with their expertise, they can save you time, money, and worry. (Check out "Using an Online or Offline Agent" later for more info.)

This section provides the necessary info to help you plan the trip on your own, including how to take advantage of airline deals and how to work directly with a hotel or resort.

Grasping group travel discounts

If you're arranging your own travel plans, be aware that you may be entitled to a group travel discount. Many hotels, airlines, and cruise lines welcome parties traveling together and often have a special department that handles buying tickets and organizing itineraries.

Depending on the size of your group, you may be able to pick up a good deal. Because selling a dozen plane tickets or rooms is more efficient for hotels, airlines, and cruise ships than selling a single one, they often pass on reduced rates or other incentives to group members. If the party you assemble is large enough and books through the same company, you may actually get a free flight or your accommodations at no cost as the bride and groom.

Scoring airline group discounts

Depending on the airline, you may be able to earn a special deal if your group travels from point A to point B together. The following are some typical offers a wedding party might use:

- ✔ **American Airlines:** Discounts are available to groups of ten or more people traveling together to the same airport.

- ✔ **Hawaiian Airlines:** When 20 guests or more book online using a special code number (assigned when you register at www. hawaiianair.com), a couple can get a one-way, first-class upgrade.

Flying first class isn't as easy as it used to be for the bride and groom

At one time, all flyers had to do to get upgraded to roomier business or first-class seats was to tell the reservationist that they were en route to their wedding or honeymoon. Alas, this has become rare. If you're determined to sit up front, you'll have to buy a ticket either with cash or airline points.

One way to fly free as a bird and high in the skies: If you know any frequent fliers with extra mileage, they may be willing to donate them to you in lieu of a wedding gift so that you can get free seats or an upgrade.

To arrange a discount, call an airline directly and tell the reservationist that you want information on group travel rates. You can access a list of airline phone numbers at http://airtravel. about.com/cs/airlines/a/phonenumbers.htm. Airline prices, although not negotiable, fluctuate day by day and hour by hour, so you ought to "test the waters" for a few days, checking several times to see what the range of rates is and buying when they're lowest.

To save additional money, look beyond the major airlines for transportation. Low-cost airlines, such as Southwest (www.southwest. com; 800-433-5368) and jetBlue (www.jetblue.com; 800-538-2583) in the United States and Ryanair (www.ryanair.com) and EasyJet (www.easyjet.com) in Europe, offer good deals. For example, Southwest offers discounts of 5 to 10 percent to groups of ten or more and awards one free ticket if your group exceeds 40 people. JetBlue extends its lowest fares available to groups of 15 or more and flies to dozens of domestic cities as well as these popular wedding destinations: Bermuda, Puerto Rico, the Bahamas, and Cancun. In Europe, Ryanair and EasyJet fares are downright cheap.

For all your wedding purchases, use a special credit card that accrues travel points. I like The Knot Credit Card from American Express (check it out at http://weddings.theknot.com/amex) because this card is designed for brides and grooms and provides a free wedding planning kit. If you buy enough stuff before you fly, you can apply points to an upgrade certificate or even redeem them for a free ticket on a choice of airlines.

Working directly with a hotel

After you find a hotel or resort you're interested in, initiate direct contact with an on-site representative. Ask to speak to the manager.

If she isn't the proper person to assist you, ask to be directed to someone who will. If you aren't helped, or are given the runaround, look elsewhere: A property that can't manage incoming calls is one you don't want to trust with your wedding party.

The Web can be a tremendous help in giving you an idea of what things cost. By going to a hotel's Web site and plugging in the dates you want to stay there, you can see the *rack rate* — the highest published rate. Consider it a starting point; when you contact a human you should be able to get the room for less by asking for the best available rate.

Always book hotel rooms by phone, rather than online. And whenever possible, call the direct number of the hotel, not the toll-free one. The latter usually takes you to a centralized reservation center, and reservationists may not be aware of the latest and lowest local rates.

When you call directly, let the representative know you're considering booking a destination wedding group with rooms for yourselves and your guests (if you've invited some) and possibly party space. The following questions are key to establishing whether a place is right for you and your gang:

- ✔ **How many rooms does the hotel have, and how many are available for the days you want?** The answer to this question tells you whether your hotel is intimate (under 100 rooms), medium-size (under 250 rooms), or large — and consequently what percentage of it your guests will fill.

- ✔ **What types of guest rooms are available?** Usually hotels have a combination of single rooms and suites with a separate living room and bedroom. If families are traveling together, they may need these bigger rooms or adjoining ones. Some resorts have private villas with multiple bedrooms, which can be ideal for a small destination wedding party.

- ✔ **What facilities does the hotel or resort have for a wedding?** Are there scenic areas, an outdoor terrace, an indoor ballroom, or special suites for smaller parties? Do they cater banquet meals?

- ✔ **Does the hotel or resort have a standard wedding package?** Can it be customized? Do you have an on-site coordinator?

- ✔ **What recreational facilities are on-site?** Is there a swimming pool? Golf course? Spa? What about tours of area attractions? Does the hotel arrange them? You may favor a resort that offers guests a variety of recreational activities during their stay.

✔ **What are the best rates available for a party of your size?** Ask the hotel whether it offers a group discount or special accommodations for the bride and groom.

✔ **Does the hotel hold a reservation?** Hotels will set aside a group of rooms for your guests to book by an established date. However, the hotel only holds those rooms for so long, so you need to find out the date by which guests must book to secure a room, when is a deposit required, and how much.

✔ **What is the cancellation policy?** What if some guests pull out? What if the event has to be postponed or cancelled? You need to know what costs you may incur if your plans change.

✔ **What is unique about your property?** This question gives the hotel or resort rep an opportunity to bring out points that you may not have been aware of and can help you in making your ultimate decision about where to stay.

Don't make the mistake of selecting a hotel based only on price. And always negotiate. When hotels put their first offer on the table, responding with "Can you do better?" never hurts. You may be surprised by how much better they can do. A hotel that truly wants your business should tempt you with a menu of amenities, discounts, and freebies. Some resorts offer a sweetheart deal to couples who return on their anniversary.

If your wedding is in a destination that has multiple hotels nearby, give guests a choice of places to stay at different price points and designate one as the main meeting place. This plan makes sense for bigger groups. If you're using a travel agent, ask her to propose a few choices.

Snagging a group deal on a cruise

Travel agents can be extremely helpful in securing cabins for you and your wedding party on a cruise and at an advantageous rate. If a cruise wedding is something you're considering, see Chapter 10.

Using an Online or Offline Agent

Turning to experts for help in planning travel is smart — especially if you can get their services for free. Travel agents receive discounted rates from hotels, airlines, and cruises, and then charge customers the same rates as they would pay if they booked a trip themselves.

If your destination wedding includes more than just a few people, a travel agent can

- ✔ **Organize everyone's travel plans.** Although buying one flight online or over the phone is simple enough for an individual, the job of coordinating multiple schedules for people flying in from different cities, at different times, and with different lodging requirements calls for help from a pro.

- ✔ **Handle travel-related problems.** If you use a travel agent, you have someone to contact when something — a cancelled flight, a messed-up reservation, a car rental overcharge — goes wrong.

If you have enough on your mind just trying to plan your wedding and don't want to hassle with making any travel arrangements, this section discusses how an online or offline travel agent can help relieve at least a bit of stress.

Making arrangements online

Have you ever booked a hotel or bought an airline ticket online? If so, you know how simple and convenient the process is. Wonder whether you can use them to book your wedding travel online, too? Expedia (www.expedia.com; 800-397-3342) and Travelocity (www.travelocity.com; 888-872-8356) make their agents available by phone — but they only book air travel for wedding parties up to six persons.

Destinationweddings.com (www.destinationweddings.com) offers services to plan, coordinate, and arrange travel to a wedding away from home. Although the company specializes in booking weddings at Sandals resorts, it can arrange travel to just about any place you want. What's more, the site's travel specialists are familiar with countries' marriage requirements. Destinationweddings.com also has a network of on-site wedding coordinators it refers customers to, provides tools ranging from a free wedding Web site to save-the-date e-mails, and offers payment plans that help make travel expenses more manageable.

Don't buy travel from any site or agent without comparing prices first. FareCompare (www.farecompare.com) and Kayak (www.kayak.com/buzz) are comparison sites that look at low airfares across the Web. TripAdvisor (www.tripadvisor.com) enables users to search multiple hotel sites for costs.

Using an online social travel planner

If the two of you are MySpace–type users who are comfortable interacting online, you should know about two relatively new sites that help you organize your group travels. As of this writing, neither site had booking functionality.

- ✔ **TripHub** (`www.triphub.com`) offers free organizing tools, can clue you in about group bookings, and lets you collaborate online with invitees. This site also has links to group reservations pages for major hotels.

- ✔ **Triporama** (`triporama.com`) lets you store, organize, and share travel research with your group.

Follow instructions on these sites to get optimal results from them, and invite all your Web-savvy friends to participate by sending them the URLs in an e-mail and scheduling a time when they can join you online.

Dealing with a corner travel agent

Establishing a face-to-face, personal connection with a reputable local travel agent can help ease the stress of planning a destination wedding. If you haven't worked with a travel agent before, the very best way to find one is through a personal recommendation. You can also search the Web sites of American Express Travel (`www.americanexpress.com/travel`) and the American Society of Travel Agents (`www.astanet.com`) to find an agent by zip code. If none of that works, pick up the Sunday newspaper and check the ads in the travel section for contacts.

To get the most out of a consultation, be prepared to share this information with any agent that you visit:

- ✔ **The dream:** Do you have a vision of what your wedding looks like? Describe the setting in as much detail as you can conjure so that the agent can understand your expectations.

- ✔ **Date:** When do you want to hold the wedding? And how many days do you expect the entire event to last?

- ✔ **Place:** Where you want to go? Do you have a specific destination in mind? Do you know what hotel or facility you want, or do you need recommendations?

- ✔ **Budget:** How much money can you afford to spend to travel? Who is paying? Are you picking up any travel expenses other than your own?

✔ **Guest list:** How many people are traveling, and do you want to help set up their itineraries?

✔ **Extras:** Are there side trips or excursions you want to include? Is additional transportation, such as airport transfers and rental cars, required?

✔ **Honeymoon:** Do you plan to celebrate your marriage in the same place and immediately after the wedding, or do you want to visit another destination?

When you begin dealing with a travel agent, he is likely to have a number of questions as well, all designed to help you narrow down your choices. When you settle on the likeliest ideas, ask for a couple of different options so that you can compare prices and other variables such as location and amenities.

Because travel agents work on commission, you may find one encouraging you to choose a specific hotel or cruise line that rewards her more than others. If that offer isn't what you want, say so — and walk out if you feel pressured.

Sending Guests in the Right Direction

Although the personal touch is lovely and appropriate when dealing with older friends and relatives who aren't Web-savvy, the Internet is now the best way to communicate travel info to your guests.

Put travel information directly in an e-mail or direct guests to visit your wedding Web site (check out Chapter 3 for info on creating and using a "wedsite") after travel plans are finalized and you have updated the information they need. You'll need to notify guests and family members who don't use a computer, either by phone or creating a travel info sheet and mailing it to them.

The following list includes major details guests need to know:

✔ **Dates:** They already may have circled the exact date of your wedding on their calendar, but now they need to know when to arrive and the day to check out.

✔ **Locations:** Announce your destination and provide Web links to appropriate tourism sites. Also note the location of the wedding ceremony itself, the reception, and the main hotel where you will be staying, with links and the phone numbers.

✔ **Travel arrangements:** If you've set up a group travel deal, post the contact information and code to use (if applicable). Let guests know whether they have a choice of hotels to stay in, and send a link to the individual properties. If everyone is expected to make plans independently, recommend airlines with the most direct routes to your destination.

✔ **Schedule of events:** This info can be a work-in-progress. Even if you don't have all the details, you can let guests know you're planning pre-wedding activities, dinner, and opportunities to tour, play beach volleyball, golf, and so on. You can include the final schedule in a newsletter you prepare for them to get when they arrive (check out Chapter 15 to see a sample).

✔ **Passport and visa info:** Leaving the country for your wedding? Guests need a passport and possibly a visa. (Review the sidebar "Securing passports, visas, and more.")

✔ **Currency exchange:** If the U.S. dollar isn't accepted as currency where you're heading, alert guests (and tell them the best place to exchange money is at an airport ATM after arrival). Chapter 4 tells you more.

✔ **Proposed packing list:** Although you may have been mentally packing (and unpacking) your suitcase for months, guests may need some reminding of what to bring (and reassurance of what's appropriate to wear). Guide them.

In your correspondence with your guests, ask them to e-mail you their travel arrangements. You can keep an eye on everyone by setting up a spreadsheet that tracks their travel plans (refer to Figure 11-1).

	Guest Name	Arrival Date & Time	Airline/ Flight #	Staying Where	Sharing Room with?	Departure Date & Time	Need Transportation	Contact #
2	John & Sue	6-26; 9:45am	American 241	Bella Mar	—	6-29; 7:30am	yes	(317) 555-1214
3	Lydia	6-26; 11am	Delta 614	Bella Mar	Julie	6-29; 9:45am	yes	(241) 555-2115
4	Barb & Stan	6-26; 12:30am	Frontier 211	Bella Mar	—	6-30; 6am	no	(416) 555-2249
5	Sam & Sandy	6-25; 10:30pm	Jet Blue 141	Sheraton	—	6-29; 10am	no	(319) 555-4622
6	Saul	6-26; 9:45am	American 241	Bella Mar	Dan	6-29; 7:30am	yes	(317) 555-2198
7	Cindy & Stew	6-25; 9:41pm	United 311	Sheraton	—	6-29; 6:49am	yes	(212) 555-0146
8	Ralph & Edna	6-26; 10:42am	US Airways 4111	Bella Mar	—	6-29; 2:41pm	yes	(203) 555-1488
9	Tammy & Tonya	6-26; 1:41pm	Continental 2141	Bella Mar	—	6-30; 7:14am	yes	(515) 555-0549
10	Dan	6-25; 11:02pm	Jet Blue 214	Bella Mar	Saul	6-29; 8:21pm	yes	(812) 555-1984
11	Laura & Leo	6-21; 8:35am	Southwest 419	Sheraton	—	6-30; 7:14am	no	(317) 555-9812
12	Chad & Michael	6-25; 5:42pm	Southwest 149	Bella Mar	—	6-29; 1:02pm	yes	(401) 555-1002
13	Julie	6-25; 8:30am	Southwest 214	Bella Mar	Lydia	6-30; 8:02am	yes	(216) 555-3142

Figure 11-1: A guest-tracker spreadsheet allows you to know your guests' travel arrangements.

Securing passports, visas, and more

If you intend to leave the United States for your wedding after June 2009, you're likely to need a passport. A visa and vaccinations may also be required; the rules vary from nation to nation. If you don't already have a passport or need to renew one, start by visiting the U.S. Department of State Web site (`http://travel.state.gov`). You can also go to a Passport Acceptance Facility; major post offices and other municipal offices are so designated and can be found on the U.S. Department of State site, too. You can also use the customer service line (877-487-2778) to help you navigate the travel documents process.

Allow the passport office at least six weeks to process your application. Expedited service, which is more expensive, delivers your passport in about two weeks. Private companies promise even quicker turnaround at exorbitant prices.

You can find visa information online at `http://usembassy.state.gov`. Click on the name of the country you intend to visit to find out whether a visa is required and how to obtain one. To determine whether vaccinations are necessary for visitors to your destination, go to `www.cdc.gov/travel/vaccinat.htm`.

This tool will be useful to turn over to any travel agent, on-site wedding planner, or event coordinator. By knowing your guests' arrival times, you can better schedule events. And if you, the planner, or someone at the hotel is managing transportation for their departures, it's important to know when they will check out.

You're the bride or groom, not a camp counselor. Still, someone needs to look after guests to make sure none feel emotionally or physically lost after making the trek to witness your wedding. For more info on how to do this, see Chapter 15.

Planning the Ground Transportation

The two of you aren't the only ones on the move during your event. Guests will be arriving, perhaps taking excursions, attending the wedding, and then making their way home. Even if the spot where you're having the ceremony and where you're all staying is the same, you still need to consider ground transportation to and from the airport. Travel agencies often offer package deals including airfare, hotel, and transfers from the airport to the hotel and back to the airport. You'll also find that many resorts provide this service at no extra charge. This section can help you square away the details.

Getting the happy couple to and from the wedding site

How do you plan to arrive at your destination wedding? Jumping off a ski lift holding hands? Rowed in an outrigger canoe by a Fijian in full warrior dress? In a carriage pulled by white steeds? In a rented Rolls-Royce or other classic car?

If your plans involve a "sand" blast, your conveyance can be as informal as the setting. A convertible can be lots of fun, and an antique boat that docks at the shoreline definitely makes a statement. Just want to get there in time? Line up a golf cart or an entire caravan of them for the wedding party; less-able guests will appreciate it.

Daunted by the expense of renting wedding transportation or having to plan one more thing? Arrive the way European couples do in the Continent's most charming villages: Walk there arm in arm.

To arrange your "special delivery," speak with your wedding coordinator or the hotel's transportation chief. The mode of transportation you choose is only limited by what's available, the cost, and your imagination.

Shuttling guests around

In addition to arranging their own on-site transportation, many couples also pick up some guests' transportation costs. Often the most confusing and distressing part of arriving in a new place is getting off the plane and wondering where to go next. You can cut down on guests' anxiety by working with your hotel to arrange for a shuttle to bring guests from the airport to your location. Imagine how relieved people will be to spot a sign that has your names and the words *wedding party* held by a driver right outside baggage claim or immigration.

Whether you help out or not with ground transportation costs, encourage guests to make the trip together to save energy and money. By referencing your guest tracker (check out the "Sending Guests in the Right Direction" section earlier), you can see who is arriving around the same time, and you can notify them to be on the lookout for one another and share a ride.

Lugging Around Luggage

The worst thing about traveling for a length of time is having to schlep luggage from place to place. And when you're having a wedding away, you aren't merely packing vacation wear. You have all your wedding gear plus the additional items you may want to import for the wedding, plus attendants' gifts, plus favors for guests. Are your arms tired yet?

Although both of you should carry your wedding garments, medications, and eyeglasses with you, consider sending other items on ahead. For example, you don't need to carry objects you intend to include in guests' welcome bags. Not only is shipping items convenient (and ensures that no one will have back strain on the wedding night), it saves you from spending even more time at the airport, clearing security and then customs when traveling back into the country. You also need to be aware of what you can and can't take onboard. (Check out the nearby sidebar "Following TSA and airline rules" for specifics.)

Using a company such as FedEx (www.fedex.com), Virtual Bellhop (www.virtualbellhop.com), or The Luggage Club (www.the luggageclub.com), your luggage and other parcels can be picked up at home, delivered to your destination before you arrive, and returned back home when you end your trip. The cost can run into the hundreds of dollars depending on the package weight, but that may be a small price to pay for the aggravation it saves.

Following TSA and airline rules

The Transportation Security Administration (TSA) has strict rules pertaining to what can be brought onboard an airplane. Your carry-on bag can contain one quart-size, clear-plastic bag that holds three-ounce (or smaller) containers of liquids or gels. Because TSA rules are known to change, check www.tsa.gov for the latest updates before you begin to pack.

Be sure to secure your airline luggage with TSA-approved locks, sold online and in luggage stores. These locks can be opened only by you and officials with a master key. Otherwise, inspectors have the right to break locks. Also check with your airline to determine the size of carry-on you may bring. On American Airlines, for example, the length plus width plus height of the bag can't total more than 45 inches. eBags (www.ebags.com) sells a garment bag that measures 60" x 22" x 3", a size that accommodates most destination wedding gowns. To bring yours aboard, you need to temporarily fold it in thirds (pack with lots of tissue paper), and then ask the flight attendant to hang it up as soon as you board.

Chapter 12

Before You Go: Putting Your Wedding Plans in Place

*A*fter you decide where to hold your destination wedding (refer to Part II for help if you haven't already made that choice) and after travel arrangements are underway (see Chapter 11), it's time to visualize your wedding style, notify guests, and pull together the elements you need to make the event a reality. Ideally you can complete as many of these tasks as possible before leaving home.

Planning a wedding, at home or away, can be a stressful event. I hope I can ease a bit of your stress with the info in this chapter, which provides info on invitations, the rehearsal (and rehearsal dinner), the caterer, decorations, photography, music, and more.

As you go through this chapter, notice that I focus on how these topics relate to destination weddings. If it's a matter of plain old wedding info you need, I recommend you pick up a copy of *Wedding Planning For Dummies, 2nd Edition,* by Marcy Blum and Laura Fisher Kaiser (Wiley).

First Things First: Choosing Colors for Your Wedding

If you didn't select colors when you were shopping for wedding wear, do it now. Everything from your invitations to your table linens will have a consistent look when you use the same shades.

Because your wedding is taking place in a very special location, why not pick colors that complement it? For example:

- **Tropical wedding:** Lemon, lime, tangerine, hot pink, turquoise
- **Garden wedding:** Yellow, pink, lavender, bright green, white
- **Mountain wedding:** Sky blue, silver, evergreen
- **Vegas wedding:** Red, black, white, silver
- **Winery wedding:** Burgundy, brown, green, gold

Deciding How Many Days to Schedule for Your Event

During the early planning process, you need to look at how many days you want to ask guests to share your wedding experience — and how many days the two of you need to spend in the location before and after. Ample advance warning enables friends and family to adjust their schedules and book rooms and flights while they're available.

Furthermore, by getting to the destination ahead of time, the two of you can ensure that all systems are go before people arrive, and then when they do, you can truly enjoy their company (for more on arriving ahead of time, head to Chapter 13). This section explains how to determine your schedule for your wedding getaway and what to consider when planning all the events.

Keeping the main events in mind

The typical destination wedding lasts three to four days over a weekend. You may want to shorten or extend the length of time, depending on the distance people have to travel, how much guests can afford to spend on extra nights' lodging, and how long you want to entertain them before or after the wedding. (Individuals who stay on after your honeymoon officially begins are on their own.)

Most couples invite guests to follow a schedule similar to this:

- ✔ **Thursday/Friday:** Arrive and check into hotel.

- ✔ **Friday day:** Relax and explore the surroundings.

- ✔ **Friday night:** Attend the rehearsal dinner.

- ✔ **Saturday morning:** Participate in a group activity with the wedding couple.

- ✔ **Saturday afternoon.** Join a second group activity (without the couple) or take advantage of some free time.

- ✔ **Saturday evening:** Take part in the ceremony and reception.

- ✔ **Sunday:** Attend a farewell brunch, check out, and depart.

Don't feel as if you have to follow the standard destination wedding schedule. No rule says you can't have the ceremony midweek (when rates are usually lower), plan for your wedding to take place at the beginning of a ten-day cruise, or even organize a villa-to-villa group bike tour that concludes with a midnight ceremony in a converted castle in Tuscany a week later. It's up to you.

Factoring in travel time

If flying to your destination involves many hours and major time changes, I advise adding a day or two to the beginning of a trip to allow guests (and yourselves) time to recover from the flight and adjust their body clocks.

Sending Invitations

How do you announce your intentions to friends and family and let them know you have something unique planned for your wedding? That's the job of invitations, and because your wedding will take guests away from home, you have additional considerations to take into account. This section gives you the quick lowdown.

Determining your guest list

Although almost every bride and groom struggles with the issue of who to invite and who to leave at home, destination couples usually have an "out." Because these weddings are typically smaller and require a substantial commitment of time and money on the part of guests, most people who are tangential to your life, such as co-workers and distant relatives, seem to understand if they're not invited. Keep in mind that your guest list should not exceed the number of people your venue holds.

After you make up your individual guest lists, review them together, asking yourselves these questions about each name:

- ✔ Is this someone we'd enjoy spending part of a vacation with?
- ✔ Can she afford the wedding travel expenses? If not, should we offer to subsidize?
- ✔ Is this person healthy enough to travel? Can we depend on him to get to our destination without help or will he need assistance?
- ✔ Will this person be comfortable in the location we've picked?
- ✔ If the guest is single, should we invite her "plus one"?
- ✔ Does this person suffer from fear of flying?
- ✔ Does our friend have special medical or dietary needs our facility can't satisfy?
- ✔ Will this person need to bring a child or children along?

One of the biggest dilemmas destination wedding couples face when deciding on their guest list is to invite or not to invite children. Kids can play one of two parts in a wedding: as guests or as participants in the ceremony. If you're planning on a pint-size flower girl or ring bearer, youngsters should be integrated into the festivities (no question). If not, you need to decide whether you want to allow children at all.

Consider welcoming children to your destination wedding if

- ✔ They're your own kids, and you can't imagine a wedding without them.
- ✔ You're happy to have them, especially because your caterer doesn't charge for guests under a certain age.
- ✔ You have someone on-site who's mature, trustworthy, and available to provide childcare when necessary.
- ✔ You choose a family-friendly resort as your destination.

You probably want to leave kids at home if

- ✔ You simply don't want them there. It's your wedding, and no excuses are necessary.
- ✔ Space is limited.

> ✔ You've selected a resort to marry at that doesn't allow guests under a certain age.
>
> ✔ You're on a tight budget, and every head counts.
>
> ✔ You've planned a sophisticated event and are aiming for perfection.
>
> ✔ The idea of finding small fingerprints smeared across your dress or on the wedding cake leaves you faint.
>
> ✔ Even their folks would rather travel without them.

Whatever policy you decide about kids, apply it to every guest. As soon as you make an exception for one, another guest who isn't granted the same may not forgive you.

Starting with a save-the-date notice

Save-the-date cards inform people well in advance to expect an invitation to a future event, allowing them to block out time on their schedules. If your wedding invitations are printed and ready to go, you don't need this item. But because many couples pin down the place and date of their wedding before they think about ordering invitations, save-the-date cards (see Figure 12-1) fill the gap.

Figure 12-1: Save-the-date cards let guests know they're in for something special at the destination you've chosen.

Some wedding guides tell you that a year, six months, or ten weeks in advance is the proper length of time to send a save-the-date notice. I say, send it out not so far in the future that you forget why you wanted that person at your wedding, and not so late that the only lodgings left will be a cot in your bridal suite.

Whether you distribute a formal, funky, or e-mail save-the-date card, that's up to you. Lots of stationers have preprinted cards designed expressly for this purpose. If you want to spread the word in a more memorable way, consider the following:

- ✔ Writing the info on the back of a postcard that shows your wedding destination
- ✔ Mailing a luggage tag with your info tucked behind the clear plastic portion
- ✔ Creating your own card with a picture of the two of you by using Shutterfly (`www.shutterfly.com`)
- ✔ Purchasing a passport holder for each guest and slipping your info into the sleeve
- ✔ Sending a pretty washcloth with a teasing note that explains they'll get the rest of the beach towel at your wedding
- ✔ Asking a friend who's good with graphics to turn a travel poster into a JPEG that's e-mailed with your information on it

It doesn't matter what form your save-the-date takes as long as it includes your names, the dates of the event, and the fact that you're having a destination wedding.

Figuring out what kind of invitation is right for your wedding

The type of invitation you send says a lot about you and your wedding. You want to pick an invitation that reflects your style. Although traditionalists still go for engraved lettering on white or ecru stock, as a destination-wedding couple you can be as casual or as formal as you like.

Depending on your budget, you can choose from the following, which are organized from the most expensive to the least:

- ✔ **Custom invitations:** These types of invites are often the most beautiful. Tiny seashells, pine cones, or even crystal snowflakes attached to paper provide guests with an enchanting preview of what's to come. Allow plenty of time for printing, plus more weeks for custom calligraphy. To be inspired by top-of-the-line design, see Red Bliss (www.redbliss.com).

✔ **Stationery store invitations:** Because as many as 25 percent of weddings today are to destinations, you can likely find a selection of off-the-rack invitations that symbolize your location at a stationery store. You can also look through sample books. If you want the info on a sample invitation to be personalized, allow several weeks for delivery.

✔ **Online invitations:** The advantage of buying from a vendor such as Jean M (www.myjeanm.com) is that you can set up stationery to your specifications, see examples of invitation wording, choose your colors and font, and proofread cards — all online.

✔ **Do-it-yourself invitations:** Office-supply stores sell blank note cards, and you can also find ones intended as wedding invitations. Using your own computer printer and a pretty font, you can save a bundle.

✔ **Hotel-supplied invitations:** In some instances, hotels and resorts include in a wedding package a specified number of blank announcements for you to customize as part of a package.

✔ **E-mail invitations:** You wouldn't be the first couple who invited guests to your wedding through e-mail, but you ought to think twice about it — especially if you're sending a text-filled e-mail rather than graphical one. Evite (www.evite.com) features free wedding invitation templates that you can customize. Still, you and your guests may prefer to treasure a real invitation you can hold in your hands.

✔ **Text invitations:** u2 won't r8 w guests if u do this.

Turning to whichever source you use for invitations to supply all your other wedding stationery needs is definitely convenient, and that way, everything matches. So as you order invitations, also consider your needs for table cards, menus, personalized napkins, matchbooks, wedding announcements (for guests who couldn't make it and others you want to notify), and thank-you notes.

Sending travel info

After you choose a type of invitation (see the preceding section), make sure you provide guests with the essential info about your ceremony and activities. Because your guests will be traveling a long distance (compared to if you were getting married at a neighborhood church), you want to spell out the following (you can mail this info in a packet with the invitation or under separate cover):

- ✔ **Destination information:** Start with a cover sheet that describes the destination. If your destination has a tourism Web site, include that URL and encourage guests to visit it to discover more about the location. You can also put in a customized map (see Figure 12-2) and travel guide to the area.

- ✔ **Hotel information:** If you want to give people a choice of hotels, provide Web addresses, price ranges, and reservation numbers. If all are expected to stay at the same resort, let them know whether you've arranged a discount rate and how to request it.

- ✔ **Flight information:** Provide the names, URLs, and phone numbers of recommended carriers and info on how to arrange a discounted flight.

- ✔ **Daily itinerary:** State what time major events — checkin, rehearsal dinner, group activities, ceremony, reception, farewell brunch, and checkout — are scheduled.

- ✔ **Airport transportation:** Tell guests how they can reach hotels. Do you recommend a shuttle, public transportation, taxi, or rental car? Supply phone numbers if guests need to arrange their own transportation after arriving at your destination.

Figure 12-2: Adding a map to your info packet, such as this fanciful one from www. stephanniebarba.com, helps guests understand your location.

> ✔ **Climate:** Give average high and low, day and evening tempera-
> tures to help them decide how to dress.
>
> ✔ **Suggested packing list:** Inform your guests what types of
> items to bring and wear before, during, and after the wedding.
>
> ✔ **Passport reminder:** Unless the wedding is in the United
> States, Puerto Rico, or the United States Virgin Islands, guests
> need their passports as ID.

Assembling the Rehearsal

Having a run-through of your ceremony allows the two of you, your
attendants, and your family members an opportunity to walk down
the aisle and understand their place in the ceremony as well as the
sequence of events. After you practice everything, you'll also want
an opportunity to thank those people who are closely involved in
your ceremony and to celebrate during a rehearsal dinner.

However, you can't throw these details together at the last minute.
This section identifies what you need to do to plan your rehearsal
and your rehearsal dinner so everyone is ready for the big event.

How to personalize your invitations

The Web is a terrific resource for finding proper and alternative wedding invitation
wording. To research the options, Google the phrases *wedding invitation language,
wedding invitation etiquette,* and *wedding invitation samples.*

Because many destination wedding couples pay for the event themselves, their invitations need not be formal (or obligatorily credit parents who are footing the bill).
Feel free to have fun with your invitation language (as long as it includes the who,
what, where, and when of the event). Some phrases you can start off with are:

✔ "Come away with us."

✔ "Grandma went to Florida, and all we got were lousy T-shirts. We're going to
the Bahamas, and you're going to get a tan."

✔ "What would Italy (Jamaica, Savannah, or so on) be without you?"

✔ "He's a prince. She's a princess. So they're getting married in a castle — and
your presence is commanded."

✔ "Salut! You're invited to toast our upcoming wedding in a winery."

✔ "Lucky in love! We're getting married in Las Vegas, and you're invited."

Arranging the final walk-through: Your rehearsal

Most destination wedding rehearsals are brief, informal affairs that take place a day or a few hours before the main event. Again, as with all things destination wedding–specific, the rehearsal is no big deal; it's just instruction on who walks down the aisle, and in what order. (I didn't even have a rehearsal for my wedding; the coordinator basically directed my husband to stand at the altar and then pushed me out the door when my processional music came on.)

Planning your rehearsal doesn't take much, but just make sure that your ceremony space is available for your "practice" day and time and that you have someone to lead the rehearsal. Everything else you can worry about after you arrive at your destination.

As you try to decide when to hold your rehearsal, consider that wrangling everyone on Saturday afternoon, especially if they've been out in the sun all morning, may be tough. Holding the rehearsal Friday before or after dinner, or Saturday right after breakfast, can increase attendance.

Planning a rehearsal dinner

Traditional rehearsal dinners are limited to immediate family and other members of the wedding party. At a destination wedding, the rehearsal dinner is more of a casual first-night get-together than a formal occasion. Friends and family have converged from near and far, and most couples want to use the time to meet, greet, and revel with all of them the night before the wedding.

Resolving where to hold the dinner: On-site or off?

If you and your guests are all staying at the same resort and it has multiple restaurants, you've got built-in choices as to where to hold the rehearsal dinner. On the other hand, if you want to experience the local flavor with your whole crew, the rehearsal dinner is the best opportunity to do so.

Check guidebooks or ask someone at your hotel who's earned your trust — perhaps a concierge, a front-desk clerk, or even the savvy lady who cleans your room — what restaurant she recommends for an authentic experience. Just make sure that whatever place you pick can accommodate your size group and will hold a table for you.

Untreated water in some Mexico destinations and other tropical countries can carry bacteria that causes gastrointestinal illness. If you have any question about your destination, check that restaurants and resorts you select have a water purification system. In case of doubt, stick to bottled water, don't use ice cubes, and avoid salad and other foods rinsed with local water.

Making your dinner fun

Any way you look at it, your first night together ought to be fun. Old friends are reunited, and new ones are introduced. Everyone will have a story about getting to the destination or settling in. However, if you want to kick things up a notch at your rehearsal dinner, consider the following:

- ✔ Give it a theme (such as Pirates of the Sea or Lucky in Love).

- ✔ Hold the dinner in an unconventional space, such as an amusement park, miniature golf course, or bowling alley.

- ✔ Use the location to its best advantage (such as a beach barbecue, clambake, or winery cheese-and-wine tasting).

- ✔ Thank each person individually for coming by sharing your connection to each guest.

The groom's parents traditionally pick up the check at the rehearsal dinner. If no representative from his side is there, the groom himself, or both members of the couple, pay for everyone's dinners.

If your guest list is so large that a rehearsal dinner creates too much expense, gather everyone for drinks instead — and then head off with intimates for a private dinner afterward.

Settling on the Food

As any experienced party-giver knows, good food and drink are essential to the success of a celebration. And you want your destination wedding reception to have that, right? Part of a wedding coordinator's job at a hotel or aboard a ship is to act as liaison to the food and beverage, banquet, or restaurant manager. If you aren't working with a coordinator, you need to directly deal with the individual in charge of the food and beverages. This section can help you settle on a reputable caterer. You can also find info on how to choose a menu for your destination wedding reception and pick the perfect wedding cake (and find the guy to make it).

Connecting with a caterer

Selecting a caterer you'll be happy with is essential if you want your reception to go off without a hitch. To make life easy on yourselves, plan to have your reception in a place that is experienced in providing good food. How can you know the food is good? Keep these tips in mind:

- ✔ **Sample the food beforehand.** Ask to try a range of items, tasting just a small portion of each. (Check out the "Tasting samples" section, later in this chapter.)

- ✔ **Rely on recommendations.** Turn to a local source such as your hotel or other travelers. Or go online and look for starred reviews at www.restaurants.com.

- ✔ **Subscribe to an online service.** For example, the recommendations at Zagat Survey (www.zagat.com) can be helpful if they cover the area you're visiting.

If you want to hold your reception in a place where food must be brought, you or your wedding planner need to work with a local restaurateur or caterer to ensure that not only will your guests be fed, but also everything from glassware to tables to servers is provided. Professional caterers should be able to furnish these items.

Ordering a menu that makes sense

Planning your wedding menu is literally an opportunity to showcase your taste and style. With people more sophisticated about cuisine these days, your menu is also an opportunity to be inventive with both food and its presentation.

How many weddings have you been to where you looked down at your plate and saw a piece of chicken covered in an unidentifiable sauce? Hopefully, not too many. Chicken is a bland and boring choice. And as a destination wedding couple, that's simply not you. You want your guests to look back on your wedding dinner and have a memorable experience, right? If so, keep in mind the suggestions in the following sections.

The type of meal affects the menu

The time of day you schedule for the reception influences the type of meal you serve and the cost. (See Chapter 4 for more on budgeting.) For example, serving brunch after a morning ceremony or a picnic lunch following a beach wedding isn't uncommon. However, because people stay the night at a destination wedding, dinner is the meal most guests expect to share with you. So even if your ceremony takes place in daylight, plan to nourish guests when darkness falls.

When you deal with a caterer, he can give you guidance on appropriate foods to serve at whatever time of day your reception takes place.

How food is presented is also a choice you need to make. You can have your guests serve themselves at a buffet line or have a wait staff serve them. The choice depends on you, your budget, and the type of meal you're having. For example, if you schedule a formal dinner and your plans involve a seating chart, you want table service so guests stay put. Less-formal affairs, and meals in outdoor settings, lend themselves to buffet service.

Tasting samples

Scheduling a tasting is one of the most fun parts of planning a wedding. Its purpose can be to help you decide on either a caterer or a menu or both. During the tasting is when you understand what type of food the caterer can supply for your event. You can tell when a caterer turns it into a bit of a celebration with flair that it's likely he will also bring that spirit to your event. To get the most out of a tasting:

✔ Give the caterer ample time to prepare for the tasting.

✔ Review menus in advance, and specify items you want to sample.

✔ Inform the caterer if you won't consider certain items such as milk-fed veal or foie gras, and ask for vegetarian options if you have guests who don't eat meat.

✔ Ask the chef to include your favorites, regional specialties, and his signature dishes.

✔ Request that she use local ingredients whenever possible; they'll be fresher and cost less than importing them.

✔ Schedule a specific time for the tasting (you're likeliest to get his full attention midday and midweek).

✔ Request to have wine matched with each course.

✔ Eat and drink in moderation in order to sample everything (and don't feel as if you must finish it all — sometimes one bite will do).

✔ Make notes after each item, rating how much you liked it.

✔ Based on your preferences, ask the caterer to submit a final menu afterward for your approval.

During the tasting, the caterer can provide you with a variety of menu items to choose. Do make your preferences known. If you don't see a dish but would like to include it or you want the jerk chicken at your wedding to conform to your Aunt Sherese's recipe, ask whether the chef is willing to cooperate.

Toasting with champagne or a custom cocktail

During the reception, toasting with champagne is traditional. The best man begins the toasting, followed by family members and then close friends. Having the groom toast the bride and vice versa is a new trend that couples find especially meaningful. Make sure you work directly with the caterer or your planner and order a beverage of your choice for your toast.

Some wedding packages include a bottle of the bubbly, along with a pair of keepsake flutes. Champagne (especially the real stuff, imported from France) is expensive, so you may want to allot two servings per guest for the toast and then switch to pouring wine and nonalcoholic beverages.

If you're not a champagne type of couple, you may want to tie the toasting drink to your location. For example, tropical drinks such as margaritas and piña coladas never go out of style in warm-weather destinations. And thanks to the martini revival, lots of destination weddings are also offering guests cosmopolitans, mojitos, caipirinhas, and custom drinks.

Choosing a cake that stands

No reception feels complete without something sweet at the end. Although a caterer may be able to supply a wedding cake — or it may even come as part of a wedding package — the cake is often a separate item that has to be special ordered from a bakery. Again, a wedding coordinator can help you locate a baker, and the baker can advise you on the size cake you need for the number of guests you have.

Although the cake is traditionally displayed in the reception area throughout the meal, if your guests are eating outdoors in the heat or in a tent that isn't air-conditioned, instruct servers to keep the cake under wraps until right before cutting into it.

Many bakers are adept at packing and shipping wedding cakes; however, this can be expensive and impractical if you're marrying far from home. You can trim costs by using a local bakery instead.

Even if you're not getting married in Las Vegas, you can find inspiration and wedding cake pictures at www.freedsbakery.com/weddings-frameset.html. (Don't look if you're hungry!) If you see something you like, print out the picture or save the Web page and show it to your local coordinator to see whether she can have it reproduced at your location.

Picking Flowers and Decor

Flowers are traditionally one of the major expenses of a wedding. Yet I have some good news: Because you're not having a traditional wedding, you may not need to buy flowers to decorate at all. For example, if you're having your ceremony in a garden setting or on a beach, recreating a floral wonderland is unnecessary. Couples who opt for a wedding package at a hotel or on a ship may find that flowers are included, especially if you're to be married in a popular, multi-use chapel, such as the one in Las Vegas where I was wed. It was already decked out with huge bouquets of fresh flowers so all I had to concern myself with was the bouquet and boutonnière.

If you do want to add some flowers or other decorations to your destination wedding, check with your hotel coordinator or your wedding planner. This section can also give you a few ideas if you're a do-it-yourselfer (DIY).

Saving money with native flowers

Although some brides (and grooms) may have their hearts set on using traditional wedding flowers, those flowers may not be readily available at your location, and you may have to pay for them to be imported. One way to save money with flowers is to choose from indigenous blooms for the bouquet, boutonnière, and decorations to keep costs down. Particularly if you're getting married in a tropical locale, you don't have to worry about their availability.

For example, orchids, hibiscus, birds of paradise, anthuriums, pink ginger, pikake, protea, and frangipani are among the flowers that bloom in humid climates and can enhance a bridal bouquet. Figure 12-3 illustrates some examples.

To get a feel for other examples of tropical bouquets, type the phrase *tropical bouquet* into an Internet search engine and then click on Images to view a variety of arrangements.

Figure 12-3: Tropical flowers are beautiful.
This bouquet mixes roses and red anthurium.

At a destination wedding, you also have the freedom to be more informal and be imaginative with the style bouquet and complementary boutonnière you select. For example, hand-tied bouquets wrapped with wired ribbon have a casual air that lends itself to destination weddings. They can be augmented with wildflowers and berries and streamers or glammed up with the addition of crystals or pearls.

Embellishing your space

If you do decide to use flowers for your decorations and you aren't using a wedding planner, you need to work directly with a florist.

The following do's and don'ts can help you make the most of your surroundings while spending the least:

- ✔ **Do look for an all-purpose florist.** One who can supply vases and props, rather than adding to your cost to rent them, is ideal.

- ✔ **Do consider the view.** What will guests be looking at (besides the two of you) during the ceremony? Devote the most attention to decorating that area.

- ✔ **Don't pick wildflowers.** Unless you want to spend your wedding night in jail, hands off the blooms. Picking wildflowers is prohibited in most places.

- ✔ **Don't go overboard prettying up the scenery.** If your setting is already gorgeous, leave well enough alone.

Floral headpieces and getting lei'd

Some destination couples decide to do away with traditional flowers entirely, opting for a floral headpiece for the bride in place of a veil or tiara and a lei for the groom instead of a boutonnière.

These options look and smell great. Just keep in mind that flowers are delicate and can bruise or turn brown if over-handled. Transport and store yours inside a foam-padded container with gel ice until you use them.

Remember that brides carry bouquets for a reason: It gives them something to do with their hands. Women who fidget when nervous may want both a floral head-piece and a bouquet. (And hey, it's your wedding. If you want a lei as well, who's to argue?)

Considering alternative decorations

If you don't have a planner and are a DIY type of couple, you can use the extra room in your suitcase to pack a few rolls of wide white ribbon. Inexpensive yet pretty, ribbon bows and trailers can be used as pew markers, stream from an altar, and be woven through a trellis. You can buy supplies online from www. weddingflowersandmore.com or at a local craft-supply store.

At the reception, you aren't limited to floral centerpieces (or cen-terpieces at all). But if tables and surroundings look naked without decoration, consider sprucing things up with these alternatives:

- ✔ **Light:** Stationary and floating candles, candelabra, lanterns, sparkle lights, and luminaries cast a romantic glow.

- ✔ **Fruit:** Tropical fruit grows in mouth-watering colors. Carve fruit baskets out of watermelons and fill with pineapples, man-goes, limes, kiwis, and bananas.

- ✔ **Paper:** Tissue-paper garlands (or beautiful Mexican *papel picado* cut-outs) are inexpensive to buy and easy to hang.

- ✔ **Shells:** They're a natural for beach weddings. In addition to the real thing, you can also find shell-shaped candles.

- ✔ **Fabric:** Tulle, mesh, swags, and draping go a long way in cov-ering up spots that are plain or ugly.

- ✔ **Leaves:** Combine leaves in an eye-pleasing pattern or tie smaller sprays with satin ribbon, arrange them on the tables, and voilà!

At hometown weddings, guests often vie to take the centerpieces when they leave. Because your friends and family are traveling after the event (and some countries ban the import of foreign plant material), you're freer to use uncommon centerpieces with fragile blooms that needn't last beyond the reception.

Working with a Photographer

Pictures provide a lasting memory of a wedding. When you're getting married in a glorious setting, you want a record of it. That's why having a reputable photographer is key. Professional photographers know the most flattering angles and pleasing compositions to shoot. The pictures won't be too dark or too light, red-eye will be banished, and you'll end up with an album that you enjoy paging through rather than a pile or file of images that don't quite capture the moment. (Friends at a wedding armed with disposable cameras may be as unlikely to create a masterpiece as monkeys in a room banging on typewriters.)

To choose a quality photographer far from your home, look for:

- ✔ An easy-to-navigate professional Web site for you to preview her work

- ✔ A gallery of photos that reflect a distinctive style (or styles)

- ✔ Someone who is easy to reach and accessible by phone or e-mail

- ✔ A photographer who doesn't book more than one wedding a day

- ✔ A businessperson who is clear about what various photographic elements cost, and the options available to you

At resorts and on cruise ships that provide photography as part of a wedding package, you may not have a say in who photographs your event. But meeting with the photographer in advance is worth your while so that you can then communicate your preferences and expectations.

To help prepare your photographer to take the best pictures, supply him with a timeline and a shot list (including special moments and people) in advance that states where the two of you can be found (along with when you don't want to be found!) during the festivities. Most good wedding photographers can provide such a list in advance that allows you to make amendments specific to your wedding.

Because you may be at your destination longer than the hours of the ceremony and reception, consider bringing your photographer in for an extra day so that he can add scenic images and casual guest pictures to your portfolio.

Whether your wedding photographer is a professional or one of your guests, keep these things in mind:

✔ You may not need a shooting schedule if you instruct your photographer to simply chronicle the natural flow of events.

✔ You can get creative with portraits by using outdoor settings and taking plenty of pictures that provide a sense of place.

✔ Using natural light is ideal (but never shoot facing into the sun).

✔ Trees or buildings can cast members of the wedding in the shadows, so try to avoid them.

✔ If you want pictures of the dress rehearsal, rehearsal dinner, hellos, and farewells in addition to the ceremony and reception, prepare to pay more or ask guests to shoot during those events.

✔ For night weddings, make sure you have more candles than you need to adequately light the space.

✔ Think multimedia: In addition to a bound wedding album, ask about having a wedding CD and slide show (accompanied by your wedding songs) created.

The Wedding Photojournalist Association (www.wpja.com) can refer you to photographers who take a photojournalistic approach to wedding photography and work around the world.

Counting on your guests to take pictures? Pack a portable printer that reads digital cameras' memory cards: HP and Canon both manufacture models that enable users to print out digital photos on the spot. You can then bring along small, colorful paper frames or mats, and you have sweet wedding favors.

If you want your video photography to say something, consider a videographer. A *videographer* uses a video camera to capture motion pictures of wedding events. Because paging through a wedding album is much easier than loading a tape into a VCR or a DVD into a computer or DVD player, many couples decide to forego a videographer to save money.

If you're determined to have a video record of the wedding, invest time screening samples from different video companies. Look for well-composed, in-focus scenes and listen for clear sound and well-edited music that matches the shots. Videographers who use at least two professional-quality cameras can cover more and yield a more finished-looking product. In the contract, make sure the number of copies and format (HD-DVD, Blu-ray Disc, DVD, or VHS) is specified. And as you want to do with the photographer, determine whether you can afford him for a longer period of time to capture all the fun of your event.

Facing the Music

To have a lively wedding, feature music. Soft music, loud music, fast music, slow music, dreamy music, dance music: Offer something to appeal to everyone. After food and drink, music is what keeps guests from slipping away too early.

Although some destination wedding couples hire live orchestras, multipiece bands, or DJs, the majority use recorded sound at the event. At any wedding, music enhances several occasions:

- **The rehearsal dinner:** Something soft and jazzy works well as background music so conversations can be heard.

- **The prelude:** As guests arrive for the ceremony.

- **The processional:** When the bride, groom, and others in the wedding party walk down the aisle.

- **The recessional:** What's played after the vows are spoken, and the couple leaves together.

- **Cocktail hour:** Lively sounds encourage mingling.

- **Reception dinner:** Music starts low in the background so guests can converse; as people finish eating, dance music comes on.

At the ceremony, classical music is the norm, but by no means the rule. If that's what you'd like to hear and you want prerecorded sound, search for *wedding music* on www.amazon.com or iTunes. You can hear snippets of songs on those sites and buy what suits your taste. This section helps you find the right music match for you and your destination wedding, whether you're having live musicians or bringing your own playlist.

Hiring musicians

Couples who book a destination resort where music is part of the ambiance may be treated to anything from a reggae group to a steel drum band to Hawaiian choristers to Fijian "warriors" chanting serenades. If you buy a wedding package from a resort or hotel, the music is usually included. If you're more of a do-it-yourself type of person and want to be in charge of your music and hiring the musicians, you can ask the hotel where you're staying or ask vendors for recommendations.

To hire your own band or figure out what to expect from the house's, demo their music. Computer users should ask potential musicians to e-mail MP3 music files to hear a sample. Otherwise, request cassettes or CDs. As with sampling food, a small taste is often enough to tell whether or not you like something.

Burning a destination wedding CD or creating a playlist

Technology has made it so much cheaper and simpler to have great music wherever you go. You can save some money and skip having live musicians or a DJ and bring some CDs or an iPod. To make sure that you can listen to sounds you love at your wedding, speak with the coordinator or banquet manager to determine the kind of sound system available.

Just about every place has a CD player and speakers. To be on the safe side, plan to bring that format with you. If you want to play a mix of tunes, you need to use a computer to burn them onto a custom CD beforehand. Otherwise, use a padded CD-holder to protect the individual disks you select to pack.

If you want to create a destination wedding playlist on your iPod, choose music that tells your love story. Whether your taste runs to modern or traditional, these romantic songs — all with a travel theme — can get you and your guests out of their seats and onto the dance floor. The easiest way to catalogue and transport songs is by creating a playlist in your iPod. To connect your iPod to speakers, acquire a stereo link cable (under $20). Tune into Table 12-1 for a destination wedding playlist.

Table 12-1:	A Great Destination Wedding Playlist		
Song Title	*Artist*	*Song Title*	*Artist*
Almost Paradise	Eric Carmen	Kokomo	The Beach Boys
America	Paul Simon	Leaving on a Jet Plane	Peter, Paul, and Mary
A Place in the Sun	Stevie Wonder	Let's Get Away from It All	Frank Sinatra
Around the World	Frank Sinatra	Let's Go	The Cars

(continued)

Table 12-1 *(continued)*

Song Title	Artist	Song Title	Artist
Beyond the Sea	Bobby Darin	Let's Go, Let's Go, Let's Go	Hank Ballard
Blue Bayou	Roy Orbison	Love Train	The O'Jays
Blue Hawaii	Elvis Presley	Mexico	James Taylor
Born to Run	Bruce Springsteen	Miles from Nowhere	Cat Stevens
Caribbean Blue	Enya	Moon River	Andy Williams
Chapel of Love	Bette Midler	One Love	Bob Marley
Come Fly with Me	Frank Sinatra	On the Road Again	Willie Nelson
Come Away with Me	Norah Jones	River Deep, Mountain High	Tina Turner
Come Sail Away	Styx	Sail Away	Randy Newman
Conga	Gloria Estefan	Sea Cruise	Frankie Ford
Daniel	Elton John	Somewhere	Phil Collins
Fly Like a Bird	Mariah Carey	South of the Border	Frank Sinatra
The Girl from Ipanema	Astrid Gilberto	The Sweet Escape	Gwen Stefani
Have Love, Will Travel	Blues Brothers	Strollin'	Prince
Islands in the Stream	Dolly Parton, Kenny Rogers	The Three Sunrises	U2
Isle of Capri	Frank Sinatra	Then We Can All Go Home	Mark Chesnutt
I Drove All Night	Roy Orbison	Travelin' Thru	Dolly Parton
I Get Around	The Beach Boys	Truckin'	The Grateful Dead
I Go to Rio	Peter Allen	You Send Me	Sam Cooke
I Love New York	Madonna	You Can Sleep While I Drive	Melissa Etheridge
I Love Paris	Frank Sinatra	Viva Las Vegas	Elvis Presley

Filling Wedding Welcome Bags

Even destination couples who are on the fence about distributing wedding favors rarely debate about providing welcome bags. A *wedding welcome bag* (see Figure 12-4) contains a combination of fun, frivolous, and functional items that you reward friends and family for coming to celebrate with you. These welcome bags can be either waiting in the room upon a guest's arrival or delivered shortly thereafter.

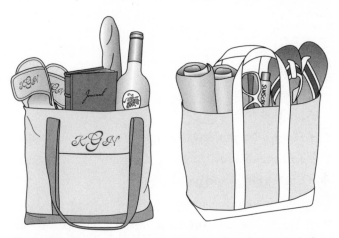

Figure 12-4: Treat your guests to a welcome bag that rewards them for making the journey.

This section identifies the kind of bags you can buy for these welcome bags and what types of items you can insert in them.

Holding it all together

The first thing you need in assembling a welcome bag is the bag itself. Most couples choose some variation on an open or zippered tote bag or miniature duffle that can double as a beach or around-town bag. Small backpacks are a good idea if scenic walks, picnics, and hikes are on your itinerary.

LL Bean (www.llbean.com) offers more than a dozen inexpensive totes that can be monogrammed. (Guests will be happier with their own monograms rather than yours.) As an alternative in the tropics, pick up inexpensive bags at a local straw market.

Don't choose a bag that is so big it will be difficult for guests to transport later or that you can only fill halfway (although crumpled tissue at the base helps in a pinch).

Adding treats for treasured guests

What belongs in your welcome bags? Items that reflect your location and your personal taste plus things that can be useful during or after group activities. For example:

- ✔ Welcome note
- ✔ Daily activities program or newsletter (see Chapter 15 for more info)
- ✔ Bottled water
- ✔ Local map
- ✔ Destination guidebook
- ✔ Beach towel
- ✔ Snorkel set
- ✔ Disposable underwater camera or single-use video camcorder
- ✔ Sunscreen and aloe gel
- ✔ Casino chips and gaming guide
- ✔ Bubble bath
- ✔ Candy, crackers, popcorn, or other wrapped treats
- ✔ Hangover cure
- ✔ Hotel spa gift certificate
- ✔ Luggage tags
- ✔ Travel candle
- ✔ Bottle of local spirits or wine and a corkscrew

Order great-looking hang tags you can customize for welcome bags (and bottled water, CDs, wine bottles, and more) at www. myownlabels.com/weddings.asp.

How much you put in a welcome bag and how much you spend on the contents is entirely up to you. Even if your budget is small, though, it's important to have something for guests to receive upon arrival that communicates how glad you are to have them with you.

Chapter 13

Setting the Stage: Your Ceremony and Reception

*T*he crowning moment of every wedding is when the bride and groom stand at the altar to recite their vows. That's when all eyes are on you, and you want that moment to be as beautiful and perfect as possible. This chapter tells you about the major elements involved in creating such a scene. As you read, you can decide whether you want to incorporate any of these suggestions. If so, you can request assistance from your wedding planner, florist, or the venue directly. You can also find info on your reception.

When you're having a wedding away, expecting to do major construction without a major budget, an event planner, and a contractor is impractical. Aside from simple decorations, do-it-yourselfers may not have much to do, either (this is a wedding, not a barn raising!). So it's best to choose a spot that is scenic, or well furnished, to begin with or one where you have access to vendors who can create the environment you envision.

Stepping into an Altared State

Prior to setting the stage for your wedding ceremony, you need to have a clear concept of where you're hosting it and how its location impacts the style you choose. Chapter 6 helps you choose the right destination. Within that destination, your ceremony's actual setting is important. The two types of settings are

✔ **Fixed:** Fixed settings tend to be indoors. In fixed settings, such as chapels, where you stand or kneel is predetermined. Often you can have a hand in floral arrangements and other décor.

✔ **Adjustable:** This type of setting tends to be outdoors. Adjustable settings such as beach and garden locations, courtyards and wineries, and outdoor hotel venues may furnish some of the elements that turn a bare space into a ceremonial one. You need to rent, borrow, or buy everything else.

With an adjustable setting, deciding on both the aesthetics and the logistics, along with how simple or elaborate you want the setting to look, is up to you, the on-site coordinator, or your own wedding or event planner.

Knowing the stage you have to work with is essential before making decisions about your ceremony's style and decorations. After you get a good feel for the type of setting, start thinking about its potential and consider the pointers in the next sections about setting the stage the way you want it.

Styling Your Ceremony

Your ceremony is where you express your love for each other in the presence of all your guests. You want the experience to be unforgettable for you and everyone else, right?

Before you start to take specific steps to create your ceremony's style, keep the following general points in mind so that everyone enjoys themselves:

✔ **When you have a choice of spots within a location, select the one with maximum eye appeal.** Examples include beside a waterfall, under a spreading tree, inside a gazebo surrounded by landscaping, or on a lawn facing the ocean. If the location is already beautiful, you'll need to do little to transform it into a ceremonial space and even less to decorate it.

✔ **Allow the natural beauty of the surroundings draw eyes, and concentrate more on lighting, acoustics, and guests' comfort.** Inspecting the spot as close to 24 hours in advance if you can is a good idea; you want to see it at the same time of day your wedding is scheduled for. At that time, check to see whether you can be heard. If not, is a quieter spot available, or should you have a microphone and speakers set up?

> ✔ **Check to see whether the sun will be in your or your guests' eyes during your ceremony.** You don't want guests having to squint and miss what they traveled all this way to witness. A change of angle or holding the wedding an hour later or earlier can fix that.

If you're having a hard time envisioning how to decorate, ask the person in charge of the site if she has photos of previous events held there. Also, whenever you see an environment you like in a magazine, tear out the page and keep it in a file. Bring it with you to use as reference. This section can also help.

Going to the altar

The wedding altar is the sacred space where you speak your vows. It can be a fixed structure, as in a church, or a piece of furniture, typically a table, and it may or may not be elevated on a step or tier. Sometimes the altar is a podium that the officiant stands behind, or it can simply be the three of you standing amidst a natural setting.

If your setting doesn't come with a fixed altar, you can do without one, create a natural one (in Hawaii, couples and the officiant are sometimes encircled by flower petals on the beach), or arrange to have a podium or table delivered. Ask a planner for help with the latter two ideas.

If you decide to use a table altar, it can look small and lonely without some form of decoration. Although much of the décor can be provided by the surroundings, you may feel enhancements are still necessary. For example, you can sheathe table legs with white fabric or in a shade that matches the wedding colors. And if wind is likely to kick up the table skirt, use double-stick tape to affix fabric to the legs. (The bride may be tempted to do the same with her gown!)

No matter what kind of altar you use, think of decorations on both sides of the altar as bookends. By keeping them symmetrical, they lead peoples' eyes to the center. Altar enhancements include

✔ Candles

✔ Fresh or silk flowers in a vase or basket

✔ Floral wreaths and garland

✔ Satin ribbons and bows

✔ Tulle or fabric table underskirt

Larger decorations and architectural pieces that some florists make available for rental to enhance the visual effect include

- ✔ Candelabra
- ✔ Easels to hold artwork or framed photos of the couple
- ✔ Pedestals and columns
- ✔ Potted plants or topiary
- ✔ Tall vases or *amphorae* (graceful two-handled jars)

Adding arches and aisles

Deciding to include decorative touches like arches and an aisle runner can instill glamour that a plainer space will benefit from. In outdoor settings, an altar often is accompanied by an arch, which acts as a frame to the scene. When a couple passes under it after the ceremony, it visually symbolizes their emergence as husband and wife. Arches can be left plain or decorated with garlands, tulle swags, satin ribbons, or even balloons.

When you decorate an arch, remember that you don't want to draw too much attention away from yourselves. That's why sheer fabrics and pale flowers are popular elements.

To add visual interest, you may also want to create a beautiful and accessible aisle. Ideally, the aisle is wide enough for the maximum number of wedding party participants who will be walking down it together without having to squeeze.

An aisle runner — the equivalent of a Hollywood red carpet for the bridal party — is another decorative option. Keep the following pointers in mind when choosing a runner:

- ✔ **Aisle runners can dress up an interior space as long as safety comes first.** Insist that any aisle runner is skid- and puncture-proof before okaying it (you don't want high heels piercing it).
- ✔ **Aisle runners may be an impediment on outside ground that's not perfectly level.** If there's any chance an aisle runner may tear or trip someone, simply do without one.

Scattering organic materials up to the altar (see Figure 13-1) — flower petals, pine needles — is preferable, especially ones that perfume the air. Lining both sides of the aisle with shells is a nice touch at beach weddings.

The task of decorating needn't fall to you; leave it to your florist or coordinator to render the arch and aisle according to your specifications.

Figure 13-1: A trail of flower petals leads the eye to a simple, symmetrical altar where the couple is the focus of attention.

Including religious and sentimental accompaniments

You may be able to customize and enhance your wedding ceremony by adding religious and sentimental accompaniments. A few examples include

- ✓ **Religious elements:** Catholic couples may request a kneeling bench; Jewish couples adhere to the tradition of breaking a glass wrapped in a napkin after the ceremony. In any case, inform the officiant and coordinator of specific requests for such items ahead of time.

- ✓ **Your own vows:** Chances are, an officiant supplied by a resort or destination has preset vows he speaks every time he marries a couple. If you want to add something special to be recited, let the officiant know, and make clear who is expected to deliver the additional material.

Go ahead and write your own vows if you like. Just keep in mind that in some destinations an officiant must follow certain guidelines about what he must say during the ceremony in order for the marriage to be legal there. One online resource where you can get inspiration is `www.beliefnet.com./UExp/ Wedding_Ceremony_Search.asp`, which is an interactive tool that suggests vow language for everyone from Zoroastrians to atheists. Remember to keep to the point. Your guests will appreciate it.

✔ **The unity candle:** A thick pillar candle lit by tapers that the bride and groom hold over its wick is a popular part of some ceremonies. Because many destination weddings aren't first marriages, and one or both members of the couple may have children already, the merging of the flames serves as a meaningful symbol of two lives and two families becoming one.

Be sure to notify whoever is helping you set up the ceremony regarding all your specific needs in advance.

Putting Guests at Ease

Long after guests forget what colors you decorated with or how the chairs at your ceremony were set up, they'll remember whether they were uncomfortable. As hosts, part of your job is to ensure there are no physical hurdles to challenge or frustrate them. This section helps you make guests' experience a smooth one.

Guaranteeing easy access for guests

Keep in mind that your guests travel a distance to celebrate with you, possibly at some physical discomfort, so choosing locations that are navigable so each person can fully participate in the wedding is essential.

Is there a friend or family member attending who has disability issues? If so, you must accommodate that person. Explain the situation to the appropriate staffers in advance so guests with disabilities can have access. Ask pointed questions such as how far is the walk to the seating area from the hotel or parking lot, and are there any steps involved or ramps available?

Attending to the bottom line: Seating for guests

As you strive to make everyone relaxed and comfortable, making sure your guests are seated comfortably is important. The length of your ceremony can determine whether you require seating at all. Provide chairs for any event that will be longer than 20 minutes or if you have guests who are elderly or suffer from a disability or illness. If you're only placing a few chairs, reserve the spots for guests who need them by putting their names on the chairs.

Spicing up your ceremony: Rentals checklist

Depending on your requirements and what your site provides, you may need to augment it with rental items. Use the following checklist to determine what you want to add:

❑ Canopy

❑ Candles (table, unity, candelabra)

❑ Chairs for guests

❑ Table for altar

❑ Table linen

❑ Tents or umbrellas

❑ Stand to hold guest book

❑ Gift table

❑ Lighting for sunset and evening ceremonies

❑ Sound equipment and speakers

❑ Heating or air-conditioning units

❑ Back-up generator

If you're dealing directly with a rental house, ask that delivery, setup, breakdown, and return fees are included in price estimates.

Tradition holds that the bride's family sits on the left and the groom's on the right, but you needn't stick to that, especially if your gathering is small. At such weddings, arranging chairs or standing in a circle or semicircle around the altar fosters an intimate feeling.

Everyone needs a restroom

No matter whether you're marrying on a remote beach, the deck of a cruise ship, or in a park setting, you want to make sure restroom facilities are nearby for you, your wedding party, and your guests. Plan ahead by having your coordinator speak with the facilities manager so that you can map out the nearest locations. Ushers, bridesmaids, and anyone else in the wedding party who may be asked where bathrooms are should be apprised in advance where to find them.

At an outdoor wedding, the restroom may be in a nearby building or even a portable toilet. Although no one in wedding finery ever looks forward to having to use a portable bathroom, it's still better than nothing. If your ceremony is going to be lengthy and held in a remote spot, out of consideration make one of these units available for each 25 guests.

Considering Mother Nature

The weather and other environmental factors can affect your destination wedding. However, you don't have to obsess about it. Indoor spaces, such as heated and air-conditioned chapels, restaurants, and hotels are safe from all but the most damaging weather. Holding your ceremony inside means one less thing to worry about. Yet many destination wedding couples still want to marry in a natural setting.

If you're getting married outdoors, hope for the best, plan for the worst, and then focus on making your outdoor setting as comfortable as possible for your party. That can include offering cool drinks and handing out fans or umbrellas when temperatures spike. At small weddings, a nearby gazebo or covered patio or porch (see Figure 13-2) may provide all the shelter you need.

© Riley Photographic, www.rileyphotographic.com

Figure 13-2: A gazebo like this shelters the wedding party from rain yet provides an open-air setting.

Flowers wilt from the heat just like people. Local varieties that can handle high temperatures and humidity hold up better than hot-house imports. In any case, keep floral arrangements, bouquets, boutonnières, and humans in the shade until the ceremony.

In the tropics, you also have to prepare for unwanted pests at your wedding — and I'm not talking about the brother-in-law you didn't want to invite in the first place. For a ceremony that's bug-free, eco-sensitive, and nontoxic to humans, place citronella candles around the perimeter and light them 20 minutes before people are due.

Moving to the Reception

After you're confident the ceremony space will be decorated to your satisfaction, you can then focus on the reception area. How you get there is a logistical issue you need to work out in advance. Will it be as easy as walking back from the beach at a resort to a terrace where hors d'oeuvres and cold drinks await? Or do you need to arrange transportation for everyone? This section covers how you, the wedding party, and guests get to the reception. It also looks at the pros and cons of having a break between the service and reception.

Determining whether you need transportation

How you travel from your ceremony to the reception can be partic-ularly an issue with a wedding away. Most travelers won't have cars, so they can't drive themselves to the reception. However, the transportation issue doesn't need to be stressful.

Although it's traditional for a bride and her dad to travel together to the ceremony and the bride and groom to travel back from it later in the same conveyance, as a destination wedding couple, you aren't expected to necessarily follow tradition. In fact, you can start your own or adapt ones from your host country or another roman-tic spot. For example, the Italian tradition of a processional walking through the village after the wedding is very charming. It can be adapted to a group beach walk or garden stroll, depending on your location. Ever hear of *second line?* That's a New Orleans tradition, where the newlyweds, holding parasols and accompanied by a few musicians, lead their party through the street to the reception spot.

Then there's the matter of transporting the wedding party and guests. Hotel shuttles, rented vans, and other multiperson conveyances are the most efficient and affordable way to move numbers of guests from one place to another. For more info on transportation, flip over to Chapter 11.

Whatever you do, don't rent a car to drive yourselves to the reception. That's what we did. My husband and I got stuck ferrying four of our relatives around in the 101-degree heat of Las Vegas after our reception. So our honeymoon had to wait. . . .

Rolling right into the reception versus taking a breather

At a wedding away, you don't have to pack the ceremony and reception into a few short hours — unless you want to. Remaining in your wedding finery and repairing to a nearby reception area directly afterwards is certainly convenient. Of course, that may feel too much like a hometown wedding for you.

As with all aspects of destination weddings, you can't find hard-and-fast rules when it comes to deciding whether to have a reception right away or delay it for a period of time. You get to choose what makes the two of you happiest and most comfortable. (Come to think of it, that's a pretty good rule for your life together.)

Plenty of couples deliberately schedule an early morning (or even a sunrise) ceremony followed by a quick change of clothes and then a group adventure, whether it's a catamaran cruise in the Caribbean or a horseback riding jaunt through the Rockies (box lunches provided). Hours later, after everyone's had time for a nap and a shower, the festivities heat up at sunset and continue long into the night. Your reception can be as far from formal as you like. Destination-authentic parties, such as luaus in Hawaii and reggae receptions in Jamaica, provide wedding guests with even more reasons to celebrate.

If you decide to go the formal route with a catered dinner, organize seating arrangements in advance and hand over your seating chart to your coordinator. And if you need to cut corners or simply prefer an informal midday meal, you can still reconvene in the evening at your hotel bar for drinks or gather around a late-night bonfire on the beach.

Chapter 14

Dressing and Grooming for a Destination Wedding

. . . .

In This Chapter

▶ Choosing a formal, semiformal, or informal look

▶ Discovering beautiful destination wedding attire for brides

▶ Determining your attendants' wedding wardrobe

▶ Deciding what the groom and groomsmen should wear

▶ Focusing on skin, hair, and makeup

. . . .

As you begin to shop for wedding wear, you quickly find abundant choices — but not all of them are appropriate for a destination wedding. Your wedding's location and the logistics of transporting fancy duds are likely to play a major role in determining what you wear.

Whether you're getting married on the beach or a mountaintop, in a church or a city, you can find clothing and accessories compatible with the setting and the style of your wedding. When they fit perfectly, convey your vision, and are within budget, you feel and look wonderful. This chapter helps you select clothing that will be right for you and for your destination.

Setting Your Dress Code

Before you run out and buy (or rent) wedding garb, consider your wedding style — which should be inspired by the location and the type of wedding you want there. Decide from among the three following dress codes for weddings early on:

> ✔ **Formal:** Same as *black tie,* formal dressing means a tuxedo on the groom and a long dress on the bride. Most formal weddings are evening ceremonies or held indoors in a religious location.

✔ **Semiformal:** No tux or long dress is required; a suit and party dress will do. Daytime semiformal events traditionally call for a suit for him and short dress or good suit for her.

Nighttime semiformal dictates that the groom's suit is a dark color and the bride wear a cocktail-length dress. But if you want to interpret semiformal to mean a traditional wedding gown for the bride and a dark- or light-colored suit for the groom, you'll be dressed in a style that many destination wedding couples are taking to the altar.

✔ **Informal:** Open to broad interpretation, informal wedding wear can range from semiformal to completely casual outfits.

The next section helps you define your own dress code, which will influence what you and your attendants wear. And as for your guests, well, unless you specify "formal," "semiformal," or "casual" on the invitations and remind them before they leave, you can expect them to show up dressed comfortably and informally.

Embracing the bride's style

Ultimately, one person designates a couple's destination wedding style: the bride. Deciding to wear anything from a traditional wedding gown with a cathedral-length train to a sequined bikini top with a sarong skirt is up to her.

As soon as the bride sets the tone with her choice of dress, the groom and the rest of the wedding party will have an idea how formal or casual their outfits should be.

Bearing your budget in mind

How much wedding wear costs depends on the style and fabric of clothing the bride chooses, its *provenance* (designer label at a specialty store versus markdown at a bridal outlet), and how elaborate the dress is. Couples who are pressed for cash but want that wedding look may even opt to rent clothing for the day.

Considering your destination

Along with the bride's style and budget, the location of the wedding can strongly influence your wedding's dress code. If, for example, you're getting married on a cruise ship, you may opt for something more informal and comfortable compared to if you're getting married in a centuries-old cathedral, where formal wear is appropriate.

The setting isn't the only part of the location that matters, however. Climate also plays a big role. What works in a cool cathedral won't do well on a Caribbean beach. No one wants to faint from the heat. Check out "Considering more than just style: Fabric, color, and size," later in this chapter, for more info.

Dressing the Bride

"The bridal dress is the third item in the food chain," says Mara Urshel, owner and president of Kleinfeld (www.kleinfeldbridal. com), the largest bridal emporium of designer merchandise in the United States and possibly in the world. "First you get the ring, then you pick the venue, and then you buy the dress."

Urshel estimates that 25 to 30 percent of her customers intend to have a destination wedding, and that number "is growing every day." "The destinations have expanded," she adds, "although most couples choose warm-weather places such as the Caribbean."

Start looking for bridal attire as soon as you decide on the venue. Many manufacturers require three to four months to custom make a dress, and some have even longer lead times. Fittings and alterations can add another one to two months to the process.

Knowing your options

When selected to be worn outdoors under a hot sun, destination wedding dresses tend to be less formal than traditional wedding gowns.

More and more destination brides are turning away from heavily beaded dresses with full ball-gown skirts that brush the floor in favor of softer and easier-to-pack fabrics, slim silhouettes, strapless bodices, and unfussy details. To make a decision you'll be happy with, explore your options for bridal attire.

Wedding dresses tend to fall into a few main categories, although some borrow elements from more than one. See which description fits you best to determine the look of bridal wear that you'll feel most comfortable in. However, you may find something that doesn't fit into any of these categories but feels right for you. You can also refer to Figure 14-1 to see examples of some destination wedding dresses.

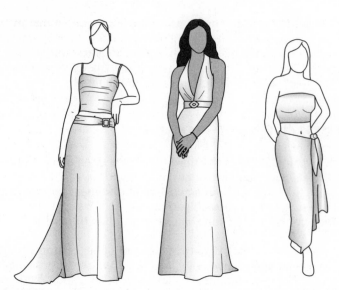

Figure 14-1: Cool and comfortable bridal wear for a destination wedding.

✔ **Traditional:** These wedding dresses are long and white, time-less and elegant, and very feminine-looking. Think princess bride. At Kleinfeld, where prices start at $2,500, customers "want long dresses," Urshel maintains. "There is something romantic about running on the sand in a long dress with the veil blowing in the wind. Imagine the photographs."

Some brides can imagine a different photograph, one that depicts the hem of a dress dragging through wet sand or imprinted with grass stains. For many destination weddings, dresses with trains, unless they can be detached, are imprac-tical. An alternative that still provides a long silhouette with-out too much drag is a *trumpet hem,* which ends at the top of the shoe in the front of the dress and extends 4 to 5 inches in the back.

The more casual a destination wedding dress is, the likelier the dress will be short. Popular short hemlines are *ballerina length* (at the ankle), *tea length* (8 to 10 inches off the floor), and above the knee.

✔ **Something nontraditional:** Nowhere is it written that a desti-nation bride must wear a wedding dress, or a dress at all. A crisp, white poplin pants suit can look chic. A short cocktail dress in white (or any color that flatters the bride) is a cool, leg-baring option.

Wearing a dress designed for your destination

Destination gowns have become a separate entity in the wedding dress category. What defines them as destination dresses is that they travel well yet allow the bride to express her own personality and style. (A bride anywhere may prefer to wear this look.) Well-known bridal design houses now offer styles specifically created for destination brides that are lighter, easier to wear, and closer to the body than formal gowns.

Brands and collections of destination wedding gowns include the following:

✔ Alfred Angelo's "Destiny" dresses (www.alfredangelo.com) are lacy, feminine designs that are priced to be affordable.

✔ Demetrios' "Destination Romance" line (www.demetriosbride.com) includes many slinky, white, strapless gowns with minimal decoration.

✔ Amy Michelson (www.amymichelson.com), a California designer whose fashions are featured at Kleinfeld, also focuses on the destination bride. Her line features sexy, flowing column and sheath silhouettes.

✔ Sandals Resorts, which hosts many beach weddings, has its own line of fluid, modern, and affordable dresses (prices start at around $500) designed with the Caribbean climate in mind (www.sandalsdresses.com). Dresses are made of lightweight fabrics and have stretch-knit linings.

✔ Recently debuted Disney Wedding Dresses are gowns based on Disney princesses. (See samples at http://honeymoons.about.com/od/destinationweddingwear/ss/disney_dresses.htm.)

On the Web, you can find many sites selling festive and inexpensive clothing suitable for a casual wedding. Tropic Bride (www.tropicbride.com) custom makes tea- and full-length chiffon dresses in colorful, lightweight tropical prints.

✔ **Beach wear:** How daring can you get? Some brides look great in a midriff-baring, rhinestone-and-pearl bikini top with a long silk skirt or sarong. Even if you decide to get married wearing nothing more than a white bikini and flip flops, you won't be the first bride to do so. And if you happen to be in the best shape of your life and the groom thinks it's a hoot, why not?

Packing and unpacking a wedding dress

Brides who buy a wedding dress from a bridal salon usually receive the finished item on a hanger in a garment bag. A molded bust form typically fills out the top of the gown. If the dress isn't new from the store, a professional dry cleaner can stuff and pack a gown for travel.

Despite post-9/11 security and carry-on regulation changes, most major airlines still allow brides to carry their dress aboard and hand it over to a flight attendant to stow in the coat closet for the duration of the flight. To be on the safe side, call and check with your airline beforehand.

If it turns out that you need to transport the dress inside a suitcase and your dress isn't already salon-packed, you can do it yourself by using generous amounts of tissue paper to line the case, stuff the bodice, and place between each layer of fabric and with every fold over.

After you reach your destination, shake out the dress and hang it up. Ideally, you can find a place that offers professional pressing. If not, your room may have an iron and ironing board, but use it with caution. If your dress is made of a delicate fabric, then using a steamer is safer; bring a portable one if your location can't furnish it. Alternatively, hang the dress in the bathroom, turn on the hot water in the shower, close the door, and let the hot vapors do their job.

Considering more than just style: Fabric, color, and size

From the clothing on her back to the shoes on her feet, the materials that a bride wears on her wedding day are far from immaterial. When selecting the bride's attire for a wedding away, consider:

- ✔ **The season and average temperature range of the destination affects which fabrics are best for a wedding dress.** Linen, chiffon, tulle, lace, and organza are all lightweight and comfortable to wear in warm spots. (If nights get cool, a bride can add a velvet wrap, pashmina shawl, or bolero jacket.) Taffeta, velvet, and satin are among the heavier fabrics that keep a bride warm in cooler climates.

    To remain as cool as possible, skip the slip. A slip adds an extra layer of warmth and weight and may be unnecessary in a lined dress (satin linings are preferable). Just make sure your dress isn't see-through in the sunlight.

- ✔ **White isn't always right.** When the destination wedding isn't the bride's first trip down the aisle (or even if she thinks white does nothing for her complexion), dresses with color — from the palest pink to fire-engine red — may be preferred over a traditional white or ivory wedding dress.

✔ **Wedding gown sizes aren't sized accurately.** In an act of incomprehensible cruelty, bridal gown sizes are uniformly inflated. Even a sylph of a size 4 may find herself incapable of zipping up any dress smaller than a 10. Every bride must deal with this sizing issue, so don't be discouraged. So when you shop for a dress, look for style, not size, and let the salesperson deal with the number on the tag.

Selecting the right (and left) shoes

Wedding shoes traditionally match the style and shade of the dress. But when the dress or destination is anything but traditional, consider where you'll be walking before deciding what to wear on your feet.

Just as with your clothing options, your shoe choices for a wedding away are endless. The following tips may help you settle on a pair you'll want to dance in all night (Figure 14-2 shows some examples of footwear for a destination wedding):

Figure 14-2: Select footwear that fits your taste, your style of dress, your location, and most importantly, your feet.

✔ **Choosing location-appropriate shoes:** If both the ceremony and reception take place indoors, select footwear that catches your fancy. Uneven ground outside, however, is a tripping hazard. When part of the wedding is slated to take place outdoors on a rugged surface, think about the ground cover before choosing shoes. Gardens are lovely, but if you're going to be walking on grass anywhere, high heels will sink into the loam, forcing an awkward gait and staining your shoes.

If you have your heart set on wearing a gravity-defying pair of shoes, ask about having a runner, platform, or moveable floor installed to level off irregular areas.

✔ **Going barefoot:** If you're getting married on a beach, you may consider going barefoot. The idea of sinking your toes into the sand at a beachfront wedding may sound wonderfully sensual.

Going barefoot isn't always practical. In fact, you may want to stamp out the idea because you can run into the following problems:

- Unless a beach area is thoroughly raked and graded beforehand, you run the risk of cutting feet on anything from a sharp seashell to a rusty nail.

- Sand gets hot in the middle of the day. Very hot. If your wedding is scheduled for noon, the last thing you want to do is hop from foot to foot throughout the vows because your soles are afire.

✔ **Toeing the line:** Some destination brides favor feminine flat-heeled shoes over pumps and stilettos. When the wedding style is informal, wearing sandals or flip-flops to both the ceremony and the reception is an increasingly popular option for brides, grooms, and their attendants.

Sandal-wearers should make appointments for pedicures no more than a week before the wedding. You don't want toenails that look like you can climb the nearest palm tree.

Color is another factor brides can consider when purchasing footwear. For example, if all-white isn't all right, you can dye shoes to match the wedding's color scheme or the natural surroundings.

Outfitting the Attendants

The bride's attire sets the tone for what the rest of the wedding party wears, but the rules may be relaxed at a destination wedding. Should the bride opt to wear a traditional long gown, attendants' dresses still may not require a cloned look. As with all weddings, if the bride asks attendants to purchase special outfits, they are expected to bear the cost for them.

When trying to determine what the attendants will wear for your wedding away, these pointers may help:

✔ **Keep attendants' attire as simple as or simpler than the bride's.** Short- and tea-length bridesmaid dresses are especially popular for weddings on location. That means a bride is likely to find a good selection of such styles to choose from. Some of these dresses are available in white as well as colors, so a bride can buy a typical bridesmaid's dress for herself for less than she'd pay for a traditional wedding gown.

✔ **Indulge attendants' personal tastes . . . to a point.** To avoid an insurrection among female attendants who express definite opinions on what they will or won't wear, brides simply can inform them of the color and fabric to shop for, or encourage them to pick a style within a collection they find.

David's Bridal offers a free, interactive Dress Your Wedding tool (`www.davidsbridal.com/dress_your_wedding.jsp`) that enables users to digitally try fashions on the entire bridal party. Another good resource for colorful, casual, lightweight gear for the entire wedding party is Island Importer (`www.islandimporter.com`).

Garbing the Groom and His Men

Traditionally (even in the most untraditional weddings), the groom's gear is chosen to match the bride's. Whether the two of you decide to take your vows in clothing that is formal, semiformal, or informal, you'll look best if your clothes are as compatible as possible, and that includes shoes.

The groomsmen's choice of attire is then quite simple: They take their cue from the groom. Groomsmen are expected to wear outfits that conform to the dress style in the colors the couple request. For more on picking groomsmen's outfits and accessories, check out *Wedding Planning For Dummies, 2nd Edition,* by Marcy Blum and Laura Fisher Kaiser (Wiley).

This section looks at the different options for clothing the groom at a wedding away and covers important stuff to consider when choosing what the groom and groomsmen wear.

Checking out your choices

Because brides have such variety and flexibility in dressing for a destination wedding, grooms do, too. When deciding on the groom's clothing, the following represent some choices. This list doesn't cover every single choice but does give you an idea of the array you have. Refer to Figure 14-3 for some examples.

✔ **Classic:** Plenty of destination grooms still don a classic black tuxedo for the wedding. A white or ivory dinner jacket (when the bride's gown is white or ivory), black trousers, and a black bowtie are equally elegant and appropriate for after-dark weddings.

Figure 14-3: The choices for what a groom wears in a destination wedding are nearly as diverse as what a bride wears.

✔ **Fashionable alternatives to a tux:** Many destination grooms opt for suitable suits instead of a tuxedo. The nontraditional style of many destination weddings opens the door for grooms to be more flexible in their choice of clothing. Fashion-conscious men who wear designer clothing during work want wedding wear that reflects the same level of taste.

The following looks can be comfortable and stylish (and if you choose any of them, you won't commit a fashion *faux pas*):

- Navy blue, charcoal, or black tropical wool suit with a white shirt and dark tie

- Linen or cotton poplin dress suit in beige or another light color with a white shirt

- Seersucker suit with edgy accessories (see the later section on accessories for more info)

- Blue blazer with khakis or light-colored trousers and crisp white shirt (tie optional)

- Neutral monochromatic outfit with same-color shirt, tie (optional), jacket, and trousers

✔ **Tying the knot without wearing a tie:** Even at the most informal destination weddings where they don't wear a tie, grooms are still concerned with style. For the ultimate in comfort in warm-weather destinations, consider these options:

- White linen shirt with dark trousers

- Solid-color shirt with linen, cotton, or raw-silk drawstring pants

- Neutral-color, natural-fiber Bermuda shorts with a solid-color shirt

- Bathing trunks to match her bikini (no Speedos, please)

Will wearing shorts on your wedding day still give you a chuckle when you look back in 20 years, or will you have wished you opted for a more classic look? Answering that question can help a man determine how to dress on his wedding day.

Because so many destination weddings take place in hot, tropical settings, picking clothing that keeps a groom and his backup team cool and comfortable is important. To ensure that he doesn't break into a sweat at the ceremony (at least not from what he's wearing), breathable, natural-fiber clothing is best. Natural fabrics don't trap sweat like synthetics. Ideal garments are made from linen, cotton, raw silk, and even lightweight wool.

Accessorizing isn't just for women

Donning accessories gives the groom and his groomsmen a way to stand out from the crowd and from each other. Small accents also help coordinate the men's clothing with the women's even further, making your bridal party look put together (and pretty snazzy, if you ask me).

According to Steve Davis, vice president of marketing for Jim's Formalwear, the accessories men use to outfit their attire are usually the same as for an at-home wedding. Davis says that many destination wedding couples opt for these accents for men:

✔ A black tuxedo with sand-colored accessories for a beach wedding

✔ Pink or spring-green accessories for a garden wedding

✔ Accessories that match the bride's flowers, attendants' dresses, or the surroundings

In hot climates, choose an adjustable-back vest rather than a full-back vest. It's cooler and more comfortable to wear.

Looking Great on the Big Day

Everyone wants to look their best when they get married, especially because wedding pictures stick around forever. In the big picture (as well as wallet-sized ones), hair, skin, and makeup are all important. So, when you're tying the knot far from home, you need to take into account how a change in environment may affect your skin and hair.

Before you leave, do the prep work. Many couples have facials a month before the wedding and conscientiously schedule dermatologist appointments, hair highlights, brow grooming, personal training, nutrition consultations, teeth whitening, and cosmetic procedures in anticipation of a day when they know they'll be photographed from every angle.

After your arrival, a great way to relax and look refreshed is by having an individual or couples massage before the main event. No matter what you do, this section gives you the lowdown on how a bride and groom can look great on their destination wedding day.

Getting that wedding glow

When you look at your wedding photos years later, you want to see a happy couple smiling, right? Make sure you prepare beforehand by following these tips to help you and your skin look its best:

- ✔ **Use an SPF-15 (or higher) lotion at all times.** Couples whose weddings are set in a sunny climate need to protect themselves from the rays, and that includes the days before the actual ceremony. Because no one wants to walk down the aisle beet red and tingling with sunburn, pack, use, and frequently apply sunblock before going outside.

- ✔ **If you sunbathe, do so evenly.** Brides who sunbathe before the wedding need to consider their shoulders. Tan lines don't flatter a strapless gown.

- ✔ **If you don't sunbathe, you can still add color.** Tanning salons are unhealthy places to get bronzed. Instead, use tinted moisturizer, find a sunless tanning product, or opt for salon airbrushing. Have the last application before you leave home; you don't want anything to stain wedding wear. And remember: Face, neck, and body should all match.

Considering renting clothes

Couples who want to deck themselves out formally but experience sticker shock after pricing wedding gear have the option of renting. Tuxedo rental shops are more prevalent than those offering gowns. Tuxedo rentals are available in many different styles. A rental company with locations in all 50 states, Jim's Formalwear (www.jimsformalwear.com) also enables customers to order a tux online by submitting measurements. If the groom and his men have rental tuxedoes, appoint the most responsible one in the crowd to collect and return them on time after the wedding to avoid late fees.

If there is a store nearby that rents wedding gowns, a bride-to-be can expect to pay about 25 percent of the retail cost — as long as she doesn't tear, permanently stain, or lose the dress. Before signing a rental agreement, ask about alterations, dry cleaning, and extra charges if the gown is returned after the deadline.

Should a bride count on renting a dress after she gets to her destination? With the exception of Las Vegas, which is well-equipped to outfit last-minute couples (quite hastily), trying to locate a perfect rental gown elsewhere is likely to take too much time.

What if, despite reminders, you've been having too much fun to slather on the sunblock and you got sunburned? Take aspirin and treat sunburn with cool, nonirritating balms. Anything from moisturizer to refrigerated plain yogurt can lessen the sting.

Making up

I made the mistake of using new products on my wedding day; in fact, I spent more money on cosmetics than on my wedding gown. Still, those weren't tears of joy streaming down my cheeks. No, my eyeballs stung from irritation.

So take it from me: Try out everything you intend to put on your face long before leaving home. High-def wedding photography and videography exposes pores and flaws. A cosmetologist can recommend products to minimize them.

Brides who schedule a wedding-day makeup appointment with attendants should put themselves first on the list; times can get backed up, and having to wait adds stress. And your wedding day is no time to experiment. You should also bring along your own products and ask the makeup artist to use them exclusively.

Consider the following suggestions when you're choosing makeup for your big day:

- ✔ **Use products that don't require frequent touch-ups.** Waterproof mascara and long-lasting lip color that will look good in pictures are best. In steamy surroundings, use powder rather than cream-based eye shadow, and keep translucent face powder nearby for shine control.

- ✔ **Consider your surroundings before applying perfume or cologne.** Marrying outdoors in the tropics? Skip the perfume. Unless trade winds carry them away, insects are attracted by fragrance.

Keeping your hair apparent

Hair that looks fine at home can rebel in a distant dry or humid climate. Dry air can attract static, making someone look as if they've stuck a finger in a light socket. Humidity can turn straight hair lank and curly hair frizzy. So before you leave for the wedding, discuss with your regular hairstylist what products and treatments to use to help hair maintain its normal appearance during your travels.

The following tips can ensure you have a good hair day:

- ✔ **If you have long hair, consider wearing it up.** Brides with long hair find it much cooler to wear an updo, and a pretty shell hair accessory at a beach wedding extends the theme.

- ✔ **If you need a haircut before the wedding, do so about two weeks before the event.** That way if the stylist makes a mistake, you still have a little time for it to grow back in.

- ✔ **Hold hometown style tryouts even if you're planning to have wedding-day hair styled by a new, on-site beautician.** Photograph the styles you like best and show them to your on-site stylist so he can recreate the look.

If you're the bride and want to see what you look like wearing different hairstyles, join www.thehairstyler.com. By uploading a head shot, you can try on some 7,000 hairstyles and 53 colors.

Part IV

Sharing the Joy at Your Wedding, Now and Later

The 5th Wave   By Rich Tennant

"I know it's a wedding present from your niece. I just don't know why you had to wear it to the Louvre."

In this part . . .

Show time! Your on-site guide, Part IV helps you with all the wedding details as soon as you're at the destination. Chapter 15 focuses on preparing for guests' arrival, what to look for when you do a walk-through, and how to make sure that you enjoy yourselves and the event, too. Dedicated to destination-wedding etiquette, Chapter 16 helps you gracefully navigate some of those sticky situations that seem to surround all weddings, plus particular issues that attach themselves to weddings away.

And because not everyone you invite can attend, Chapter 17 provides innovative and joyful ways for those who can't make it to the ceremony to still share in the celebrations. Think of Chapter 18 as the icing on the (wedding) cake — your honeymoon. I help you decide when is the right time to go and guide you to the ideal honeymoon for the two of you.

Chapter 15

After You Arrive: Leading Up to the Big Day

*T*he moment you reach your destination, the prospect of getting married starts to feel real and very exciting. Whether you have a lot of work to do before guests arrive or plenty of time for fun, walking through the event both physically and mentally is a good idea.

What can you do to prepare for the main event? The list may seem endless, but don't worry. If you can visit key locations — sample a guest room, look at the rehearsal dinner location, and see the ceremony space and reception area — you'll have the main tasks covered. Introduce yourselves as you go, and let staff members in these places know how much you're looking forward to having them be a part of your wedding.

Fortunately, many destination weddings are turnkey affairs where everything you need is assembled for you so you may not have to do much checking or choosing. Couples having more-elaborate weddings normally have a coordinator to supervise the details. Still, you're bound to have some details to oversee, if only to put your mind at ease. This chapter offers suggestions for the productive and fun ways to spend the time before your wedding.

Finalizing All the Details On-Site

Whether you're on your own, have a planner in tow, or a mother hen is clucking around you, you still have tasks on your to-do list.

Are you wondering where to start with this list after you arrive at your destination? This section covers the major details to finalize so that everything goes as hoped.

Acquiring a marriage license

Step one in getting a license — familiarizing yourselves with the requirements to make sure you can get legally married — needs to be done long before you leave home (see Chapter 6 for background). Arriving with proper paperwork and ready to meet those requirements, your first order of business — the one all others depend on — is obtaining the marriage license. On-site wedding coordinators at resorts typically help couples deal with the paperwork, and some escort them to the license facility.

Places that issue marriage licenses and hotel zones aren't always in proximity to one another. If you're going on your own, ask the clerk at your hotel's front desk to recommend the best way to reach the issuing office. Don't forget to check its hours (and days) of operation and get the address. And find out before you go whether you need to pay with local currency and how much the license costs.

Doing the front-desk drill

Before guests arrive, visit the concierge or hotel manager to go over last-minute details. If the property has an on-site wedding coordinator, connect with her first; some of these responsibilities can be borne by her. Whether you're on your own or she lends a hand, the to-do list will likely include most of the following:

- ✔ **Provide your credit card.** Allow the clerk to take an imprint. Give clear instructions on who may charge to your account and what expenses should be billed to guests. Specify a cut-off date after which only the two of you are allowed to charge.

- ✔ **Confirm guest rooms.** Double-check not just the number but also the location. At larger resorts, having your party's rooms clustered on the same floor or wing is preferable. Also check on any handicap-accessible rooms you may have reserved; make sure they're available, close to an elevator, and have the necessary facilities.

- ✔ **Double-check rehearsal dinner plans.** Confirm the time your party will arrive at the dinner and the number of people attending. If you've requested a private room or special menu, remind your contact. And if you're planning an informal outdoor event such as a luau, clambake, or barbecue, check the weather report in case you need to make adjustments.

✔ **Book excursions.** Want to take the gang on a sunset cruise or a jeep tour of the surroundings? (Check out the section "Promoting Activities to Keep Everyone Busy," later in this chapter, for some ideas.) If you haven't made reservations in advance, visit your hotel's activities desk now. If the hotel doesn't offer activities, ask the front desk clerk who provides such services.

✔ **Set up transportation.** Do you need rides to the rehearsal dinner venue? From the ceremony to the reception and back? Airport pickup and delivery? Tours? Book it all at once to save time. (Refer to Chapter 11 for more on transportation concerns.)

Inspecting your ceremony space

Are you seeing your ceremony space for the first time, or do you need to choose between a few potential sites? Take a good look around. Ask yourself the following types of questions:

✔ **Is the site as private as you would like?** Or is it accessible to public traffic and views? If so, you may be able to mark off the space with temporary stanchions or screens, which have to be rented, delivered, and retrieved after the ceremony. Consult with the facilities manager or your planner for guidance.

✔ **Is the site groomed and trash-free?** Focus on cleanliness during your walk-through of the ceremony and reception areas. If not, ask the property manager when they plan on tidying up.

Also discuss with the planner or facilities manager how you want seating set up, the proximity of nearby restrooms, where guests can retreat for shade if needed, the time that decorations will be delivered and in place, and whether you must abide by any sound, curfew, or photography restrictions.

If you're hoping to have a confetti-like send-off, make sure guests will be supplied with birdseed, rice, butterflies, blossoms, jars of soap bubbles, or the projectiles of your choice. An attendant or planner can assist with this.

Rehearsing with or without your officiant

Resorts that host many weddings often have an officiant they regularly call upon. He may or may not be available to be a part of your rehearsal. If he's not around, the on-site coordinator or a local planner can put your group through its paces.

Before your rehearsal, be sure to give your crew a few repetitions of the time and place to meet for the rehearsal, but don't expect military precision after they're in vacation mode. (In fact, it's not unusual for at least one member of the wedding party who's hung over from having too much fun to blow off the rehearsal entirely.)

During the rehearsal, you can handle these tasks:

- ✔ **Confirm whether you need witnesses.** If so, recruit guests or attendants, or round up staff members who are willing to sign your wedding certificate.

- ✔ **Reiterate requests to personalize the ceremony with the officiant.** If you want to use your own spoken vows, a poem, music, include the lighting of candles, or ask to have a few words said to honor people who aren't with you, make sure you share this info with the officiant so she can plan on incorporating them into the service.

  Even if the officiant isn't at your rehearsal, and you can't speak to her in advance to put in requests, you'll still have a chance to meet her before the actual ceremony, if only very briefly. Talk to her at that time.

At even the most casual rehearsal, you still ought to make sure the person leading the rehearsal accomplishes the following:

- ✔ Makes sure the wedding party knows when to walk in and walk out and where to stand.

- ✔ Goes over the schedule for the day of the ceremony.

- ✔ Reminds you to double-check that you have the right shoes. At a beach wedding, it's better to wear flats or even flip-flops than struggle with high heels.

If you purchased a wedding package, you need not pay the officiant (although tips are usually appreciated). However, if you didn't buy a package, officiants are normally compensated for their services by a donation from the groom or a designated member of his team. Amounts vary from $50 to $500, usually depending on the size of the wedding. Officiants also should be compensated for travel expenses.

Readying for the reception

Key elements to every successful reception are intelligent seating, pleasant décor, tasty food, and entertainment that guests appreciate. Ideally, you've organized all these details before you left home. (Check out Chapter 12 to make sure your reception is planned accordingly.)

When refining your choices, use this time for the following:

✔ **Check your seating chart.** If your party is large and you have a seating chart, how does it work in the actual room? Anything from the location of windows and air conditioners to the proximity of tables from the music or food to the two guests who just stopped speaking to one another, may inspire you to tweak the chart.

✔ **Inspect and approve table settings.** If you've selected specific colors, are you happy after seeing them in person? Reception halls may have a stock of table linens in standard colors. Should all else fail, switch to all white — you can't go wrong with that.

✔ **Taste what's on your menu, remind the staff if you or your guests have any dietary restrictions, and check on the wedding cake.** Obviously you can't taste your actual cake in advance, but the baker could provide you with a sample of the cake and frosting. When you contact her, make sure to remind her of the delivery time for the cake and who will receive it.

If your time on the ground is limited, or you simply don't have the inclination to sweat every detail, you may not end up overseeing these decisions. If that's one of the reasons you decided to have a destination wedding in the first place, then just go with the flow.

Focusing on perfect pictures

You want photos that you can look at and recall how wonderful your wedding was, right? After you arrive, devote a little time to address photography issues. Some destination wedding couples don't get to see their venue until they arrive for the wedding. In those instances, decisions about photography and videography may need to be made on the spot. Either the coordinator or a member of the wedding party can take on the responsibility of communicating with the lensmen, making sure they know the VIPs who need to be photographed. (Check out Chapter 12 for more info.)

Watching the Webcam

If your facility guaranteed Webcam coverage of your wedding, now is a good time to investigate the setup. (A *Webcam* is a camera that captures images and sends them over the Internet in real time; refer to Chapter 17 for info on Webcams at weddings.)

1. **Ask at the facility whether a human operates the Webcam or whether it's attached to a fixed place, such as a wall or beam, and is trained on the spot where the couple is expected to stand.**

2. **Depending on the answer, verify the camera is positioned correctly.**

   If a human is behind the controls, you can request that certain people and parts of the ceremony are covered the way you want. You can also request that the cam operator focus on your best angles.

   If the Webcam is in a fixed position, here's what to do: Use a stand-in to preview the angle of the camera frame. That way, you know what mark to hit, or you can adjust your wedding party's positions until you approve of the view.

3. **Confirm how the video of the event will be archived and ask for a copy.**

   Because you're the stars of the live Webcam show, you'll certainly want to view it afterward, so ask the operator about your archiving options. You may be able to arrange for the facility to e-mail the broadcast to you as a RealPlayer or QuickTime file or burn it onto a CD or DVD so that you have a permanent copy.

Via e-mail, notify friends and family of the hour your wedding will take place (take time differences into account) and include the Web address where they can view it live.

Surveying the small details

Lesser details, especially ones that show your taste and personalities, are what make your wedding a real reflection of who you are. You can do the following tasks yourselves, ask one of your attendants to help out, or hand them off to your wedding planner:

✔ **Music:** Using the house band? Make sure they know your favorite songs. If you're supplying your own CDs or MP3 player for the ceremony and/or reception, deliver them to the person in charge with a written note describing what's on the playlist and the order you want followed. And don't forget to stress what you want to hear for your first dance. See Chapter 12 for a great destination wedding playlist.

If bringing a homemade CD, test the CD on the equipment beforehand. Don't hand over your CDs to anyone without first clearly marking at which point in the wedding each disc and selection is to be played. Write instructions directly onto the

CD with a marker and provide a detailed schedule of events to the person you put charge of the music.

- ✔ **Hair and makeup:** Has the bride booked salon time for herself at a salon on or off the premises? Confirm it, along with transportation, if needed. If your whole group is getting beautified, make sure the bride goes first.

- ✔ **Flowers:** Sometimes couples don't choose flowers until the last minute because that's when they find out what's in season and in stock. View sample arrangements, make your choices, and confirm prices, quantity (if centerpieces are needed), and delivery time. (Check out Chapter 12 for more info.)

- ✔ **Wedding rings:** Were you hoping to buy your rings at your destination? If so, purchase from an established jeweler who gives you a money-back guarantee, and hold on to the receipt. Keep the rings on you, with a trusted guest, or locked in the room safe until the wedding. If your room doesn't have a safe, ask the front desk to store the rings in the hotel's safe. Get a receipt.

- ✔ **Wherever bag:** Because unexpected things can happen at a wedding, especially a wedding away, having a fix-all bag nearby is a good idea. Pack the following items and keep the bag nearby at the ceremony: water, tissues, safety pins/sewing kit, tampons, deodorant, comb, toothpaste and brush, floss, mints, aspirin, and local currency.

Scheduling Time for Yourselves

As the wedding gets closer, you may start to feel tension build. That's natural. But you also owe it to yourself and your partner to make the effort to stay calm. Trust the people you've chosen — your attendants, the officiant, vendors, the people at your facility — to rise to the occasion and do their jobs. For better or worse, they will.

The following activities can help you to relax and de-stress:

- ✔ **Exercise.** Go for a walk, a run, or a swim, or use the gym in your hotel.

- ✔ **Get massages.** Arrange in-room or in-spa treatments by setting up an appointment with the hotel spa.

- ✔ **Take a drive.** Don't have a car? Hire a cab by negotiating an hourly rate, and explore your surroundings.

- ✔ **Start on thank-you notes.** Addressing envelopes can be a perfect task because it requires concentration without taxing the brain.

✔ **Reflect on your love.** You're on the cusp of a great life change together; the time is perfect to express what you value and love in one another.

Later, after your quality time alone together, you'll feel refreshed and ready to meet your guests as they arrive.

Welcoming Guests (And Keeping Them Out of Your Hair)

Although travel sounds glamorous, it can be grueling and expensive. Your guests may have come a long distance to celebrate with you, and they most likely want to unpack and freshen up. They also want to feel welcomed and get their bearings. This section explains how you can make guests feel welcome and keep them occupied without blowing them off.

Ideally, you or someone from your wedding party can be present to greet and help orient arrivals. Otherwise, alert the front desk as to who is expected. Ask that your friends and family members be shown to their rooms quickly.

Appointing a second-in-command

You can't do it all — nor should you. Having a second-in-command who can meet and greet guests when they arrive can give you more time to wrap up last-minute details and relax before the ceremony.

You can call on anyone who you trust and is reliable. Ask one of the dads, moms, the maid of honor, or a close friend who is qualified to be your proxy. That person can keep their eyes on things, hold onto your valuables, and communicate your wishes with the photographer or musicians. If you have a wedding coordinator, you can also lean on her.

Arranging a hospitality suite

Consider booking a hospitality suite at your hotel for guests to gather in. The advantage of these spaces — usually a meeting room or empty guestroom — is that friends and family have a central place to gather, mingle, and leave messages. If yours are staying at multiple hotels, such a spot can be especially useful.

Normally refreshments such as cold sodas, bottled water, and
cookies and brownies are furnished. You can order healthier items
and specialties by making arrangements with room service or the
banquet staff.

Notifying guests of optional and required events

Deciding how loose or structured you want the wedding weekend
to be, and which events require optional or mandatory attendance,
is up to you. (See the section "Promoting Activities to Keep
Everyone Busy," later in this chapter, for activity ideas.) What you
need to do is make sure your guests are informed about the events.

To keep everyone in the loop, provide an itinerary in your wedding
newsletter (see Figure 15-1). A *wedding newsletter* is a document
with an agenda that's typically included in a guest's welcome bag
or separately delivered to their room. Leave extra copies in the
hospitality suite (see preceding section) and at the front desk so
guests are never at a loss for what to do or where to find you.

Figure 15-1: A sample wedding guest newsletter.

Giving gifts and thanks

It's customary for the bride and groom to receive wedding gifts.
And it's also customary at a destination wedding for the couple to
give gifts to each other, to their attendants, to their parents, and

even to guests. (Check out Chapter 16 about gift-giving etiquette.) So when do you hand out the goods? This section gives you the scoop.

Guest welcome bags

When your guests arrive, have welcome bags ready for them. (Chapter 12 deals with selecting appropriate contents.) If you've planned well, you've already shipped the bulk of the goodies and the bags to contain them.

Your coordinator or attendants can handle filling guest bags. If neither is available, offer to compensate staff members to help. It's best to work at a long table in a room that can be locked. Line up bags, followed by items in the order they need to be placed inside. Use paper (or real luggage) tags to identify the guest and room number for each bag delivery. After the welcome bags are packed and labeled, you can arrange delivery with the bell or service desk.

Wedding-party gifts

If you've brought a gift meant to be used at the wedding, such as a fine new watch for the groom, pearl earrings for the bride, silver bracelets for the bridesmaids, or money clips for the groomsmen, distribute them before the wedding so they can use them at the ceremony. A good time to distribute gifts is at the rehearsal dinner or any other occasion before the wedding when attendants are present — as long as everyone receives something.

Promoting Activities to Keep Everyone Busy

Scheduling group events helps guests bond before the wedding. If you have a crowd that's up for just about anything, suggest a variety of events and then allow things to take their course.

Weekend wedding activities that involve physical activities are especially good at getting guests to relax, have fun, and interact. Beach volleyball games and team events like scavenger hunts and destination wedding "Olympics" with a series of competitions (with gag prizes for winners) are usually a blast.

Adventures that the two of you participate in with your guests — group kayaking trips, shopping expeditions, winery tours — are bound to become memorable experiences for all. So you definitely should set up at least one or two such events. Realize that differences in age, interests, and energy levels may cause guests to split into smaller groups. This section provides some ideas to keep everyone busy.

Who pays for these extra activities? No strict rules here. But in general, picking up the cost of group activities that at least one of you attends is good form. Individual guests usually bear the cost of sports and activities they pursue on their own. (Check out Chapter 4 for more info on what guests are responsible for.)

Having fun with the guys

When pre-wedding tension mounts, the sexes may prefer different ways to let off steam. Guys appreciate having an activity to burn off energy. Rigorous land and water sports are a good idea. Horseback riding, paintball, snorkeling, golf, and windsurfing may be options. Check with your hotel's activities desk for ideas.

Scheduling spa sessions for the gals

Females who prefer pampering, a massage, facial, body wrap, or hydrotherapy treatment can leach away stress in a spa. Some facilities also offer yoga and meditation classes. These activities are always more fun when you do them together (and a couple of guys come along)!

Whether or not you're picking up the bill for salon and spa visits, request in advance that a group discount price be applied to the cost of services for your guests.

Individual pursuits

If your guest list consists of individualists, suggest ways for them to entertain themselves while you attend to wedding business (or slip off to join them).

Present activity options in your newsletter or include brochures with details in the welcome bag. You'll also want to inform guests about who to talk to in order to get more info or make arrangements. Because this is free time for your guests, you aren't responsible for doing the planning.

Your friends, the individualists, can be inspired to participate in

> ✔ **Activities for early risers:** Your hotel may schedule a morning hike or personal training session; sometimes these activities are posted in the lobby.

✔ **Sports:** Snorkeling excursions and golf and tennis tournaments are good ways for sports enthusiasts to dive into the action.

✔ **Zip-lining:** Whizzing from treetop to treetop platform while securely rigged to a zipline is thrilling in tropical jungle areas.

✔ **Reaching for the sky:** Flight-seeing and sunrise champagne balloon flights are pricey but unforgettable experiences.

For cultured guests, the following activities may be fun:

✔ **Guided tour:** Historic sites, museums, and landmarks are a big draw.

✔ **Tastings:** Propose a sampling at a local winery.

Laid-back guests may enjoy these types of activities:

✔ **Cooking class:** If one of the chefs on staff at your hotel appreciates an audience, you may be able to press him into service to share the secrets of his specialty.

✔ **Shopping expedition:** Have the concierge or front desk provide directions and arrange transportation to the local market or shopping area if it isn't within walking distance.

✔ **Cruise to nowhere:** Some resorts have boats that ferry guests to nearby islands to swim and sun. Let your group know where they can sign up and get a picnic lunch.

Late-night lovers can have fun doing the following:

✔ **Take a gamble.** Las Vegas, many islands in the Caribbean, and several European capitals have casinos (for more on these locations, see Part II). Texas Hold'Em poker is an increasingly popular game where lots of people can fit around a table. So ask the casino manager whether a dealer can give your group instruction. And don't forget the Cuban cigars: Outside the United States, they're perfectly legal to smoke.

✔ **Make music.** No live professionals around? Find out where to rent a karaoke machine. Or hire a local band and hand out extra tambourines, bongos, and other music-makers for an outdoor concert. Otherwise just kick back and enjoy the music the pros make.

✔ **Create sparks.** Send guests off after evening meals with lanterns or sparklers, build a beach bonfire, or even arrange for fireworks.

Chapter 16

Minding Your Manners: Destination Wedding Etiquette

*W*hether it's the fancy new clothing you're wearing, the scrutiny of family and friends who have traveled to celebrate with you, or just the disorientation of being away from home, something about destination weddings makes a couple wonder whether behavior that they've considered perfectly acceptable all along suddenly isn't good enough for such a special occasion.

Although certain rules of behavior are best left unchallenged (no matter what, tell the bride she looks beautiful, no fighting in the aisle, and send a timely thank-you note for every gift), destination weddings tend to be more informal than those at home, so the rules are more flexible. Because destination weddings are still a fairly new phenomenon, there are few set-in-stone ways to behave. That said, you're the hosts of this event, and as such it's part of your responsibility to make sure your guests are comfortable and don't regret the time, effort, and money they spend traveling on your behalf. This chapter focuses on some of the major issues that arise around a destination wedding and smart ways to handle them.

Inviting Guests but Not Disaster

One of the touchiest topics in planning any wedding is deciding who to invite. For a destination wedding, it's a little different, which can work to your advantage. In fact, crowd control is one reason couples opt for a destination wedding (for more reasons, see Chapter 2).

Most people perceive destination weddings as smaller events, limited to your nearest and dearest, so they understand that your guest list is limited. Most people also realize travel expenses are involved. So you need not mask your excitement at work: Your co-workers aren't likely to expect an invitation.

However, *most* people isn't *all* people. Inviting guests (or uninviting them) can become an exhausting task — if you let it. This section explains how to handle uninvited guests, how to persuade guests to leave the kids at home, and how to deal with guests who can't afford to come. (Chapter 12 takes a closer look at creating the invitations and figuring out who to invite.)

Dealing with unwanted guests

An *unwanted guest* may be your partner's ex, an obnoxious uncle, or the best friend from childhood that you no longer have anything in common with. For whatever reason, you can't imagine hosting this person at your wedding. An unwanted guest can also be someone you genuinely like but aren't close enough with to want to spend a significant amount of time together.

What to do? The simple answer is, don't invite him or her. If you're footing the bill for the wedding, that should put an end to the discussion. However, if your parents are helping to fund it and insist on Aunt Buzzkill coming along, put your foot down: Your destination wedding isn't an event that will be over in five hours. It's more like going on vacation with someone. If you explain it that way, it's likely you can keep unwanted guests off your list.

What if someone who hasn't been invited to your wedding rudely confronts you with "I've always wanted to see Jamaica (or Italy or wherever) and this will be the perfect time!"? Or even politely asks whether they can come? Rather than make apologies, inform the person that your guest list is set and the travel arrangements have been completed. If they press the issue, politely but firmly stick to your guns. Ask your significant other for backup if you feel you need it. But keep your eyes on the prize: This is your wedding, and you deserve to have it your way.

Confession: When we got married, we wanted to keep it small, and we hoped that certain people wouldn't make it to our wedding. As we anticipated, choosing Las Vegas as our destination successfully kept them on the East Coast, far from our celebration.

A difficult decision to make for any wedding, but especially a destination wedding, is whether or not to include that "and Guest" on the envelope of your single friends' and family members' invitations. Try to remember that not all your single friends will be comfortable traveling alone. Because most hotels charge the same rate for a single or double room, let those friends know it's fine to bring a plus-one if you can afford to host the companion at your reception and related events. But what if you aren't crazy about your friend's "plus one?" Then you have to take a calculated risk: Invite the friend alone, and realize that she may not want to travel by herself and may decide not to attend.

How to graciously not invite kids

Allowing children at a hometown wedding is somewhat common; parents can easily remove rambunctious ones from a chapel or a reception to prevent them from disturbing the event and take them home if necessary. But when a family is hundreds or thousands of miles away from home at a destination wedding and kids get sick or act out, it's not so easy.

If you have children of your own or know others that you couldn't imagine a wedding being complete without, by all means include them. However, if you decide you'd rather not have children present, that's your prerogative. Because keeping children off your guest list can be a touchy issue, a couple needs to handle it diplomatically, so apply the same rules to everyone.

In the past, it was considered bad manners to include a line on an invitation such as "Adults only, please." However, I wouldn't trust anything as subtle as not including "and family" on the envelope to get the message across these days. By being straightforward and apprising guests of your decision in advance, you allow parents who want to attend ample time to make babysitting arrangements.

Addressing guests who want to come but can't afford to

Send an invitation to everyone you want at your wedding, even if you know they may not be able to attend. If it's a matter of cost and you can afford to subsidize someone's travel, let him know how important he is to you and offer to help. For more about this, see Chapter 17.

If that person declines to come, let him know whether he has other options to celebrate with you, whether it's watching your wedding on a Webcam (read Chapter 3 for more on this) or attending an at-home reception planned after your return.

Holding Showers and Other Pre-Wedding Celebrations

Destination brides- and grooms-to-be who are planning a small, out-of-town affair may wonder whether they're entitled to the traditional parties that surround weddings held closer to home. Will friends and family members who either weren't invited to the wedding or can't attend resent having to participate beforehand?

You have one way to find out: Ask. You may be surprised to find out that although everyone in your circle won't be at the wedding, most still would be glad to celebrate with you beforehand.

Your wedding may be small but your shower doesn't have to be

Typically the responsibility of arranging the bridal shower falls to the maid of honor. Have her contact key people (your friends and family) to see how they feel about coming to a party.

If your wedding is going to be so small that you don't have attendants, then a close friend may be willing to host your shower. (It's considered bad form for a family member to do so because that can be interpreted as shilling for gifts.) And just because your wedding will be small doesn't mean you have to limit the number of guests invited to your shower.

To make it clear that your bridal shower isn't a ploy to extract gifts from people who won't be attending your wedding, you can ask whoever is sending invitations to include a line such as "Your presence — but not your presents — is requested."

At my bridal shower, which I asked a friend to hold in her apartment, none of the women who came were invited to my tiny wedding. (And most of them were relieved I didn't expect them to travel to Las Vegas for the event!) Yet they graciously sent me off in style.

Bachelor and bachelorette parties

Bachelor and bachelorette parties have become a rite of passage, a night (or weekend) of revelry that marks your transition from sin-glehood to marriage. Typically no gifts are exchanged at these events, so even less pressure is on guests.

Although it's acceptable to have a bachelor or bachelorette party at your destination wedding location, it's a better idea to do the celebrating before you leave. That way, people need not spend more time away, and the pre-wedding event won't overshadow the main one. Plus, you can include friends from home who aren't attending the wedding.

If you decide to have it on-site, avoid scheduling it for the night before the wedding. The last thing you want to be is hung over when you stand up to get married. Instead, plan your pre-wedding blast around an activity, whether it's on the slopes, at sea, or at a spa.

Playing the Host

In addition to the myriad details and concerns you have about your own role as bride or groom, you're also the co-host of your destination wedding event. The most important responsibility as host is taking steps to put guests at ease from the time the first ones arrive until you leave for your honeymoon.

You want friends and family to have a wonderful time, so take time to consider each guest's comfort level and what you can do to keep it high. A few things to focus on to make your guests feel wel-come and comfortable include the following:

- ✔ Provide full details about traveling to the destination well in advance, plus contact numbers to call for questions.

- ✔ E-mail an annotated guest list a week or so before the event (for example: Jen Smith, my college roommate; Mark Goodstein, our first boss at the company where we met).

- ✔ Make introductions after guests arrive. Although you know everyone, they may not.

- ✔ Distribute an agenda that informs guests when and where they need to be during their stay so they don't miss the main event or any fun activities.

- ✔ Place in their rooms a fun and practical welcome bag (find ideas to fill it in Chapter 12) with a copy of your agenda.

The job as greeter need not fall squarely upon you. Check out Chapter 15 for more info on appointing a second-in-command. The bottom line is that no one who travels to your wedding should suffer the discomfort of feeling lost, out of place, or disconnected to the festivities.

Tipping Points

At home, adding a 15 to 20 percent tip to a bill is customary. At a destination wedding, giving tips to certain service providers is also expected. For instance, the officiant is entitled to an honorarium or a donation. A minimum of $100 is considered appropriate. If the officiant has spent significant time with you or traveled a long distance, giving more is fair.

Some of the helpers you may encounter expect a tip for good service, as you can see in the following list. The amounts reflect the minimum. Inflate these amounts in big cities, at four- and five-star hotels, or for people who go out of their way for you.

- ✔ Bellboy: $2 per bag
- ✔ Cab or limo driver: 15 percent
- ✔ Parking valet: $1 per car
- ✔ Chambermaid: $2 per a day
- ✔ Restroom attendant: $.50 per visit or $1 per guest
- ✔ Rental setup hands: $5 each

If you've worked with an on-site wedding coordinator who is paid by your hotel but has gone above and beyond the call of duty for you, she deserves to be acknowledged. Thank her for her service with a tip or a send a personal gift with a thank-you note after you return home.

Before you leave a tip (or hand cash to Dad or the best man in labeled envelopes to take care of this for you), make sure a service charge isn't already included in the bill. Anyone who receives a negotiated fee doesn't require a tip. Adding an amount beyond the fee for superior service is strictly at your discretion.

Overseas tipping customs vary. In general, people don't expect to be as highly rewarded for service as in the United States. To avoid making a *faux pas,* ask a local representative or contact the tourism office of the country to ask what percentage is appropriate.

Gifts You Give and Gifts You Get

I had this dream before my destination wedding: I was seated on a bench next to my best friend. We were surrounded by hundreds of people bearing exquisitely wrapped and beribboned presents. Over the loudspeaker, a voice repeated: "Please! Step up to the transom, deposit your gift, and step aside. . . ."

Although my wedding didn't play out that way, weddings can engender a frenzy of gift-buying and gift-giving. Traditionally and realistically, weddings of all kinds are an occasion to give and receive, and it is thoughtful, considerate, and good etiquette to thank everyone who makes the effort to acknowledge your union. This section covers basic gift etiquette.

Attending to your attendants

Rewarding the friends and family members who come to stand up for you at your wedding is good form. Not only do they provide moral support and make a destination feel more pleasant, they also typically bear the expense of their trip and buy a special outfit for the occasion.

Bridesmaids, moms, and honor attendants — especially ones who have traveled a distance — deserve big thanks from the bride, which is why it's traditional to give them a gift before the wedding. If time and funds allow, host an all-girls lunch and present gifts at that event. Because everyone is traveling and no one likes to add weight to her luggage, something lightweight and compact (such as a pendant, earrings, or a small leather item) is usually appreciated.

Brides having a wedding at a resort with a spa may opt to gather the wedding party and treat them to treatments. In addition to it being a female bonding experience, they'll look rested and glowing at the ceremony and in photographs. The groom also needs to take care of the best man and ushers. While the females are in the spa, he can treat his buddies to a round of golf or a half-day chartered fishing expedition. Great guy-to-guy thank-you gifts that are small and light include engraved silver luggage tags, flasks, and money clips. At informal destination weddings, you can give something local, such as a bottle of bay rum aftershave or a box of Jamaican jerk spice seasonings to be used at barbecues at home.

Thanking everyone for their gifts

No matter what presents you receive for your wedding, every gift merits a thank-you note. Make sure you budget for thank-you notes when buying wedding stationery. And although guests have up to a year to send a present, don't let more than three months pass before responding to their generosity.

Dealing with Bad Behavior

What can you do if you anticipate that one of your guests will act out and put a damper on the celebration? The simple answer: Don't invite that person. Of course, it's not that easy when the offending party is a parent or a close friend. If, say, divorced parents remain enemies, you need to speak to them in advance and let them know that you're counting on them to be civil. Seat them as far away from one another as possible, and have someone keep an eye on them.

What if you have a friend or family member who drinks too much? Some people consider a wedding at a resort where everyone stays overnight and no one has to drive an invitation to overindulge. To avoid a drunken scene, you can do a couple of things:

- ✔ **Don't have an open bar.** Set specified times, such as during a cocktail hour, when the bar will be open.

- ✔ **Limit drinks to beer, wine, and champagne.** Provide low-alcohol-content beverages rather than hard liquor.

- ✔ **Offer nonalcoholic alternatives.** Piña coladas and other fruity tropical drinks are still delicious without rum, and hot coffee should always be available.

- ✔ **Get the bartender on your side.** An alert bartender can be your best ally: Ask her to keep a close eye on anyone who's starting to get sloppy, halt service at a certain hour, and stop pouring drinks for any person who is obviously inebriated. Service like this merits a tip beyond the caterer's fee.

The last thing you want is to have something occur at your wedding away that would merit an embarrassing cameo on one of those wedding-disaster TV shows. In case no one's told you this yet, you can't control every aspect of your wedding, nor are you obliged to. But you can take precautions.

If a guest has the bad manners to start feuding with another or becomes an obnoxious drunk, ask someone in the wedding party to handle the situation. Don't attempt to engage them or rectify the situation yourself. If you're at a resort, call security. If you're at a different location or don't have security nearby, know in advance how to reach police, firefighters, and emergency medical assistance. Just in case. Find out more about dealing with emergencies in Chapter 19.

Chapter 17

Making Friends and Family Feel As If They Were There

In This Chapter

▶ Streaming your wedding on the Web

▶ Collecting and circulating photos and keepsakes

▶ Hosting a post-wedding bash

*O*ne of the realities of having a destination wedding is that not everyone you want to celebrate with may be able to make the trip. Fortunately, you can use different means to involve the people who are separated from you by distance. This chapter tells you how to use the Internet to span the miles while you're away, what you can do to transport the essence of your destination home to loved ones, and how to share the joy when you arrive home after the wedding.

Staying in Touch in Real Time

All brides and grooms are stars on their wedding day and those couples who want to share their performance can use technology to enable people they know in faraway places to witness the event as it happens. (As long as those folks have a computer and Web access.) This section explains how you can keep in touch by using a Webcam and a guest blogger so loved ones at home don't feel left out.

Putting your wedding on a Webcam

The *Webcam* (a digital camera that streams live video over the Internet) is one of the biggest boons to hit destination weddings, reducing any residual guilt a couple may have over getting married far away. From a facility that has a Webcam, your friends and family (and perhaps an ex who just happens to stumble across it) can watch your ceremony on the Internet.

Places that host many destination weddings every year — ranging from the Viva Las Vegas Wedding Chapel on the Las Vegas Strip to Princess Cruises' *Golden Princess* at sea to Frenchman's Reef & Morning Star Marriott Beach Resort in the Caribbean — have Webcams built into their chapels that couples can employ to transmit pictures of their weddings in real time anywhere in the world.

When you decide where you'll marry, ask the wedding coordinator whether a Webcam is available. If the answer is yes, sometimes there will be a fee; other times it is part of a wedding package. Typically a wedding Webcast is hosted on the facility's Web site for at least a month, and you can request to have a copy for yourselves burned onto a DVD or CD.

To help guide people how to watch your wedding on a Webcam, you need to e-mail them a link to the Web page that hosts the images and tell them what time to click on the link to watch your wedding live.

If your destination wedding location doesn't have a Webcam, you can take advantage of the technology by contracting with an outside company to provide this service. Ask a local planner for a recommendation. Prices start at about $400 for the Webcast plus 30 days of access to view your wedding on a company's site.

Getting geeky with a guest blogger

A *blog,* also known as a *Web log,* is a personal online journal. (Check out Chapter 3 for more specifics on how to use a blog.) You can have a close friend or family member live-blog during the ceremony, so folks at home can follow the event play by play, as in the following example:

> ". . . the flower girl just started down the aisle. Lisa's grandmother is crying, but her grandfather is laughing. A couple of wedding guests just tried to sneak in late and unnoticed. HEY Chris and Ashley! Where were you two?? . . ."

If you want to have your ceremony live-blogged, pick someone who can type quickly (and coherently) and has a reporter's eye. She needs to have started a blog in advance plus that person will need a portable computer with a wireless card, a good line of vision, and a place to sit and input observations. (Just make sure that the property has Wi-Fi range that extends to where the blogger is seated.)

If you're including live-blogging at your destination wedding, notify people well in advance to save the time, and be sure to inform guests in absentia of the specific URL they need to log onto in order to read in real time.

Collecting Memories Before You Depart

Even those who couldn't celebrate with you still may want to see and hear all about the location, the ceremony, and the activities. Being able to share memories of your wedding away (along with your own desire to later revisit the experience) provides impetus to collect and capture mementos before you head home. This section helps you gather ideas for photographs, scrapbook items, and souvenirs so you can share them with friends and family who couldn't attend.

Shooting stars

Pictures of the two of you, dressed for your wedding and dressed for fun, guest gatherings, meals and excursions, even your room and the place where you stay deserve to be captured on film.

At a typical hometown wedding, a photographer is booked for a limited number of hours during the ceremony and reception. However, because your destination wedding may last a couple of days — and different events (his attendants' kayaking expedition, her bridesmaids' mani-pedi session) may take place at the same time — one pro can't possibly capture the complete destination wedding experience and the price could be stratospheric.

 To solve this dilemma, ask friends to bring their cameras and shoot even if you have a photographer booked for the formal part of your event. You can never have enough pictures of your own wedding. If friends' cameras are digital, ask them to burn the shots onto a CD or e-mail them to you right after the wedding. If not, offer to pay for a duplicate set of prints or ask for copies of the negatives.

You can also distribute one-time-use video cameras or disposable waterproof cameras (with postage-paid returns to you) in guests' welcome bags, along with a request to take memorable pictures of their experiences. After you have a chance to go through all the photos, choose the best ones and upload them to your wedding Web site and make prints for your photo album as well as for people who couldn't attend. (Framing and sending one great shot to each guest who did come as thanks is a nice touch.)

Collecting scrapbook-worthy items

Photographs and postcards aren't the only mementos of a destination wedding worth collecting. If you intend to create a digital or paper scrapbook or if you want to compile a keepsake box to hold meaningful items, gathering the following can help to revive memories in years to come:

- ✔ **From your wedding stationery:** Save copies of your wedding invitation and announcements.

- ✔ **From the front desk:** After the wedding, stash a copy of the hotel brochure and other brochures that describe activities your guests took part in.

- ✔ **From the bar:** Pick up matchbooks, napkins, and anything else that has the property's name on them . . . except the bartender's uniform. (At least not while he's still in it.)

- ✔ **From your hotel room:** Many resorts issue nonreturnable plastic room keys with a pretty design or picture of the hotel on the front. And don't forget to nab the Do Not Disturb sign.

- ✔ **From your welcome packet:** Did you prepare an agenda, program, or newsletter for guests? Keep a few copies.

- ✔ **From pre-wedding events:** Admission tickets, postcards, even promotional materials may be worth saving.

- ✔ **From the ceremony:** If you issue a program, include this. And preserve some petals from the bride's bouquet.

- ✔ **From your guests:** You want to save all the wedding gift and greeting cards you receive from well-wishers. Also put aside any silly notes and doodles guests may leave you during the trip. (See Figure 17-1 for some examples.)

> Mazel tov! Getting married is a big deal. Getting Dana on the plane was an even bigger one! (But definitely worth it.) Glad we could share in your happiness,
>
> Robin & Jordan

> If we had it to do over again, we'd do it your way. Love, long life, and happiness to both of you,
>
> Mom & Dad

> Jess, I know you're expecting us at the rehearsal dinner, but Sharona broke her ankle on the hike and I have to act as The Iceman Cometh. She says not to worry; she still plans on wearing heels at the ceremony . . . even if it's heels and crutches.
> –John

Figure 17-1: Don't forget to include notes from wedding guests in your scrapbook.

As soon as you get home, scan in all important paper and flat objects for your digital scrapbook before they have a chance to be misplaced. After you've gathered all the items, check out the "Creating your own look book" section, later in this chapter, for tips on putting everything together.

Shopping for meaningful souvenirs

If you shop for souvenirs during your time away, consider picking up small gifts for the dearest friends and family members who couldn't attend. Gifts needn't be expensive or showy; just select something that shows you know what they like.

Choosing a gift that is unique to your wedding location is a good idea. If your destination wedding takes place in Jamaica or Hawaii, for example, a container of homegrown coffee is a natural choice. Taking your vows in Vegas? Play up the kitsch with an Elvis-related goody, or please people with a box of sweets from the city's own Ethel M. Chocolates.

Traveling home from Europe? If you splurged on gifts for yourselves and others there, make sure to gather up your VAT (value-added tax) receipts and turn them in for a refund at the designated spot in the airport.

Spreading Cheer After You Return Home

Although the wedding may be over, opportunities to celebrate your marriage with friends and family members who couldn't attend need not be. This section highlights a few ways to reach out to them and share memories.

Making the big announcement

If you didn't have destination wedding announcements printed up beforehand and mailed from the location after the ceremony, consider doing so now. They're a gracious way of telling folks that the event took place. Depending on your taste, announcements' fonts, design, and language can be formal sounding, folksy, fun, or funky. Mail the announcements from your destination or as close to your arrival home as possible.

Announcements go out after the wedding and are primarily for people you didn't invite (like business associates, co-workers, and distant relatives) and those who you did invite but who didn't attend.

Be sure to include the following information in your wedding announcement (refer to Figure 17-2 for some destination wedding announcements):

- ✔ Your names
- ✔ Where you were married
- ✔ The date you were wed

Figure 17-2: You can send a destination wedding announcement to anyone you think would be pleased by the news after you return home.

Creating your own look book

Pictures are worth a thousand words, and nothing tells the story of a wedding better than a beautiful and well-organized book or digital document that tracks your event from beginning to end.

After you have all your wedding photos and scrapbook items gathered from the different sources contributing them, decide how you want to present and preserve them for your own enjoyment and that of your circle. This section shows you a few options. (Check out *Scrapbooking For Dummies* and *Digital Scrapbooking For Dummies*, both by Jeanne Wines-Reed and Joan Wines [Wiley].)

Getting an album to have and to hold

Most couples prefer to have a physical wedding album. If your photography package didn't include one, or you'd like to upgrade, consider purchasing a photo album and putting it together. You can find a variety of styles at camera and gift stores as well as at www.weddingalbumdepot.com.

Going for a digital display

The advantage of making wedding pictures and mementos available online is that regardless of how far away friends and family are, they can access your treasures after you put them online.

Some photographers include an online album in their services that can be accessed via password, and photos can be purchased directly online or downloaded for the user to print herself. If this applies to you, let people know it's available to them by e-mailing the link and password to them.

If you're the one posting your photos online, consider the following options:

✔ **Use a free photo-sharing site, such as `www.flickr.com` or `www.kodakgallery.com`.** Choosing this method is a simple way to get your digital wedding pictures seen quickly. After images are posted, all you need to do is send out an e-mail with the address of your site and invite friends to take a look at your photos and register so that they can leave comments.

✔ **Try Microsoft PowerPoint.** This program isn't only for business presentations. You can use it to create a wedding album or slideshow by importing a sequence of images and adding headlines and comments. To make sure the widest number of guests and nonguests who have a computer can easily view it, save your PowerPoint album as a PDF file and then e-mail it to them as an attachment.

Going from pixels to a printed book

There's nothing like having a rich-looking photo album that you can hold in your hands — especially when you want to point out particular pictures to a couple of friends at your side.

Here's good news: You can have your pictures preserved both digitally and printed. iPhoto software, which is bundled with all new Apple computers, enables you to organize your best photos into a great-looking photo album that can be professionally printed. Picaboo (`www.picaboo.com`) enables Windows XP users by allowing you to download the appropriate software to do the same. And you can buy multiple copies of the album or share it online for free.

Updating your wedsite

If you created a wedding Web site, known as a *wedsite* (turn to Chapter 3), updating it when you get home from your wedding is worth the effort. Even if you never touch the site again (and many couples do abandon theirs after the wedding), your words and pictures that describe the ceremony, reception, and related events can create a satisfying conclusion to the first chapter of your married life together.

Additional elements that you may want to include are links to related Web sites that show off where you traveled to and photos of the wedding. If you spent your honeymoon elsewhere, include photos and a narrative of that trip on your wedsite as well. If your wedding was captured on video, you may want to post some of it on your site. Ask your videographer to provide you with a digitized version that you can upload.

Holding an at-home reception

You can't find a rule that says couples who have a small destination wedding can't still host a celebration at home. In fact, many newlyweds do just that. Having a post-wedding celebration is a great way to let friends and family who couldn't travel witness you now as a married couple. No one expects a re-creation of the wedding (although that's what some couples attempt). Because you pick up the tab, you can keep your event modest and still be comfortable.

When should you schedule the party? Again, nothing is written in stone. Most couples aim to have their party within a month of their return, while memories are still fresh (as long as their pictures are back from the photogapher by then). But if you had a winter wedding away, you can wait until summer and throw a backyard barbecue then. If funds are tight, you can even wait for your first anniversary to roll around.

At one point during the event, invite guests to gather in front of your TV or a screen you rent for the occasion. Arrange to have your best man, maid of honor, or another person run a slide show or video while the two of you sneak away until he or she announces, "Ladies and gentlemen, it gives me great pleasure to introduce to you. . . ." And then the two of you can make an entrance, even wearing your wedding attire if you like.

To help your hometown wedding reception feel different from an ordinary party, enhance it by giving the event a destination theme that's carried through to the drinks and decorations. Be sure to have your look book (see the section "Creating your own look book") available for viewing. Consider blowing up some of your favorite photos, framing them, and arranging them in a wall gallery for party guests to admire as you tell about your amazing wedding trip.

Chapter 18

Beginning the Honeymoon

. . . .

In This Chapter

▶ Deciding where and when to go

▶ Choosing a honeymoon or romance package that suits you

▶ Knowing what to pack

▶ Guaranteeing your privacy as Mr. and Mrs.

. . . .

*I*n the storybook fantasy, a honeymoon begins that moment after the wedding when a couple disappears into the sunset, and they live happily ever after. In reality, honeymoon happiness takes a bit of planning for that to occur. Traditionally it was the groom's responsibility to organize the honeymoon. Because your wedding and honeymoon may be rolled into one extended getaway, you likely will want to decide together where to go.

Whether you make your honeymoon part of the destination wedding or take it at another time, this chapter can help you to plan a first vacation together as Mr. and Mrs. that is as rapturous as the fantasy.

The Best Is Yet to Come

Having a wedding away is fabulous, but for some couples the ceremony's merely the prelude to an even bigger thrill: going on the honeymoon. If you intend to take a post-wedding twirl, you have three choices: Stay on in the place where you wed, head someplace else directly after the wedding, or return home and take your honeymoon at another time.

Deciding whether to go or stay

When figuring out your honeymoon plans, remember that remaining in one place has certain advantages:

✔ You're likely to find pricing deals that make it tempting to stay put.

✔ You can immediately start to relax after the wedding and not have to deal with making additional travel connections.

✔ You don't have to pack or unpack.

✔ If you want to vacation with your wedding party, staying put makes it easy.

The majority of couples who have a destination wedding at an all-inclusive resort combine it with a honeymoon at the same spot or one in close proximity. For example, Sandals Resorts, which coined the term *weddingmoon* (a combination wedding and honeymoon) offers honeymooners at its Jamaican properties privileges to use facilities at other Sandals on the island, which can add variety to a getaway.

On the other hand, a property that worked wonderfully for a wedding may not be as desirable as a honeymoon spot. Or perhaps you've got a touch of wanderlust and would prefer to visit more than one destination during your time away from home. Whatever the case, investigating different options before you make a commitment is worth the effort.

Going on close calls

Some of the smartest destination weddings and honeymoons combine two different types of trips within close proximity to one another. That way, not much traveling is involved, but you have the excitement of visiting a fresh venue.

If you want a slightly different experience with your honeymoon than you did with your wedding, look to the surrounding areas. When you make the plans, consider nearby locations that would make a great getaway but don't require much travel time. Many travel guidebooks feature info on day trips from the primary destination. Or you can simply eyeball a map to see what's nearby. But before making plans, find out what type of transportation is available from Point A to Point B.

Taking the honeymoon later

Not every couple goes on their honeymoon directly following the wedding, and you may find advantages to postponing yours. Perhaps you don't have much extra money after paying for your wedding, or your work schedule just doesn't allow for you to take an extra week for your honeymoon.

Rather than rushing through or skimping on your honeymoon, you can find good reasons to justify taking a honeymoon later:

- ✔ **You can spread out the fun.** Go home and relax after the wedding, savor the memories, and then take your honeymoon when you really need a break.

- ✔ **You can save up.** Maybe you always dreamed of a honeymoon in Paris, or on safari in Africa, or even a cross-country drive. After funding the wedding, you may not have the money for that dream honeymoon.

- ✔ **You can head off in another direction.** Winter-wed couples can warm up by honeymooning on a tropical island; summer ones can hit the slopes. City couples may enjoy active outdoor adventures.

- ✔ **You can take "mini-moons."** Instead of having just one honeymoon, plan for a year of them, taking off on a series of long weekends that lead to a variety of places and experiences.

Having the Honeymoon You Want

Just as with the wedding, you probably harbor an image of what your honeymoon should be like and where you want it to take place. What makes this more than an ordinary vacation is that two of you, with two different visions, need to communicate and compromise so that your post-wedding getaway fulfills as many of both of your desires as possible.

Don't think you can afford a honeymoon? If you'd rather receive travel gifts in lieu of household items, consider signing up with a honeymoon registry service, such as www.giftpile.com. Guests can contribute any amount they want, which can be applied to your airfare, accommodations, tours, special dinners, and other honeymoon delights.

In order to have a honeymoon that you both remember fondly, this section helps you identify some different types so you can customize yours. Whether you remain at the destination wedding site or take your honeymoon at a different time than the wedding, knowing your honeymoon "personality" as a couple will lead you to select a place where you can be happiest. And there's nothing wrong with picking a honeymoon destination first . . . and afterward determining a suitable spot to hold a wedding there.

Knowing your honeymoon type

Where you go on your honeymoon should reflect the kind of couple you are and what you like to do on vacation. These categories can help point you in the right direction and provide some ideas.

For the active, sports-minded couple

Are you and your betrothed constantly on the go, playing golf or tennis, skiing, sailing, biking — you name it? You can find resorts throughout the United States and the rest of the world to concentrate on that activity to your heart's content. Keep in mind that a nearby spa is a good complement to vacation exertion.

Consider the following honeymoons if you're active:

- **A golf or tennis getaway:** Florida is the state with the most golf courses (California comes next), and tennis courts are plentiful. Full-service resorts offer play time, instruction, and other activities.

- **A ski trip:** For great skiing, consider the Rocky Mountain and New England states, Canada's Laurentians, or Argentina's slopes in summer.

- **A sailing tour:** Sailors appreciate the world-class experience of Newport, Rhode Island, as well as in the British Virgin Islands, only reachable by boat. You can skipper your own skiff or rent one with a crew and relax.

- **A bike trek:** Like to bike? Riding around on bicycles is a great way to see a country. For example, Switzerland rents bicycles at all major train stations and allows renters to bring bikes aboard.

For the sophisticated couple

Dynamic cities appeal to stylish couples. Look for destinations that primarily appeal to adults (casino resorts are one option) and have nightlife and good entertainment available. Consider these options:

- **New York City:** If you've never been to New York, Gotham is a terrific place to honeymoon. World-class theater, shopping, restaurants, and hotels all draw lovers.

- **Santa Fe:** Out West in New Mexico, Santa Fe's laid-back vibe, spicy Southwestern fare, and vital art scene make it a favorite with romantics.

✔ **Paris:** A honeymoon in France is still the gold standard for some couples. You can also combine it with side trips to romantic Bruges, Belgium, and heady Amsterdam.

✔ **Eastern Europe:** Although Western Europe is expensive, Eastern Europe is less so. Emerging countries such as Croatia and the Czech Republic have excellent hotels and spas.

For the couple with kids

Even if children are along, your getaway should still feel like a honeymoon and allow you time alone. Look for family-friendly resorts and all-inclusives that have children's programs and babysitting services. Also, you may want to consider a cruise on one of the Disney ships because they're geared to youngsters but also have spas and some adult-oriented activities.

For the couple who simply wants to kick back

Go ahead. Pamper yourselves: You've earned it. If you don't feel like doing more than lifting a finger to summon a waiter to bring another margarita, who's to say no? Find honeymoon bliss on holidays like these:

✔ **Caribbean islands:** Surrounded by the sand, baked by the sun, and cooled by the sea, you'll get back in touch with your senses in the tropics. Younger couples and inexperienced travelers appreciate the security of all-inclusive resorts; older ones may find other places where they are less cut off from the local culture more appealing. (Check out Chapter 8.)

✔ **Cruises:** The original no-stress vacation, a cruise takes you from port to port without the hassle of repacking. And all the major costs are paid upfront, which makes it easier to stick to a budget. (Chapter 10 has more info.)

✔ **Spas:** Sleep right through the optional 6 a.m. hike and head out after breakfast for a bike ride or dual hot-stone massages. Look for spa resorts that have a menu of couples' services that you can enjoy together in a couples treatment room; outdoors in a private, shady spot; or en suite.

Honeymoon romance packages: What you can expect

Reveling in the amenities in a romance package can make a honeymoon feel blissfully different from a typical vacation. Typically the package cost is in addition to the daily room rate, although it may be bundled together. Goodies in such packages, like the following treats, vary from place to place, but often include

✔ Room upgrade

✔ Champagne, flowers, and/or fruit basket upon arrival

✔ Couples massage

✔ Candlelight dinner

✔ Rose-petal turndown

✔ Breakfast in bed

✔ Late checkout

Hotels and resorts that truly cater to honeymooners often have a dedicated staff person, such as a romance concierge or butler, who you can call upon to orchestrate extraordinary experiences such as a sunrise hot-air balloon ride, a gourmet picnic at a secluded spot, and a moonlight cruise.

Packing for Your Honeymoon

How much you need to pack for a honeymoon depends on how long you will be gone from home and the type of honeymoon you plan to take. Some brides plan to wear a different outfit for every day, plus different sexy lingerie every night (and sometimes in between). Other couples like to travel as light as possible, especially if they will be carrying their own bags and visiting multiple destinations.

Should you take one big suitcase or two smaller ones? Everyone has a different packing style. If each of you is doing your own packing, you may be happiest to have one suitcase apiece. To be on the safe side, though, tuck a day's underwear and socks into one another's bags. And putting a layer of tissue paper or plastic between items cuts down on wrinkling.

You can find a comprehensive honeymoon packing list on my Honeymoons/Romantic Getaways from About.com site at `http://honeymoons.about.com/cs/travelplanner/a/Packing_List.htm`. In addition to travel documents and whatever clothing you bring along with you, consider the following essentials:

Sundries

❏ Medications

❏ Sunscreen with SPF

❏ Travel toothbrush with toothpaste and floss

❑ Birth control

❑ Personal lubricant

Miscellaneous

❑ Quart-size, zip-top plastic bags

❑ Daypack

❑ Cell phone (check coverage area) with charger

❑ Current-converter plug (if traveling overseas)

❑ Custom-fitted sports gear

❑ Extra contacts or eyeglasses

❑ Address list to send postcards

❑ Scented travel candle

What you leave at home can be as important as what you travel with if you experience a loss. Before you go, make photocopies of your passport and all your credit cards (back and front) and leave them with a trusted friend or family member. If you're using traveler's checks, give that person the serial numbers too. Keep a copy of everything with you as well, in a different place from the originals.

Bidding Guests Good-Bye

Joy-filled days surround a destination wedding, but sooner or later the party is over. If you're staying on at the destination, it's thoughtful to appear at the send-off to personally say good-bye to everyone who attended and thank them for coming. When guests decide to stay on after the wedding (after all, you picked a blissful spot for them to travel to), you have two choices — spend time with them or make a graceful exit. This section examines those options.

How to make a great escape

The wedding festivities are over, and the two of you now want to relax at your destination. However, some of your loved ones have decided to also stay at the destination for a couple of days. No matter where you go — to the pool, to the spa, or to dinner — you keep running into your sister and her new boyfriend.

If you want to spend some time with them, then communicate to them when you're available. Focus on something you want to do anyway — take out kayaks, try a new restaurant — and invite them to come along for an activity that has a clear beginning and end. That way you can have quality time together and won't be impolite when you take your leave.

If after the festivities you don't want to be bothered, how can you let hangers-on know when it's time to give you privacy? Mention on the agenda tucked into their welcome bag at what point you'll be going into seclusion, hang a do-not-disturb sign on your door, and instruct the operator not to put any calls through to your room. If you have a persistent family member who's just not catching on, you can change rooms, switch to a nearby hotel, or simply take off on an excursion and return when the coast is clear.

The buck stops here

After the wedding is officially over and guests remain, charges may still accrue. Who pays for guests' food and drinks then? In two words: They do.

To clarify that message, you can include a small area on your wedding Web site, in a travel-info mailing, or on the welcome-bag agenda that spells things out. For example:

> *We are thrilled to have you as our wedding guests. The rehearsal dinner and drinks, everything at the reception, the trail ride, and the farewell brunch are all complimentary, our gift to you. Unfortunately, we cannot fund additional meals, activities with fees, and airport transportation; they will be charged to your credit card.*

Confirm that the front desk has taken a credit card imprint from each guest. Make clear to management whether anyone besides the two of you may add to your tab after the wedding. And before the first guest leaves, give your own bill the once-over to make sure there are no unauthorized or misappropriated charges.

As you're checking out, if you notice extra fees, such as your Uncle Harry's back waxing from the spa on your bill, direct the front desk to reassign the charge to the correct account; they'll still have Harry's card on file.

Part V
The Part of Tens

In this part . . .

*E*very *For Dummies* book concludes with quick tips and practical suggestions designed to help and inspire you. Chapter 19 covers what to do when unexpected emergencies arise (closing your eyes and counting to ten won't help). Finally, Chapter 20 is a goldmine of money-saving ideas that can help you spend less on airfare and lodging, curtail reception costs, and look great on a budget. It also clues you in to the wedding stuff you can skip (and no one will even notice is missing) and still have a fabulous event.

Chapter 19

Ten Emergencies You May Face and How to Handle 'Em

*R*are is the destination wedding that goes off without a single hitch. Although brides and grooms don't go looking for trouble, it can still show up like an unwanted guest. Fortunately, most wedding emergencies are temporary and manageable.

Expect the unexpected — and prepare as best you can by following my four "S" system for handling unforeseen problems:

✔ **Stress safety.** Whatever the situation, put people's safety first.

✔ **Stay calm.** People look to you in a crisis. Act confidently and decisively, even if you have to fake it initially.

✔ **Show sensitivity.** It's your day, but everyone involved — from your guests to the serving staff — wants it to turn out well. Appreciate their efforts and understand that cultural differences can cause confusion. The words *please* and *thank you* in any language go a long way toward maintaining harmony.

✔ **Smile.** A situation can seem like a disaster at the moment, but in retrospect, you may be able to laugh about it. Should it continue to hurt forever after, at least you'll be smiling in the wedding pictures.

Although anything can happen at a wedding, this chapter covers some common disasters large and small that couples fear most and how to handle them.

Someone Gets Sick

The number-one destination wedding fear couples have is some-one getting sick. Buying insurance can contribute peace of mind (so can packing all necessary medications and carrying them with you). *Wedding insurance* can cover the cost of postponing the event if key people can't attend due to sickness or injury. *Trip insurance* extends your health insurance coverage to another country and can fund emergency transportation home or to a reputable local medical facility. Talk to an insurance agent to get more info on these types of policies or visit www.wedsafe.com or www.insuremytrip.com on the Web.

If the bride or groom is ailing (or another member of the wedding party), as long as she or he can stand and speak, go through with the ceremony and deal with the situation afterward.

Mother Nature Doesn't Cooperate

Skies can open even in the sunniest venues, so if you're planning a beach, garden, or other outdoor wedding, think ahead and have an indoor space or tented area available as a backup. If minor show-ers are expected, ask one of the staff or wedding-party members to round up enough umbrellas for everyone.

If you're trying to decide whether to move the ceremony indoors, my rule of thumb is this: If the weather is going to seriously detract or distract from the wedding, you need to go indoors.

Luggage Is Lost

To avoid having your most important items lost in transit, be sure to carry your wedding gear with you. Everything else is replace-able. (Check out Chapters 11 and 18 for more info about packing.)

If your luggage goes AWOL, fill out and submit a claim form at the airline's baggage service desk before you leave the airport and hold onto your claim tags. Understand that most airlines endeavor to return missing bags within 24 hours, so make sure your carrier knows where you can be reached if the address is different from the one on your luggage tag.

A Fashion Disaster Occurs

Sometimes the fashion gods aren't on your side. What do you do if someone steps on your dress and it tears or you spill a little red wine on your guayabera shirt? No worries.

Every bride and groom needs an emergency kit that includes safety pins, needle and thread, and stain remover. If a wardrobe malfunction is beyond help, go to your room and change — and encourage everyone else to take a break and get comfortable, too.

Vendors Are No-Shows

Aside from the two of you, everyone else at your wedding is replaceable — and the show must go on. What happens, though, if the following people don't show?

- ✔ **Your officiant MIA?** Seek out a civil authority to conduct the ceremony.

- ✔ **No musicians?** CDs can serve as backup.

- ✔ **Caterers kaput?** In a pinch, pick up takeout.

The key word is *improvise*.

Uninvited Guests Arrive

Hotels and resorts all have security details, which is a good thing since the movie *Wedding Crashers* gave some people the wrong idea. If you spot a stranger helping himself to the crab dip or hitting on the bridesmaids, notify security and ask to have that individual escorted away from the party.

At a public facility such as a beach or park, couples are more vulnerable and need to depend on the persuasive powers of a dad or the best man to keep riff-raff away. You may also consider hiring an off-duty policeman to work security.

A Fight Breaks Out

What happens if the groom's cousin Mel starts fighting with the new boyfriend of his ex-girlfriend? No bride or groom should have to be put in the position of a referee. One way to limit the possibility of this happening is by keeping feuding friends and family members off the guest list. Should tempers nonetheless flare, have someone separate and isolate the party poopers. And don't fan the flames with more alcohol; stop serving drinks.

The Ceremony Is Interrupted

Some things you can plan for — others you can't. However, you can take steps to ensure that your ceremony isn't interrupted by certain distractions, such as the following:

- ✔ **Sirens:** To avoid the blaring sound of sirens, don't stage the ceremony within hearing distance of a hospital, firehouse, or police station.

- ✔ **Public announcements:** Outdoors on a ship, ask that loudspeaker announcements be postponed until after the ceremony.

- ✔ **Construction noises:** At a hotel or public spot, find out whether construction is taking place nearby. If it is, request from the person in charge that the noise abate during a specific time (a gift of cash can make such a request that much more urgent) or try to juggle the ceremony schedule to coincide with lunch hour or after quitting time.

In the case of unanticipated interruptions, allow a short time to pass until everyone regains their composure and continue with the ceremony as planned.

The Wedding Ring Is Missing

What if the groom or best man can't locate the wedding bands? This emergency is easy to solve (at least for the ceremony): Borrow a ring from a married guest. Afterwards you can take the necessary steps to find the missing ring.

The Cake Collapses

Someone jolts the table holding the wedding cake, and the cake falls over in slow motion while everyone gasps. Or the whipped cream topping or buttercream frosting doesn't hold up under extreme temperature and starts to melt. Instead of an elegant cake, you've got . . . mush. What should you do? Salvage and serve what you can. If a bakery or supermarket is nearby, send someone to buy a substitute cake. And if all else fails, remember that everyone loves ice cream for dessert.

Chapter 20

Ten Ways to Save Money on Your Destination Wedding

In This Chapter

▶ Getting the most out of a destination

▶ Saving money without sacrificing style

▶ Flying, dressing, and dining smart

*Y*ou may find it mind-boggling that the typical wedding costs as much as a new car. But it doesn't have to. By controlling the size of your guest list, buying locally, and forgoing some unnecessary frills, you can pull off a fabulous destination wedding at a fraction of that cost.

Don't lose sight of the fact that destination weddings are big business: It should come as no surprise that as soon as *wedding* is affixed to a product's description — as in *wedding invitation* or *wedding favor* — another 25 percent or so gets tacked onto the price. Counter that by assuming everything is negotiable.

Subsidizing the wedding industry or paying more than your fair share to have a memorable event certainly isn't your responsibility. Of course, no one wants an event where corners obviously have been cut and guests can't fully enjoy themselves (example: the cash bar). On the other hand, being clever about destination wedding costs can ensure that you, like your money, go farther than you ever dreamed. This short chapter can help you save money without sacrificing.

Book a Location Off-Season

Destinations have popular and not-so-popular seasons. For example, every April 15, hotel rates in the Caribbean plummet, and come summer, you can find bargains at mountaintop ski resorts, too. By choosing to hold your wedding in a place out of season, you can avoid both crowds and higher prices. What's more, you're likely to receive more personal attention when staff isn't harried and overworked.

 In addition to traveling off-season, consider adjusting the day of the week and time of day for the wedding. Saturday night is prime time; everything else is cheaper. And an event that takes place in daytime hours is less expensive than one that begins at or after sunset. (For more info on booking a location, check out Chapter 11.)

Invite Fewer Guests

More guests means higher expenses. Scrutinize your list for people who aren't essential. Do all your work colleagues need to be invited? What about the best friend you had when you were 7 years old and promised you'd go to each other's weddings but only exchange Christmas cards with now?

 As you consider each name, ask yourselves, "Is this someone we not only want at our wedding but would also like to spend our vacation with?" (Refer to Chapter 12 for figuring out who to invite.)

Skip the Paid Wedding Planner

Keep the wedding small and simple, and you can do the planning and organizing yourselves. Have confidence that the pros you hire can operate without being supervised by a middleman: It's more than likely that your recommended printer understands what a deadline means; your florist knows how to acquire, arrange, and deliver bouquets to the right place and on time; and your baker has made more than a few wedding cakes in her day. (See Chapter 3 for how you can organize a memorable event.)

 Depending on where you hold the wedding, you may be entitled to use a wedding coordinator at no cost. If you choose a hotel that maintains an on-site coordinator, her planning services are typically included in the wedding package price.

Save on Airfare

Look beyond the major airlines for transportation. Low-cost airlines, such as Southwest and jetBlue in the United States and Ryanair and EasyJet in Europe, offer great deals. For example, you won't find Southwest on Expedia or Travelocity; the airline only sells flights online from its Web site (www.southwest.com).

Also, if you know any frequent fliers with extra mileage, they may be willing to donate them to you in lieu of a gift (another great money-saving alternative).

Get Dressed for Less

You have many alternatives to paying retail when dressing for a destination wedding. Keep the following suggestions in mind:

- ✔ **Look for sales and discounts.** Small-size brides can score big at sample sales. Brides of all sizes can find deals online at eBay (search for wedding gowns that are "NWT" — new with tags), www.preownedweddingdresses.com, and Craigslist (www.craigslist.com).

- ✔ **Check the newspaper's classified section and keep an eye out for local bridal shows.** Vendors may offer a discount to brides who buy that day.

- ✔ **Wear a used dress.** If you don't mind something preworn, borrow from a friend, haunt upscale thrift shops, or consider retailoring your mother's wedding dress.

Frugality doesn't have to end with the dress. Carry a silk rather than a live-flower bouquet. (It will look the same in pictures, and you can treasure it forever.) And make your own bridal veil, which consists of little more than tulle and a comb or headband. Anyone who can sew a button on neatly is qualified to create one of these. Find complete free instructions at www.wegotgame.net/jen/veils.html.

Employ the Talents of Friends and Family

Do you have an artistic friend who can design invitations? Who takes the most interesting (and in-focus) photographs in your group? Can someone arrange flowers elegantly? By engaging the skills that amateur but able friends and relatives have, you can save money and have a wedding in which those guests take special pride. (For more tips on collaborating with friends and family, see Chapter 5.)

If you're crafty yourself, adding the prefix DIY (do it yourself) to what you want to make in the Google search box can yield free advice on how to create everything from DIY invitations to DIY centerpieces to DIY wedding favors.

Buy Locally Rather than Bring It with You

Purchasing wedding supplies locally is cheaper and more ecologically sensitive than bringing everything with you. Plus, using anything from indigenous flowers to local musical talent underscores a destination wedding's sense of place while supporting the local economy.

Celebrate in a Restaurant

Scout out the best family-owned restaurants at your destination. Having a reception at a place with the owner on the premises and that is 100 percent dedicated to serving food means you don't have to deal with caterers, rentals, and basically reinvent the wheel. Try to schedule at least one tasting, and consider places that specialize in regional cuisine. Many eateries have private rooms for parties, and smaller ones may close their doors to host your party.

Forgo the Program and Favors

If your wedding is small, you don't need a program to identify the players and spell out the scenario. Those details can go in a welcome-bag newsletter. As for favors, either make something by hand or skip them entirely. Put things guests will really use and appreciate in the welcome bag. (Check out Chapter 12 for more info.)

Sacrifice Extra Desserts

Of course you want a wedding cake. (Although you can save by having a small one for show and another that's a sheet cake, cut and plated in the kitchen.) No one will think less of you if you don't have a Viennese table or sweet little cookies to send them off — especially if you're all gathering for breakfast the next day.

Index